Reverence for ALL Life

By

John Webster

and

Ty F. Webster

Reverence for ALL Life

First Edition

Cover illustration of Albert Schweitzer and his pet pelican, Parsifal, by David Andrews.

"Earth Tree" illustration on back cover by Megan Gjersvig.
Photos of Albert Schweitzer on back cover and spine by Erica Anderson, used with the permission of The Albert Schweitzer Fellowship. Other photos on back cover are the authors' own.

ISBN 1-889406-42-2

Published by

Prell Books & Multimedia
18989 Hilltop Road
Sparta, WI 54656-8104
www.prellbooks.com

Dedicated to the Memory of Albert Schweitzer

1875 - 1965

Photograph by Dr. Schweitzer's granddaughter Christiane Engel
(Courtesy of Rhena Schweitzer Miller)

May his message of Reverence for Life live forever.

Acknowledgments

Grateful acknowledgment is made to the following people for permission to use the following materials:

Rhena Schweitzer Miller for copyrighted materials written by Dr. Albert Schweitzer; Congressman Dennis J. Kucinich for the full transcripts of his speeches "Peace and Nuclear Disarmament," "Prepare for America's Future," and "A Second Renaissance;" John and Deo Robbins for excerpts from John's books *Diet for a New America: How Your Food Choices Affect Your Health, Happiness and the Future of Life on Earth* and *The Food Revolution: How Your Diet can Help Save Your Life and Our World*; Charlotte Aldebron for her essay "What the American Flag Stands For" and the transcripts from her speeches "Is Anyone Listening?," "Take a Look at Me," and "Do We Really Have Free Speech?;" Justin Walker for his article "Compassion for a Homeless Man;" Dr. Edwin A. Schick for passages from his composition *Albert Schweitzer: A Voice for the Twenty-first Century*; Phyllis Hiller for the words to "Love is a Circle;" Ed Garvey for blogs from his website; the political watchdog organization BushGreenwatch for quotes from their website; Bree Breckel for her poem "Flow;" Christine Meisenheimer for her poem "Peace Is;" Linda Jenkins for "Enjoy Your Moments…," and Jo Meyer for her painting "Peace on Earth."

The authors also wish to thank Jay Webster, Forest Jenkins, and Kestrel Jenkins for contributing original material for publication in *Reverence for ALL Life*.

iv

In Recognition and Honor
of
Rhena Schweitzer Miller

Daughter and only child of Helene and Albert Schweitzer

Photograph by Erica Anderson (Courtesy of Rhena Schweitzer Miller)

Rhena, pictured here with her father, spent several years working at Dr. Schweitzer's hospital at Lambarene, Africa. She helped develop and was in charge of the pathology laboratory. In 1965, Dr. Schweitzer named Rhena to take over the direction of his hospital after his death, which occurred later that year.

Later, Rhena worked with her husband, Dr. David Miller, assisting native people in the countries of Egypt, Ethiopia, Vietnam, Yemen, Pakistan, and Haiti.

Rhena has worked diligently to perpetuate her father's ethic of Reverence for Life by writing numerous articles about her father's life, participating in Albert Schweitzer organizations worldwide, and by the very life that she lives.

The authors thank Rhena for her encouragement and suggestions in our attempt to share her father's important message with our readers.

Contents

vii

Preface

Several years ago my son, Ty, suggested that I write a book about experiences and concepts I felt were significant. My initial reaction was to dismiss the idea, as I felt I had neither the expertise nor the urgently important message that would justify such a project.

A few years later I became familiar with the life, work, and message of Dr. Albert Schweitzer. I was particularly grasped by Schweitzer's ethic of "Reverence for Life," and soon realized I had found the important message I had been seeking. With this realization came the desire to share Dr. Schweitzer's message in the form of a book, with the hope that I could play a role in spreading his ideas in a world that too often seems to have forgotten them.

As the book began to take shape, Ty—an English major and free-lance writer—became involved in the project as editor, correcting and refining the mechanics of my writing. To my good fortune, as work on the book progressed and Ty became more familiar with Schweitzer's ethic and philosophy, he agreed not only to edit, but actually to co-author the book. In this capacity, Ty brings his own unique ideas, observations, experiences, and expertise to the pages of our book. Thanks Ty.

I also owe a debt of gratitude to my wife, Elizabeth, for her endless support and encouragement and her invaluable services as proofreader of the book. Thanks, Liz.

~ John Webster ~

Introduction

By John Webster with Ty F. Webster

During my school days long ago, I learned about a man named Dr. Albert Schweitzer. I discovered who he was and what he was doing. As time passed I proceeded to forget most of this information. However, one detail that stayed with me over the years was that Schweitzer was a doctor in Africa who would let ants crawl across his desk and not kill them. In fact, he would sometimes actually encourage the ants by leaving a few cookie crumbs lying around so he could watch them carry the crumbs back to their homes.

This remembrance intrigued and haunted me through the years when ants crossed my own desk or other places in the houses I have lived in. Why would anyone *not* want to kill an ant that was invading his or her territory?

In recent years I have become re-acquainted with the life, work, and words of Albert Schweitzer. I have read a number of books by and about him and given much thought to his message. As a result, I have come to personally experience the attitude of life that enabled Dr. Schweitzer to be so kind to ants and all other creatures—human and non-human alike.

Two of the concepts in Dr. Schweitzer's ethic have particularly inspired me:

1.) The Will to Live.
2.) Reverence for Life.

One of the unique aspects of Schweitzer's ethic is that it strives for the well-being not only of human life, but of all life. He said that the most immediate fact of man's consciousness is the assertion: "I am life which wills to live, in the midst of life which wills to live." In other words, just as I possess the will to live, so too does every other form of life. This assertion lays the foundation for the idea of "Reverence for Life." When we become aware of the fact that all life possesses the same desire and right to live as we have, we then realize that we should do everything within our power to assist and enhance all life everywhere at all times. In short, we come to realize that we should have reverence for *all* that lives.

I feel that Dr. Schweitzer's personal history and message are very inspirational and am firm in my conviction that they have the power to transform the world and make it a better place. I also feel that many people today have never heard of Dr. Schweitzer or are like I was and remember only a small part of his story. Therefore, I felt a challenge to write a book that would introduce (or re-introduce, as the case may be) Dr. Schweitzer's message to a wider audience and apply it to our modern times. Because of what his message has meant to me, I have dedicated this book to Dr. Schweitzer and his ethic of Reverence for Life, which—as you might guess from the title—will be the book's central theme.

The will to live filled with reverence for life is something we all need. The purpose of this book is to urge us to think about our world and about what we can do to incorporate Dr. Schweitzer's ethic into our everyday existence in order to help make it a better place for all that lives.

This is a very urgent and important task for all of us. Our fragmented world is badly in need of people who are willing to think for themselves and give it some tender loving care. During the last 100 years, our world has been torn and devastated as it struggled through the terror and destruction caused by two world wars, a cold war, a number of smaller very hot wars and now a seemingly endless war on terrorism. We now need to move quickly toward a world beyond war, where the concept of non-violence lies at the center of our being. Our natural world, too, has been abused and degraded horribly in recent times. Our continued existence depends on our successful transformation to a universal ethic of Reverence for All Life.

This transformation can only happen with the efforts of individuals like you and me. All too often, people allow organized groups such as clubs, churches, corporations, or especially governments, to tell them what to believe and what to do. Governments should be serving all the people of the world and not just some of the people within their own boundaries. It is time for individuals to think for themselves and help transform our societies into entities that serve the well-being of all that live. To quote Dr. Schweitzer: "Remain men in possession of your own souls! Do not become human things which have offered hospitality to souls which conform to the will of the masses and beat in time with it." In other words, dare to be different and stand up for what you believe in. Only in this manner can true change come about.

In this book the authors will use Dr. Schweitzer's ideas to suggest that we all have many partners, that in fact everything that lives is our partner in this great process of creation. The theme might be stated as follows: "I am your partner. You are my partner. The birds and the trees, the flowers and the bees are our partners. Everyone who lives, everything that lives is our partner." As we walk through the world filled with our partners, their lives stream like a flood into our own. We become one with all that lives. In short, we attain Reverence for All Life. This feeling of oneness can bring us great joy. But it also presents a great challenge to dedicate our lives to becoming living examples of this ethic in order to benefit all life.

In following pages we will share what the life and thought of Albert Schweitzer has meant to us with the hope that it might also be meaningful to you. We will start with a short biography of Dr. Schweitzer's amazing and inspirational life, followed by a brief summary of the profound message he brought to the world. We will then present, in our own words, some ideas about how we feel Schweitzer's message applies to our modern world. We will also present viewpoints from several other people whose ideas mesh with this message.

In particular, we will present the message of Dennis J. Kucinich, a Congressman from Ohio who was a candidate for the Democratic Presidential nomination in 2004. Kucinich is one of the woefully few people active in the political arena of today's world who dares to be different and stand up for what he believes. His life's story and message have the spirit and power to enable us, our nation, and our world to move toward a still more excellent way that is in tune with the concepts of Reverence for All Life.

xi

His willingness to represent us in Congress, and perhaps one day in the White House, deserves our attention and consideration. We would like to present a vision of the Kucinich message of peace and hope by including several of his speeches in this book. We will end the book with a call to action, urging all readers to do everything possible to implement the concepts of Reverence for Life into their own lives. We will urge everyone to contemplate this meaningful, challenging ethic, and we will supply some concrete suggestions of ways that we all can work together to bring about a better world. Our hope is that you will be inspired to follow some of our suggestions and do what you can to bring about a more peaceful, caring world. We invite you to explore with us what Dr. Schweitzer's ethic means for our daily existence as men and women who can have reverence for life and know that *all life* has the same will to live that we do. We hope you will join us in what we feel will be an exciting adventure in striving for and participating in the "Realm of Reverence."

A Song of Reverence

By John Webster

Deep respect, love and wonder, for all that lives.
Deep respect, love and awe, for all of life.
I am life which wills to live, in the midst of life which wills to live.
Think of it! Think of it!
You are life which wills to live, in the midst of life which wills to
live.
Think of it! Think of it!
We all are life which wills to live, in the midst of life which wills
to live.
Think of it! Think of it!
We are one! We are one!
We are one in relationships.
We are one with the universe.
We are one in our origins.
We are one in our destinies.
We are one! We are one!
It is good to help all life.
It is bad to hinder life.
The will-to-live filled with **Reverence for Life** is what we need.
Who is my partner? You are my partner.
Who is your partner? I am your partner.
Everyone who lives, everything that lives is our partner.
The birds and the trees, the flowers and the bees are our partners.
The will-to-live filled with **Reverence for Life** is what we need.
Deep respect, love and wonder, for all that lives.
Deep respect, love and awe, for all of life.
We are one! We are one!

The Village of Günsbach

1

Dr. Albert Schweitzer:
A Life of Reverence

By John Webster and Ty F. Webster

Albert Schweitzer was born on January 14, 1875, in Kaysersberg, a small village in a region of Europe known as Alsace. This region of small towns and pastoral countryside runs from the crest of the Vosges Mountains on the west, to the shore of the Rhine River at the border of Germany and France on the east. Due to its strategic location, the region has been the site of many bloody battles over the years. It has belonged alternately to the two countries, depending on the outcome of the most recent conflict. This fact would be cause for great strife in Schweitzer's personal history, and is the reason that, although Alsace is today part of France, Schweitzer was born a German citizen.

When Albert was several months old, his father, Louis—a Protestant pastor—and mother, Adele—the daughter of a pastor—moved the Schweitzer family to Günsbach, a small village in Alsace's Münster Valley, where houses are clustered around the picturesque, centralized church like chicks around a mother hen. Louis was pastor at the Günsbach church for the next fifty years, until his death in 1925. It was only natural, then, that Albert would grow up in and around the church, and that the church would become a vital and meaningful part of his life.

Günsbach lies in close proximity to the surrounding countryside with its abundant examples of nature's beauty: vineyards, forests, and pastures full of farm animals. It is a short walk to the valley or hillsides, and Albert enjoyed being so close to the mysteries of nature and the changing of the seasons. At a young age he gained strong feelings of respect for and kinship with all the various life forms that he encountered. It was here that the seeds of his great philosophies were planted, as evidenced by a wonderful prayer that he created before he was even able to read and write.

Albert did not understand why, during bedtime prayers with his mother, they prayed only for humans. The young lad thought it would only be right to add a prayer for all of God's creatures, and—as Schweitzer recounted in an autobiographical account of his formative years, *Memoirs of Childhood and Youth*—he did just that:

It was quite incomprehensible to me...why in my evening prayers I should pray for human beings only. So when my mother had prayed with me and had kissed me goodnight, I used to add silently a prayer that I had composed myself for all living creatures. It ran thus: 'O, heavenly Father, protect and bless all things that have breath; guard them from all evil, and let them sleep in peace.'(1)

The Early Years

Schweitzer was privileged to grow up in a progressive, open-minded family. He was openly exposed to information and was free to question ideas and use reason in the formation of his own ideas. His mother, Adele, had a passion—inherited from her father and passed on to her children—for keeping up with world events and new information. It is said that she was always annoyed when the daily newspaper was not available.

Another influence on the young Schweitzer was an openness in the Günsbach church, symbolized by the fact that the same building was used for both Catholic and Protestant services. This practice had been going on for many years, and (somewhat to the amazement of this retired American pastor) is still happening today.

Albert proved to be a prodigy in the field of music. His father and maternal grandfather were both able to improvise magnificently at the piano and organ; Albert inherited this ability and shared his gift with listeners throughout his life. He was only five years old when his father began giving him piano lessons. At age eight—his feet barely able to reach the pedals—he began to

2

play the organ. At nine he was proficient enough to take the place of the organist for a service at the Günsbach church. When Albert reached school age, he began attending Günsbach's village school. He was not a very inspired student and not very happy about going to school, because it limited the time that he could spend out-of-doors enjoying the beauties of the natural world. He spent much of his time in school daydreaming about being a swineherd, sailor, or outdoor adventurer.

At age nine, Albert entered the "Realschule," or secondary school, at Münster, two miles from Günsbach. His favorite part of the day was the walk to and from school. Although most of the students from Günsbach would take the lower, more direct route along the road between the towns, Albert took the path over the hills so he could be alone to enjoy the changing seasons. He long remembered this as one of the happiest years of his youth because of the daily opportunity it afforded him to be so close to nature.

At about this same time, an event took place that made a deep and lasting impression on Albert. On a Sunday morning toward the end of Lent, a friend suggested taking slingshots up the hill outside of Günsbach to shoot birds. Albert did not like the idea but went along for fear that he would be laughed at if he did not.

The two soon spotted a leafless tree with a number of birds singing beautifully in its branches, oblivious to the encroaching hunters. The friend stooped down, loaded a stone in his sling and nodded at Albert to do the same. Schweitzer felt a terrible twinge of conscience; but for fear of disappointing his friend, he took aim, intending to shoot when his companion did. Schweitzer was not to become a killer of birds, however. As recounted in *Memoirs:*

At that very moment the church bells began to ring, mingling their music with the songs of the birds and the sunshine. It was the Warning-bell, which began half an hour before the regular peal-ringing, and for me it was a voice from heaven. I shooed the birds away, so that they flew where they were safe from my companion's catapult, and then I fled home. And ever since then, when the Passiontide bells ring out to the leafless trees and the sunshine, I reflect with a rush of grateful

3

emotion how on that day their music drove deep into my heart the commandment: 'Thou shalt not kill.'(2)

Secondary School at Mulhouse

In the autumn of 1885, when Albert was ten, he entered the "Gymnasium" at Mulhouse to continue his secondary education. He lived with his Uncle Louis and Aunt Sophie, who offered to give him free room and board. This was an unhappy change for Albert for several reasons. Mulhouse was an industrial city and lacked the beauty and proximity to nature that he so loved. Also, his aunt and uncle—who were elderly and never had children of their own—established strict rules for Albert's daily life, and he dearly missed the freedom of his home life in Günsbach. Eventually, though, Schweitzer was able to appreciate his relatives' efforts. As he stated in *Memoirs,* "How great the benefit was which Uncle Louis and Aunt Sophie conferred upon me by thus taking me in I only realized later; at first I was conscious only of the strictness of the discipline under which I came."(3)

Albert's grades during his first years at Mulhouse were a cause of constant concern for his parents. The boy continued to daydream in class and was not very attentive. His aunt constantly had to drag Albert to the piano to practice. At times he was amazed that his parents did not give up and bring him home.

When he was fourteen, however, the young student experienced some rather dramatic events that awakened his will to learn and desire to excel. The first of these related to a new schoolteacher, Dr. Wehmann. Albert quickly noticed, through the mist of his dreaminess, that this new teacher always had every lesson carefully prepared and handed back all of the homework papers right on schedule. As told in *Memoirs,* Schweitzer was duly impressed:

> Experience of this self-disciplined activity had a distinct effect upon me. I should have been ashamed to incur [Dr. Wehmann's] displeasure, and he became my model. Three months later when my form, the Quarta, got its Easter report, I was one of the better scholars,

although my Christmas report had been so bad that my mother had gone about the whole of the Christmas holidays with eyes that were red from crying. (4)

The young Schweitzer's will to learn, question, explore, make discoveries, and excel were awakened and would never again be silenced during his long life.

Schweitzer's musical interest experienced an epiphany at about the same time. Like many young music students, he found it difficult to truly express himself through music. While at Gymnasium, Albert would often come to his music lessons ill-prepared because he had spent his practice time improvising or sight-reading a number that had caught his fancy. .

One day his music teacher, Eugene Munch, assigned Albert a song by the German composer Felix Mendelssohn, saying: "Really you don't deserve to have such wonderful music given to you to play. I suppose you'll spoil this like everything else. If a boy has no feeling, I certainly can't give him any." Albert was hurt but decided that he would prove his teacher wrong. For once he practiced all week with great care. At the next lesson he gave his teacher a pleasant surprise by playing the assigned song with skill and feeling. From then on, teacher and student were colleagues in the world of music.(5)

Soon Schweitzer began organ lessons at a local church where Eugene Munch was organist. By the age of sixteen, Albert was filling in for his teacher at services. Eugene Munch also imbued Albert with an enthusiasm for the music of German organist and composer Johann Sebastian Bach, and Schweitzer later rose to great heights in the music world as a Bach specialist, playing Bach's organ music throughout Europe and authoring several volumes of books on the music and history of Bach.

Strasbourg University and a New Life Plan

In 1893 Schweitzer graduated from the Mulhouse Gymnasium and began his studies in philosophy and theology at

5

the University of Strasbourg. His academic and musical talents continued to thrive. He excelled as a student under the tutelage of the university's liberal faculty, and he made frequent trips to Paris to receive instruction from Charles Marie Widor, the most famous organist in France at that time. Widor recounted his initial interaction with Schweitzer in the preface to the German edition of Schweitzer's first volume of books about Bach:

> In the autumn of 1893 a young Alsatian presented himself to me and asked if he could play something on the organ to me. 'Play what?' I asked. 'Bach, of course,' was his reply.
>
> In the following years he returned regularly for longer or shorter periods, in order to 'habilitate' himself—as they used to say in Bach's day—in organ playing under my guidance.(6)

At the age of twenty-one, Schweitzer created a new plan for his life path. He had often given much thought to ideas that had long troubled him: how good life was for him and how very bad it was for many other people. Schweitzer recounted the dilemma in his autobiography, *Out of My Life And Thought*:

> It struck me as inconceivable that I should be allowed to lead such a happy life while I saw so many people around me struggling with sorrow and suffering…At the university, enjoying the good fortune of studying and even getting some results in scholarship and the arts, I could not help but think continually of others who were denied that good fortune by their material circumstances or their health.(7)

On one occasion in particular, the problem especially troubled Schweitzer, and consequently, he made a very important decision. As told in *Life and Thought*:

> One brilliant summer morning at Günsbach during the Whitsuntide holidays—it was in 1896—as I awoke, the thought came to me that I must not accept this good fortune as a matter of course, but must give something in return.
> While outside the birds sang I reflected on this thought, and before I had gotten up I came to the conclusion that until I was thirty I

6

could consider myself justified in devoting myself to scholarship and the arts, but after that I would devote myself directly to serving humanity. I had already tried many times to find the meaning that lay hidden in the saying of Jesus: 'Whosoever would save his life shall lose it, and whosoever shall lose his life for My sake and the Gospels shall save it.' Now I had found the answer. I could now add outward to inward happiness. What the character of my future activities would be was not yet clear to me. I left it to chance to guide me. Only one thing was certain, that it must be direct human service...(8)

With this decision made and tucked away in his own mind, Schweitzer went on with his studies. What he managed to accomplish between the ages of twenty-one and thirty is incredible to think about, and perhaps more than even he dreamed was possible. Following is a summary of only a portion of what Schweitzer did in those years:

- Earned the degree of licentiate in Theology (an academic degree between bachelor and doctor).
- Was ordained and served as a minister at the St. Nicholas Church in Strasbourg.
- Earned the doctorate of philosophy degree at Strasbourg University.
- Was appointed principal of St. Thomas theological seminary in Strasbourg and lectured in theology at Strasbourg University.
- Spent time in Paris and Berlin studying organ and philosophy.
- Worked on his books, including *The Mystery of the Kingdom of God, The Quest of the Historical Jesus*, a book on Bach, and others.
- Was an organist for many different events.
- Became an expert on the construction of organs and spent many hours trying to save old church organs, as he found them to have a much better tone than the newer ones.

How was it possible for one man to do so much? In large part it was due to the fact that Schweitzer could function with less sleep than most people. Often he would get only a few hours of sleep a night. He knew how to relax and sleep as he traveled on trains and was refreshed after short naps he would grab whenever the opportunity presented itself. When counseling students at the seminary, he would sometimes say, "I am tired, come back in twenty minutes." He would take a short nap in his office and be refreshed and ready to continue his day.

Marriage and a New Calling: Doctor of Medicine

While racking up such an incredible array of accomplishments throughout his twenties, Schweitzer never forgot his vow. At the age of thirty he would devote his life to the direct service of mankind. But what form would his service take? As he neared thirty, he pondered a number of different options, but none seemed the right one.

Then one evening in the autumn of 1904 he found on his desk a magazine in which the Paris Missionary Society reported its monthly activities. An acquaintance of his had placed it there, knowing that Albert was interested in the society. As he set the magazine aside to begin his work, Schweitzer mechanically opened it. As he did so, an article titled "The needs of the Congo Mission" caught his eye. The article contained a complaint that the Mission lacked sufficient workers to carry on its work in the Gabon, the northern province of the Congo Colony. It concluded with the words, "Men and women who can reply simply to the Master's call, 'Lord, I am coming,' those are the people whom the church needs." After finishing the article, Schweitzer quietly began his work with the knowledge that his search was over.(9)

On Schweitzer's thirtieth birthday, January 14, 1905, he continued to ponder his plan. He knew that the Missionary Society desperately needed medical help. If he could apply as a doctor of medicine, surely he would be accepted by the society. The idea seemed practical, except that he had never studied medicine. He was thirty years old. How long would it take to learn to be a doctor? Could he do it, starting so late in life? Such were the concerns that he had to consider. By the end of the day, he had made his decision. He would step down from the professorial ranks and become a student again at the start of the next university year, when the medical course began, and in due time offer his services as a doctor to the Paris Missionary Society.

For another nine months he worked secretly on his plans, continuing his many tasks as before, sharing his plans with no one except one special friend. Although he never revealed the identity of this person, it is now believed that it was his future wife, Helene Bresslau. The daughter of a Strasbourg historian, Helene was a special person. Like Schweitzer, she had decided to devote her life to social service. She once helped to found and operate a home for unwed mothers—something that "nice, young women" of that day did not tend to do.

Albert and Helene developed a special and somewhat secret relationship during the ten years leading up to 1912. As they were living in different locations during much of that time, much of their communication was through letters. A number of these were found many years later by their daughter and published, giving the world a greater awareness of the depth of their relationship. Helene was willing to share Albert's African adventure, and she acquired a nursing degree in order to assist Albert in his efforts. The two were married on June 18, 1912.

On October 13, 1905, Schweitzer officially disclosed his plan to the other important people in his life. Into a Paris mailbox he dropped letters that would inform his parents and some select acquaintances about his intention to begin studies as a medical student at the beginning of the winter term in order to become a doctor and subsequently use his medical skills to assist natives in equatorial Africa.

From 1905 to 1912 Schweitzer studied medicine while continuing many other activities. He continued to preach at St. Nicholas Church and to lecture at the University. And he was more active than ever playing the organ at special events, as he needed money to continue his studies. He wanted to complete all of his unfinished projects before he left for Africa. In February of 1913, having completed his full-year medical internship and finished his thesis, Schweitzer received the degree of Doctor of Medicine from Strasbourg University.

Off to Africa

On the afternoon of Good Friday, 1913, Albert and Helene Schweitzer left Günsbach by train and began their long journey to Africa. They traveled to Bordeaux, France, where they set sail aboard the steamship *Europe,* eventually reaching their destination, a small village called Lambarene in the jungle along the Ogowe River in equatorial Africa.

The Schweitzers immediately had their work cut out for them. There were not yet any medical buildings for them to use; but word of their arrival spread quickly, and a number of patients gathered under the trees seeking treatment for various ailments.

As soon as possible, hospital and support buildings were built. In addition to his medical duties, Albert oversaw and assisted in the construction of the buildings. Word spread far and wide about the new facility at Lambarene, and the Schweitzers had their hands very full. During their first nine months in Africa, Albert and Helene treated nearly 2,000 patients. The chief ailments they battled were malaria, leprosy, sleeping sickness, dysentery, and phagedenic ulcers (skin sores).(10)

An Ethical Dilemma

Dr. Schweitzer was always a deep thinker and a man of many pursuits. Although he devoted much time attending to his patients and maintaining and improving the hospital facilities at Lambarene, he also spent a lot of time following more philosophical pursuits: thinking about such weighty issues as modern civilization and the role of humans in the modern world.

Much to his dismay, Schweitzer soon had more than ample time to devote to these ideas. On August 5, 1914, news came to Lambarene that war had broken out in Europe. That very evening, the Schweitzers were informed that, because they were German citizens working in a French colony, they were prisoners of war. They were placed under house arrest and not allowed to treat any patients.

To pass the time during his arrest, Albert deeply contemplated the problems of modern civilization. As early as his first years at Strasbourg, he had begun to feel misgivings about the generally accepted opinion that mankind is constantly progressing. He could not ignore the fact that in many cases it did not seem so. He could not understand, for instance, why public opinion did not reject ideas that were largely inhumane but instead often accepted them and approved of inhumane courses of action taken by their national governments.

He furthered this line of thought during the days of his house arrest and continued it after the end of November, when the Schweitzers were released from their internment and again allowed to tend to the sick. Albert pondered the downfall of civilization and wondered what might put humankind back on the road to progress. He concluded that the essential nature of civilization is ultimately ethical. He felt that there must be a guiding principle that would expound this view; but what could it be?

Reverence for Life

In the summer of 1915 Dr. Schweitzer and Helene spent some time in Port-Gentil on Africa's Atlantic coast because Mrs. Schweitzer's health was suffering from the stresses of the African jungle climate. In September they received word that the wife of a Swiss missionary had fallen ill 120 miles inland up the Ogowe River and needed Dr. Schweitzer's medical attention. The only means of transportation Schweitzer could find was a small steamer boat towing a barge full of cargo. Schweitzer was still very engrossed in thinking about a philosophical worldview of civilization. He resolved to devote the entire trip to contemplation of the problem of how a culture could be created that possessed a greater moral depth and energy than the current one. In *Life and Thought*, Schweitzer described the trip and his state of mind:

> While in this mental state I had to take a long journey on the river…Slowly we crept upstream, laboriously navigating—it was the dry season—between the sandbanks. Lost in thought I sat on the deck of the barge, struggling to find the elementary and universal concept of the ethical that I had not discovered in any philosophy. I covered sheet after sheet with disconnected sentences merely to concentrate on the problem. Two days passed. Late on the third day, at the very moment when, at sunset, we were making our way through a herd of hippopotamuses, there flashed upon my mind, unforeseen and unsought, the phrase "reverence for life." The iron door had yielded. The path in the thicket had become visible. Now I had found my way to the principle in which affirmation of the world and ethics are joined together!(11)

Schweitzer had his answer and the foundation for a novel, compassionate ethic. It became obvious to him that the only hope of attaining a level of greater good in society was by means of Reverence for Life: developing a deep-seated respect for *all* living things. In "Albert Schweitzer Speaks Out," an article published in the *World Book Year Book of 1964*, he elaborated on the significance of his discovery:

…the phrase 'Reverence for Life' struck me like a flash. As far as I knew it was a phrase I had never heard nor ever read. I realized at once that it carried within itself the solution to the problem that had been torturing me. Now I knew that a system of values which concerns itself only with our relationship to other people is incomplete and therefore lacking in power for good. Only by means of reverence for life can we establish a spiritual and humane relationship with both people and all living creatures within our reach. Only in this fashion can we avoid harming others, and, within the limits of our capacity, go to their aid whenever they need us.(12)

The discovery would affect Schweitzer for the rest of his life (and perhaps will influence your life, as it has ours). As the months and years went by, Schweitzer continued to develop and communicate the ethic of Reverence for Life in the books he wrote, the sermons he preached, and the very example he set in the way he lived his life.

As fate would have it, that same month—September 1915—a huge battle raged between French and German troops in Schweitzer's Alsatian homeland. Some 30,000 men died, and the military situation remained unchanged. How desperately the world then needed, and still needs, the spirit of Reverence for Life!

Return to Europe

The War continued to have a direct and negative effect on the Schweitzers' lives. In September of 1917, Albert and Helene were taken to Europe and detained in prisoner-of-war camps. While in the camps, Albert developed a severe case of dysentery, which plagued him for many months. He fully recovered only after several surgeries and much suffering.

Health was not his only problem. When the war ended in 1918 (and the Schweitzer's became French subjects, as Alsace now belonged to France) Albert was faced with a dire situation. He had amassed great debts in building the hospital in Africa and had no means of repaying them. The situation in his homeland had changed dramatically because of the war, and his reputation as a noted scholar, author, and musician was useless. His dream of returning to Africa and reestablishing his hospital seemed impossible.

1919 was perhaps the most quiet and unexciting year in Schweitzer's entire adult life. He worked at the hospital and church in Strasbourg, but in his seclusion he felt "rather like a coin that has rolled under a piece of furniture and has been forgotten there."(13) His body suffered from the lingering effects of an internal abscess from his bout with dysentery, and his spirit suffered from a deep, post-war depression. A lone bright spot occurred on January 14, 1919—Albert's forty-fourth birthday—when Helene bore him a daughter, whom they named Rhena. Schweitzer's fortunes began to turn at the end of the year.

A few days before Christmas, he received an invitation from the Archbishop of Sweden, Nathan Soderblom, to deliver lectures at the University of Upsala after Easter the following year. This proved to be just the change of scenery that Schweitzer needed to recover his health and vision for the future. For the next several years, he traveled in countries such as Switzerland, Sweden, Denmark, and England, giving lectures and concerts and working on his book, *The Philosophy of Civilization*, which was published in 1923. Doing so allowed Schweitzer to earn enough money to pay off his debts and realize that his dream of returning to Africa was alive.

Return to Lambarene

On February 21, 1924, Dr. Schweitzer departed Bordeaux for his return trip to Africa. This time he made the journey without his wife. Helene stayed behind in the Black Forest area of Germany and cared for Rhena.

For the next three years, Schweitzer was hard at work in Africa. He began to rebuild the hospital buildings, which had decayed and collapsed during the seven years of his absence, tending to the medical needs of the natives all the while. After a year of rebuilding, Schweitzer realized it would be best to move the hospital to a larger site several miles up river, where there would be room for an isolation ward for infectious cases and more accommodations for mental patients. On January 21, 1927, the transfer of patients to the new hospital began. By the middle of the year, the new facility was able to accommodate 200 patients and the friends and family that accompanied them.

Schweitzer spent most of 1927-1929 back in Europe, giving lectures and organ recitals. When he was not traveling, he lived with his wife and daughter in Königsfeld, Germany, or at Strasbourg. Because his father had died in 1925, Albert no longer had a place in Günsbach to call home. So after being awarded the

Goethe Prize by the city of Frankfurt, Germany, in 1928, he used the award money to build a house in Günsbach. It would be his European home for the rest of his life. Between 1929 and 1939, Dr. Schweitzer continued to enlarge the facility at Lambarene. Throughout the process, his philosophy of Reverence for Life guided him and helped him to create a truly unique medical facility. In reality, the place became more like an African village with a clinic than a traditional hospital. In tending to the sick, Schweitzer and his medical assistants had a unique approach that included the patients' families. When invalids came to the village, often their whole family accompanied them. Lodging was made available for the families, who then assisted in the care of their sick loved ones.

In a *Life* magazine article published in 1965, Schweitzer explained the policy. "Here we permit the families to come and stay with the patients," he said. "This lessens the shock of the people who come from deep in the jungle, and their convalescence is better. Furthermore, the family serves as nurse and provides meals. Thus, we can care for many more patients than would be possible otherwise."(14) Schweitzer's hospital was not a place of sickness and despair, but a healing ground, where the circle of life and death was integrated as a complete whole.

And, true to his philosophy, the doctor did not limit his compassion and assistance to humans. He was famous for tending to injured or orphaned animals. Word spread of his practices, and natives began to bring him animals of all kinds. They always expected some form of payment for their efforts. Although this troubled Schweitzer somewhat, he would always pay out of fear that if he did not, the natives would take the animals away to a lesser fate. Lambarene became home to quite a variety of animals such as goats, chickens, turkeys, chimpanzees, monkeys, antelope, dogs, cats, wild pigs, pelicans (including Parsifal, the pet pelican that guarded Schweitzer's hut for many years), and gorillas—in which Schweitzer was particularly interested. Once a visitor to the hospital exclaimed, "Why, this is a regular zoo." The Doctor's response was, "Yes, and I am the head gorilla."

Fame

Dr. Schweitzer was responsible for raising the revenue necessary to finance the hospital complex, as no particular organization or company funded it. Therefore, he made a number of trips back and forth to Europe, where he could raise money for the hospital by lecturing and playing the organ. He always traveled by boat, even after airplanes began to land regularly at Lambarene, because these journeys afforded him much of his only free time. He would use the time on the boat trips to answer some of the many letters that he received.

When World War II started, Schweitzer could no longer travel to Europe to raise funds. For a while it looked as though the hospital was in danger of closing. Fortunately, word of Dr. Schweitzer's incredible project was spreading far and wide, and gifts of money and medical supplies began to arrive from the United States. The hospital at Lambarene could continue to serve the local people.

After the war, Schweitzer's popularity and fame grew by leaps and bounds. *Life* magazine ran a major article on October 6, 1947, titled, "The Greatest Man in the World—that is what some people call Albert Schweitzer, jungle philosopher."

In the summer of 1949 Dr. Schweitzer made his only visit to the United States. He traveled to Aspen, Colorado, to speak at the Institute for Humanistic Studies on the occasion of the bicentenary of German author Johann Goethe's birth. While he was in the States, his picture appeared on the cover of *Time* magazine and articles about him ran in a number of other publications.

As his fame spread, Schweitzer was approached by numerous moviemakers and drug companies offering him great profit to make films about his life or use his name in advertisements. He could easily have raised enough money to build a large, modern hospital at Lambarene. To every offer he responded with a resounding "No!"

In his excellent book, *Albert Schweitzer: A Biography*, James Brabazon reasoned that the doctor knew this money would bring with it a flood of western doctors who would force their spartan clinical approach to medicine on the natives at Lambarene: "The Africans would have been separated from their families, forced to eat unfamiliar food cooked by strangers, and imprisoned in impersonal wards functionally designed not for living in but only for being ill in...His creation was not just a hospital, which could be improved by spending money, but a way of life."(15)

Dr. Schweitzer was recognized for his great accomplishments at Lambarene and for his efforts to spread his message of peace and reverence for life throughout the world when he was awarded the Nobel Peace Prize for the year of 1952. Schweitzer announced that the prize money, about $36,000, would be put toward the expenses of constructing a hospital especially for the treatment of leprosy patients at Lambarene. On November 4, 1954, Schweitzer went to Oslo to deliver his Nobel Peace Prize address, "The Problem of Peace in the World Today."

The Later Years

Although Schweitzer spent much of his later life in the African jungle, he always kept abreast of world events and did whatever he could to spread his message. Even after turning 80 years of age, he did not relent in his efforts. Throughout the last ten years of his life, he spoke out concerning the horrors of the nuclear arms race and the testing of nuclear weapons. He wrote letters to world leaders and wrote radio addresses that were broadcast around the world. Many people listened, and worldwide public opinion slowly started to support a ban on the testing of nuclear weapons. Sadly, nuclear weapons, testing, and waste are still very much a problem in today's world. We, like Dr. Schweitzer, must speak out to help stop this terrible noose around our necks from choking us and all of creation.

Albert Schweitzer died in Lambarene on September 4, 1965, at the age of 90. He was buried on the hospital grounds beside his wife, Helene, who had died in 1957. Several weeks before his death, Dr. Schweitzer announced that his daughter Rhena would be responsible for the hospital after his passing. Today, the Albert Schweitzer Hospital at Lambarene, in what is now the independent African nation of Gabon, is busier than ever. Tens of thousands of patients make use of the hospital's services annually. Today's hospital is larger and more modern than in Dr. Schweitzer's day, but the spirit of the "Old Doctor" and his message of "Reverence for Life" are still very much alive there.

"No one has ever come back from the other world," Schweitzer once said. "I can't console you, but one thing I can tell you, as long as my ideals are alive I will be alive."(16) It is up to us, all of us who have heard and realized the importance of the message of Reverence for Life, to be sure that Dr. Albert Schweitzer and his ideals remain a vibrant part of our world.

Notes

1.) Dr. Albert Schweitzer; *Memoirs of Childhood and Youth* (1963); p.47.
2.) Ibid. p. 47-48.   3.) Ibid. p.54-55.
4.) Ibid. p. 65.   5.) Ibid. p. 67.
6.) Schweitzer; *J.S. Bach: Volume I*; (1952); p. viii.
7.) Schweitzer; *Out of My Life and Thought* (1998); p.82.
8.) Ibid.   9.) Ibid. p. 85-86.
10.) Ibid. p. 137.   11.) Ibid. p.154-55.
12.) Schweitzer; "Albert Schweitzer Speaks Out," *World Book Yearbook of 1964*; p. 142.
13.) *Life and Thought*; p. 185.
14.) "The White Wizard's 90th: An Inquiring Visit to Dr. Schweitzer;" Hugh Moffet; *Life*; February 19, 1965; p. 92.
15.) James Brabazon; *Albert Schweitzer: A Biography* (2000); p. 413.
16.) Schweitzer; *The Words of Albert Schweitzer*; Selected by Norman Cousins; (1984); p. 69.

2

The Great Ethic

By John Webster and Ty F. Webster

"I can do no other than be reverent before everything that is called life. I can do no other than to have compassion for all that is called life. That is the beginning and the foundation of all ethics."
--Albert Schweitzer; A Place for Revelation: Sermons on Reverence for Life.

"Reverence for Life" is one of the most important messages in the history of language. Dr. Albert Schweitzer brought us the concept as a result of a flash of inspiration at sunset one day while on a boat journey up Africa's Ogowe River in September of 1915. Into his awareness came the phrase, "Ehrfurcht vor dem Leben," and suddenly he had the foundation for his great ethic. Schweitzer recorded the experience and his message in German. It comes to us through translation into English. In any language, it holds great significance for all of us.

In English language dictionaries—such as Webster's New World Dictionary, Second College Edition—the word "reverence" is defined as "a feeling or attitude of deep respect, love, and awe." So "Reverence for Life" is a feeling or attitude of deep respect, love and awe for every living being. It should not, however, be interpreted as an inactive feeling. Dr. Lachlan Forrow, president of The Albert Schweitzer Fellowship, has suggested the English translation does not quite capture the full weight of the German original: "For me, 'reverence' has too passive of a feeling, like the quietude of being in church, almost afraid to make a sound. My sense is that the German word 'Ehrfurcht' has a much more dynamic feel, and for Schweitzer the energy of what we call 'Reverence for Life' was clearly not a quiet thing at all."(1)

Dr. Edwin A. Schick, professor emeritus at Wartburg Theological Seminary in Dubuque, Iowa, makes a similar point:

> Something has been lost in translation. Reverence for Life isn't quite up to the German original, *Ehrfurcht vor dem Leben*. . . . 'Ehrfurcht' is more awesome than 'Reverence,' and 'vor dem Leben' is more direct and intimate than 'of life.' We stand in awe not of life <u>out there</u> but of life <u>right here in us, in front of us, and all around</u>. Being deeply respectful of that life and fearful of showing disrespect for any form of it, and finally feeling the inexpressible mystery of it all—this is Ehrfurcht vor dem Leben.(2)

There can be no doubt that Reverence for Life involves a dynamic reality that not only calls us to have respect, love, and awe for all that lives, but also energizes us to become caretakers of one another and of all life within our circle of influence. Indeed, what separates Schweitzer's ethic from most ethical systems throughout history is that while others have tended to apply only to human beings, his ethic also takes non-human life into consideration. Reverence for Life is an ethic to guide us not only in our relations with other humans, but in our relations with all that lives. In order to be more fully human, Schweitzer's ethic tells us, we must realize and act upon the will to love all that lives and continually work to create a more sustainable environment for all of the inhabitants, human and non-human, of our world.

Schweitzer was perfectly aware of his system's deviance from traditional ethics. In fact, the deviation was intentional. He viewed the inclusion of non-human life as a necessity for an ethical system. This is evident in a passage in his autobiography, *Out of My Life and Thought*:

> Until now the great weakness in all ethical systems has been that they dealt only with the relations of man to man. In reality, however, the question is, What is our attitude toward the universe and all that it supports? A man is ethical only when life as such is sacred to him—the life of plants and animals as well as that of his fellow men—and when he devotes himself to helping all life that is in need of help.(3)

The Will to Live...

Schweitzer based his ethic on the simple yet profound concept that all forms of life share one basic trait: the desire to survive. He would have us begin to conceptualize this idea by thinking about our own lives and realizing what lies at the heart of our own experience. He asserts that when we do so, we quickly become aware of our own desire for survival. He presented this view in an article in *Christendom* magazine titled, "The Ethics of Reverence for Life:"

...if we ask... 'What do I self-consciously know of myself, making abstractions of all else, from childhood to old age? To what do I always return?' we find the simple fact of consciousness is this, *I will to live* [Schweitzer's emphasis]. Through every stage of life, this is the one thing I know about myself. I do not say, 'I am life'; for life continues to be a mystery too great to understand. I only know that I cling to it. I fear its cessation—death. I dread its diminution—pain. I seek its enlargement—joy.(4)

...In the Midst of Will-to-Live

Having become aware of the basic idea of our own will-to-live—our personal drive to survive under any circumstance and the desire to maximize enjoyment in our own lives—the next step in Schweitzer's ethic is to extend our awareness to all other life forms. We should consider our fellow humans, each and every one, but we must also consider all the various creatures of the plant and animal kingdoms and come to view them all as extensions of the life force that exists within ourselves. Schweitzer asserts that just as we know that our own lives have value, so too, should we conclude that all other lives are valuable. In *Life and Thought*, he states his position:

The most immediate fact of man's consciousness is the assertion: 'I am life that wills to live, in the midst of life that wills to live,' and it is as will to live in the midst of will to live that man conceives himself during every moment that he spends meditating on himself and the world around him.

We can easily recognize and understand our own desire for survival. We do everything in our power to continue to live and to live well. We seek pleasure; we try to avoid pain. Schweitzer calls us to recognize that all living beings have the same goals, whether or not they possess the ability to tell us so. He continues his point in *Life and Thought* in this manner:

As my will to live includes an ardent desire to perpetuate life and for the mysterious exaltation of the will to live, which we call happiness, and while there is fear of destruction and of the mysterious damage of the will to live which we call pain, so too is this will to live in those around me, whether it expresses itself to me, or remains mute.(5)

In short, Schweitzer maintains that all life forms are intricately linked to one another, and he beseeches us to recognize this basic fact. In "Ethics," he explains the interconnectedness of all life forms:

The important thing is that we are part of life. We are born of other lives; we possess the capacities to bring still other lives into existence. In the same way, if we look into a microscope we see cell producing cell. So nature compels us to recognize the fact of mutual dependence, each life necessarily helping the other lives which are linked to it. In the very fibers of our being, we bear within ourselves the fact of the solidarity of life. Our recognition of it expands with thought. Seeing its presence in ourselves, we realize how closely we are linked with others of our kind. We might like to stop here, but we cannot. Life demands that we see through to the solidarity of all life which we can in any degree recognize as having some similarity to the life that is in us.(6)

Reverence for All Life

Schweitzer was very aware of the human tendency to view *Homo sapiens* as a superior and most important life form. But he did not agree with this practice and viewed it as a flaw that limits us from reaching our full potential for humanness: for compassion and fulfillment. He felt that mankind needed a wider-ranging ethic, an ethic of Reverence for Life. Returning to "Ethics" we find these words:

Ordinary ethics seeks to find limits within the sphere of human life and relationships. But the absolute ethics of the will-to-live must reverence every form of life, seeking so far as possible to refrain from destroying any life, regardless of its particular type. It says of no instance of life, 'This has no value.' It cannot make any such exceptions, for it is built upon reverence for life as such. It knows that the mystery of life is always too profound for us, and that its value is beyond our capacity to estimate. We happen to believe that man's life is more important than any other form of which we know. But we cannot prove any such comparison of value from what we know of the world's development.(7)

Schweitzer knew that his view would be perceived as unusual, but he was firm in his belief. In *Life And Thought*, he elaborated on the topic and explained the danger of elevating humans to a higher level of importance than other beings:

The ethic of Reverence for Life is judged particularly strange because it establishes no dividing-line between higher and lower, between more valuable and less valuable life. It has its reasons for this omission.

To undertake to establish universally valid distinctions of value between different kinds of life will end in judging them by the greater or lesser distance at which they stand from us human beings. Our own judgment is, however, a purely subjective criterion. Who among us knows what significance any other kind of life has in itself, and as a part of the universe?

From this distinction comes the view that there can be life which is worthless, which can be willfully destroyed. Then in the category of worthless life we classify various kinds of insects, or primitive peoples, according to circumstances.(8)

Schweitzer calls us to whole-heartedly examine our relationship to all that exists in nature, to conclude that we are inter-related with all that lives, and to deepen our respect for all life. In an article titled "Religion and Modern Civilization," published in *The Christian Century* magazine, Schweitzer wrote:

The deeper we look into nature, the more we recognize that it is full of life, and the more profoundly we know that all life is a secret and that we are united with all life that is in nature. Man can no longer live his life for himself alone. We must realize that all life is valuable and that we are united to all this life. From this knowledge comes our spiritual relationship to the universe.(9)

Putting the Ethic into Action

According to Schweitzer's ethic, once we have recognized that all life is valuable and has the same will-to-live as we do, we must subsequently take one additional, crucial step: put this recognition into action in our everyday lives. Because we know that all life shares our own inherent will-to-live, we must do everything in our power to sustain and encourage life in every form and everything in our power to avoid harming any life form. We should live our lives—at every moment, in everything we do— with an attitude of Reverence for Life. Schweitzer's ethic calls us to treat all that lives with the care and respect that we want for ourselves. In "Ethics" Schweitzer says:

What shall be my attitude toward other life? It can only be of a piece with my attitude towards my own life. If I am a thinking being, I must regard other life than my own with equal reverence. For I shall know that it longs for fullness and development as deeply as I do myself. Therefore, I see that evil is what annihilates, hampers, or hinders life. And this holds good whether I regard it physically or spiritually. Goodness, by the same token, is the saving or helping of life, the enabling of whatever life I can influence to attain its highest development.(10)

It is not enough merely to hold the belief. We must act on that belief. We must, according to Schweitzer's ethic, incorporate our knowledge into our every-day existence and act accordingly.

24

We must use our spiritual relationship with the world around us as a guide and do everything within our power to assist all living beings whenever possible. In a sermon preached at St. Nicholas Church in Strasbourg on February 23, 1919, Schweitzer made the following statement: "...the presupposition of morality is to share everything that goes on around us, not only in human life but in the life of all creatures. This awareness forces us to do all within our power for the preservation and advancement of life."(11)

By acknowledging and sharing the wills-to-live of other beings, Schweitzer tells us, we give our own lives more value. In *Life and Thought*, he wrote: "Affirmation of life is the spiritual act by which man ceases to live thoughtlessly and begins to devote himself to his life with reverence in order to give it true value. To affirm life is to deepen, to make more inward, and to exalt the will to live."(12)

Will to Live Divided Against Itself

Schweitzer knew full well, however, that it is impossible to preserve life in every case at all times. He was profoundly aware of the true nature of existence: the undeniable fact that life continues to live and thrive at the expense of other life. In *Life and Thought* he says: "The world, however, offers us the horrible drama of will to live divided against itself. One existence holds its own at the cost of another."(13) But he subsequently points out that humans are the only creatures able to become aware of and assist in the will-to-live of other life forms. He acknowledges the reality that we cannot live without harming some life sometimes, but he compels us to do all within our power to limit the harming, and promote the benefit, of all life whenever possible. It is in this manner that we separate ourselves from the lower life forms and become more truly human. The passage from *Life and Thought* continues:

Only in the thinking man has the will to live become conscious of other wills to live and desirous of solidarity with them. This solidarity, however, he cannot completely bring about, because man is subject to the puzzling and horrible law of being obliged to live at the cost of other life and to incur again and again the guilt of destroying and injuring life. But as an ethical being he strives to escape whenever possible from this necessity, and as one who has become knowing and merciful, he tries to end this division of the will to live insofar as it is in his power. He aspires to prove his humanity and to release others from their sufferings.(14)

"...Never From Thoughtlessness."

An article published in *Life* magazine in 1965 summarized Schweitzer's view in this fashion: "He is in favor of 'nonkilling' and 'nonharming,' but he also goes to great pains to point out that there are times when, bowing to the laws of necessity, you must kill, sometimes even making the grand decision as to what will be killed and what saved."(15)

According to Schweitzer, these decisions should never be taken lightly. They must always be made in accordance with the ethic. In *Life and Thought* Schweitzer expressed the view with these words:

Standing, as all living beings are, before this dilemma of the will to live, man is constantly forced to preserve his own life and life in general only at the cost of other life. If he has been touched by the ethic of Reverence for Life, he injures and destroys life only under a necessity he cannot avoid and never from thoughtlessness.(16)

In every case when it becomes necessary to make a choice that for some being will be a life-or-death decision, we must take full responsibility for our actions. Elsewhere in *Life and Thought* Schweitzer makes the following statement:

Man makes distinctions only as each case comes before him, and under the pressure of necessity, as for example, when it falls to him to decide which of two lives he must sacrifice in order to preserve the other. But all through this series of decisions he is conscious of acting on subjective grounds and arbitrarily, and knows that he bears the responsibility for the life that is sacrificed.(17)

Schweitzer continues this narrative by giving two direct examples of his own actions in the face of the dilemma. "I rejoice over the new remedies for sleeping sickness, which enable me to preserve life, where once I could only witness the progress of a painful disease," he writes. "But every time I put the germs that cause the disease under the microscope I cannot but reflect that I have to sacrifice this life in order to save another."

He continues with the second example: "I bought from some villagers a young osprey they had caught on a sandbank, in order to rescue it from their cruel hands. But then I had to decide whether I should let it starve, or kill a number of small fishes every day in order to keep it alive. I decided on the latter course, but every day the responsibility to sacrifice one life for another caused me pain."(18)

"...A Genuine Experience of Life."

Undoubtedly, incorporating Schweitzer's ethic into our day-to-day existence is a daunting task. The responsibility involved in living with Reverence for Life is immense. Certainly it is easier to live solely for ourselves and those nearest and dearest to us. To heck with the rest of it! But as Schweitzer points out, the reward for incorporating Reverence for Life into one's own life is great. For an existence filled with reverence is an enlightened existence. It is a life filled with the great reward of knowing that one has risen to a higher level of awareness—that one has overcome the ignorance and narrow-mindedness of living only for oneself. It is an existence filled with the glory of knowing that the individual is not merely an isolated fragment struggling for survival in an uncaring universe, but rather an important piece of the greater whole. It is an existence that knows the comfort of being at one with all of creation. Schweitzer said it magnificently in his sermon at St. Nicholas Church on February 23, 1919:

The world given over to ignorance and egotism is like a valley shrouded in darkness. Only up on the peaks is there light. All must live in the darkness. Only one creature can escape and catch a glimpse of the light: the highest creature, man. He is permitted to achieve the knowledge of reverence for life. His is the privilege of achieving the knowledge of shared experience and compassion, of transcending the ignorance in which the rest of creation pines. And this understanding is the great event in the evolution of life. Through it truth and goodness appear in the world. Light shines above the darkness. The highest form of life has been attained, life sharing the life of others, in which one existence feels the pulse of the whole world and life becoming aware of its all-embracing existence. Individual isolation ceases. Outside life streams like a flood into our own.(19)

Schweitzer points out that Reverence for Life is such a powerful concept it has a tendency to take a strong hold of those who are introduced to it. Once we have been awakened to the idea and gained a heightened awareness of the will-to-live of all beings, we cannot help but incorporate this profoundly intriguing mode of thought into our lives. In *The Philosophy of Civilization* Schweitzer wrote:

Even if the phrase reverence for life sounds so general as to seem somewhat lifeless, what is meant by it is nevertheless something which never lets go of the man into whose thought it has made its way. Sympathy, and love, and every kind of valuable enthusiasm are given with it. With restless living force reverence for life works upon the mind into which it has entered, and throws it into the unrest of a feeling of responsibility which at no place and at no time ceases to affect it.(20)

When we open ourselves to the concept of Reverence for Life, we cannot help but incorporate it into our own lives. But this is not a bad thing. There are great riches to be gained. The beauty is that with this large dose of responsibility comes an infinite measure of fulfillment. Said Schweitzer in *Life and Thought*:

Once man begins to think about the mystery of his life and the links connecting him with the life that fills the world, he cannot but accept, for his own life and all other life that surrounds him, the principle of Reverence for Life. He will act according to this principle of the ethical affirmation of life in everything he does. His life will become in every respect more difficult than if he lived for himself, but at the same time it will be richer, more beautiful, and happier. It will become, instead of mere living, a genuine experience of life.(21)

May every one of us strive to comprehend this profound ethic from this great man and fully incorporate it into our own life. May we all come to live with a spirit of Reverence for Life!

Notes
(All sources authored by Dr. Albert Schweitzer unless noted.)

1.) Dr. Lachlan Forrow; E-mail to the authors. 08-08-2005.
2.) Dr. Edwin A. Schick; *Albert Schweitzer: A Voice For The Twenty-First Century* (2005); p. 41. (Used by permission.)
3.) *Out of My Life and Thought* (1998); p. 157-58.
4.) "The Ethics of Reverence for Life;" *Christendom*, 1936 vol.1, no. 1; p. 225-39.
5.) *Life and Thought;* p. 156.
6.) "Ethics."   7.) Ibid.
8.) *Life and Thought*; p. 235.
9.) "Religion and Modern Civilization;" *The Christian Century*; vol. 51, November 28, 1934; pp. 1519-21.
10.) "Ethics."
11.) *Reverence for Life* (1969); p. 119.
12.) *Life and Thought*; p. 157.   13.) Ibid. p.158.
14.) Ibid.
15.) "The White Wizard's 90th: An Inquiring Visit to Dr. Schweitzer;" Hugh Moffet; *Life;* February 19, 1965; p. 94.
16.) *Life and Thought*; p. 236.   17.) Ibid.
18.) Ibid.
19.) *Reverence*; p. 121-22.
20.) *The Philosophy of Civilization* (1987); p. 311.
21.) *Life and Thought*; p. 233-34.

3

Living the Philosophy:
Dr. Schweitzer's Reverence in Action

By John Webster and Ty F. Webster

The greatness of Schweitzer rests not just on what he has done but on what others have done because of him. What has come out of his life and thought is the kind of inspiration that can animate an age. He represents enduring proof that we need not torment ourselves about the nature of human purpose. His main achievement is a simple one. He has been willing to make an ultimate sacrifice for a moral principle. Because he has been able to make the supreme identification with other human beings, he has exerted a greater force than millions of armed men on the march.
--*Norman Cousins; Introduction to* The Words of Albert Schweitzer.

The body of thought Albert Schweitzer introduced to the world is a great one with a deep message for all who listen to it. What separates Schweitzer's ideas from so many others' is that although Schweitzer's concepts are deeply profound, one does not need a dozen doctorates in order to decipher them. They present a message that speaks clearly to people everywhere. As Schweitzer biographer James Brabazon points out in the epilogue of *Albert Schweitzer: A Biography*, Schweitzer's ideas may not satisfy all of the experts, but they are widely accepted because they are so firmly grounded in common sense. Brabazon writes:

His theology will probably never satisfy the theologians; it ignores all the fascinating blind alleys they love to explore. His philosophy will never satisfy the philosophers; it fails to put the universe in its place, and it fails to pursue verbal distinctions down long dark burrows leading nowhere. It speaks to the whole man, not to the intellect alone.

Even his ethics will never satisfy the students of ethics. They fail to lay down clear and definitive regulations as to what to do in all circumstances. . . . On the other hand, the ethics of the ethicists, the philosophy of philosophers, and the theology of the theologians will never satisfy ordinary people. Schweitzer's might.

The things that Schweitzer believed and fought for are believed by millions and millions of people already. Is there anything startlingly new in the proposition that life is to be preserved and encouraged, and death, disease and human destructiveness to be fought against?(1)

A Living Example

What makes Dr. Schweitzer extraordinary is that he became a living example of his philosophy and ethical system. It is one thing—albeit a very great thing—to develop a new, profound system of thought and present it in a comprehensible fashion to the world at large. It is all together another to incorporate that philosophy into everything one does. This is precisely what Albert Schweitzer did in his lifetime. In no way did he live a "do as I say, not as I do" existence. He did not merely offer Reverence for Life as a good idea. He lived the idea. And his example calls us to do all that we can in our own lives to adhere to the philosophy of Reverence for Life.

The jungle hospital at Lambarene was the greatest manifestation of Schweitzer's incorporation of his ethic into physical reality. From the day he arrived on the site beside the Ogowe River in the African jungle with his wife in 1913, Schweitzer did everything within his physical power to make the place a working example of his philosophy. Despite the necessity of devoting vast amounts of time to constructing hospital buildings on the site, Schweitzer—with Helene's help—treated over 2000 natives in his first nine months in Africa.

Schweitzer worked diligently at the hospital for much of the next four years, doing all within his power to ease the pain and suffering of the thousands of people who came to the hospital seeking medical treatment. When he returned to Lambarene from post-war Europe in 1924, he picked up right where he had left off in 1917. He rebuilt the dilapidated buildings and again attended to the desperate medical needs of the native Africans. Here and at the new, larger facility opened in 1927 several miles upriver from the original site, he put into action his philosophy of Reverence for Life. The medical hospital, mental hospital, and leper colony treated and housed countless thousands of native and non-native patients over the course of Schweitzer's life, immeasurably reducing the suffering and increasing the well-being of many people.

The results of Schweitzer's medical practice were not all that bore witness to how the doctor incorporated his philosophy into his daily life, however. His conduct within that practice also reflected his commitment to always act with reverence for all. There are countless stories that bear witness to the level of reverence he had for his patients.

Dr. Louise Jilek-Aall, a medical doctor who worked with Schweitzer at Lambarene for a time in 1961, told one such very pertinent story in her book, *Working with Dr. Schweitzer*. Told to Dr. Jilek-Aall by a native African who worked for many years as a medical orderly on the wards at the hospital, this story relates how Schweitzer went about his work with great compassion even in the face of hopelessness and with no thought to the risk of damage to his own reputation. It also shows how his work was an inspiration to others:

One evening I walked past the hospital on my way home. I saw a light in one of the rooms. There were only a few kerosene lamps available for the whole hospital, so I went back to see if something was wrong. I stopped when I discovered that it was Dr. Schweitzer himself who used the lamp.

Through the open door I saw him bending over a patient and helping him to some water. I knew the patient; a hopeless case of sleeping sickness already in the last stage of the illness, even too weak to lift his head. We had warned Dr. Schweitzer to leave this patient be! In

32

my people's view, a medicine man who continues to treat a dying person loses his power as a healer and becomes the laughing stock of the entire village. Annoyed, I was about to turn away when Dr. Schweitzer lifted his head and looked into the dark. There I stood, nailed to the ground. The light of the kerosene lamp shone upon his face and there was something in his sorrowful look that touched my heart. It flashed through my mind: 'compassion.' My legs became weak and as I sank to my knees, the spirit of compassion took hold of me and I knew that I would never be the same person again.(2)

Schweitzer's limitless concern for his patients was apparently not lost on them. Elsewhere in her book, Dr. Jilek-Aall wrote about the patient-doctor relationship: "It almost appeared to me that patients who saw Dr. Schweitzer sad and worried when one of them got worse, mustered all their willpower to get well just for the sake of making their beloved old doctor happy again."(3)

Reverence for Non-humans

True to his philosophy at every turn, Schweitzer did not limit his reverence to the human realm. Examples of reverential treatment of non-human life are abundant in Schweitzer lore. An article about the Doctor in the July 11, 1949, issue of *Time* magazine gave several. "In his daily life Schweitzer takes his own injunction to revere life so seriously that it sometimes astonishes those around him," the article says. "He himself reports that the natives consider his views impractical and perverted when he tells them they must transplant young palm trees instead of cutting them down when a clearing is to be made. A Lambarene colleague reports that when a grapefruit was brought to Schweitzer as he worked late at night, he would always drop a spoonful of the juice on the floor beside him for the ants. 'Look at my ants,' he would say. 'Just like cows around a pond.'"(4)

A story by Erica Anderson, who filmed the Oscar winning biographical documentary, *Albert Schweitzer*, gives another great—though by no means out-of-character—example of the

Doctor's endless reverence. Recounted in her book, *Albert Schweitzer's Gift of Friendship*, the anecdote tells of Schweitzer's reaction when some natives brought a wounded, wild pig to Lambarene one day while she was there. Injured animals were frequently brought to the hospital, as the natives knew that Schweitzer would care for the animals and that often he would give a small reward.

On this particular day, Schweitzer was busy preparing a speech for a radio show when he was interrupted by the commotion of the natives bringing in the injured animal. Immediately, he went to the animal's aid, putting it in an enclosure, giving it food, and speaking comforting words to it. Later, when the animal had calmed down, he returned to give medical attention to its wounded leg and build a shelter to protect it from the jungle rains. Anderson, in quiet amazement, watched him work and subsequently described the proceedings:

Schweitzer goes to work. A shelter for a sick, wounded pig must be built. For the moment, his health, the speech he is working on, all other considerations are irrelevant. The animal was brought to him by people who have learned and accepted the fact that among them is a white man who takes care of every man or beast, whatever the need...

I stand there, my face pressed against the wire enclosure, in the pouring rain of the African jungle. I look down on the man busy with a shovel, busy with his hands creating a shelter, busy in his heart, in his great and peaceful heart, with the pain of a wounded animal.(5)

An Eye on World Affairs

Dr. Schweitzer did not limit his reverential actions to Lambarene, however. From his jungle outpost and during his trips to Europe Schweitzer kept himself well informed about world events. He was very concerned about the course of world history. Although he took pains to remain politically unaffiliated, he tried to promote Reverence on a worldwide level. He used his power as an esteemed public figure in his later years to call on individuals to do their part to promote world peace.

In his Nobel Peace Prize address, presented in Oslo, Norway, in 1954, he called for a new, ethically based approach to life:

I am well aware that there is nothing essentially new in what I have been saying about the problem of peace. I am profoundly convinced that the solution is this: we should reject war for ethical reasons—because, that is to say, it makes us guilty of the crime of inhumanity...The only originality which I claim for myself is that not only do I affirm this as true, but I am convinced, intellectually convinced, that the human spirit in our time is capable of creating a new attitude of mind: an attitude based upon ethics.(6)

In the following years, Schweitzer did his part to bring about such an attitude. After being convinced that his stature as a world-renowned voice of reason could assist in the implementation of a worldwide nuclear weapons test ban, Schweitzer agreed to write messages for broadcast via radio around the world in hopes of raising public consciousness of the issue. This came at a time when the world's superpowers—the United States, Great Britain, and the Soviet Union in particular—were carrying out extensive nuclear weapons tests while doing all they could to perpetrate the myth that such tests were both necessary and safe.

Schweitzer hoped that his message would persuade knowledgeable scientists and, especially, concerned citizens around the world to speak out against the tests. He felt that popular sentiment would be a most valuable tool in convincing world leaders to act more sensibly. A passage from a letter to his friend Norman Cousins explained his willingness to give the radio addresses: "This crisis intimately concerns the individual. The individual must therefore establish a connection with it...The leaders will act only as they become aware of a higher responsibility that has behind it a wall of insistence from the people themselves."(7)

He chose Radio Oslo for the broadcasts, wanting the message to come from the Peace Prize City. The first message, titled "Declaration of Conscience" hit the airwaves on April 24,

1957, and three more speeches, "The Renunciation of Nuclear Tests," "The Danger of an Atomic War," and "Negotiations at the Highest Level," were broadcast in April of 1958. The addresses helped build his sought-after wall of public insistence on the issue and fuel the worldwide campaign for nuclear disarmament. International polls showed that the number of people in favor of nuclear tests had dropped dramatically following the broadcasts, and the testing of nuclear weapons was soon suspended.(8)

Reverence to the End

Throughout his adult life, in obscurity and later in great fame, Schweitzer's greatest passion—his life work—was the hospital at Lambarene. Unsurprisingly, Schweitzer continued to practice Reverence for Life at his jungle hospital right up until his death. *Life* Magazine correspondent Hugh Moffet went to Lambarene in 1965 to do a story on the occasion of Schweitzer's 90th birthday. Moffet found a vast hospital complex where approximately 950 operations were performed and between 300 and 400 babies were delivered annually. Although Schweitzer was no longer practicing medicine, he was still very much in charge of the place, and still very obviously conducting his life with great reverence for all living things. While showing Moffet around the hospital complex, Schweitzer passed a group of meandering chickens. He produced a bag of rice from his pocket and scattered the contents among the birds while telling the reporter, "If you write anything about the chickens, be kind to them."(9)

Yet, it was for the natives' benefit that Schweitzer had come to Lambarene, and it was they whom Schweitzer diligently served for over half a century. Although accurate records of the numbers were not kept at the hospital, it is estimated that over half a million patients were treated at Lambarene during Schweitzer's lifetime. It is no wonder then, that the natives came to have great reverence for the man who had such reverence for them.

The amount of respect that Schweitzer received from the natives and the world at large is greatly evident in the report of

36

Schweitzer's death published in the American Schweitzer Fellowship's newsletter, *Courier*:

On Sunday 5th September at 5:30 in the morning the big hospital bell tolled and was joined by the bell from the leper village to signal the death of the "Grand Docteur." The tom-toms of the natives began to mingle with the bells to spread the sad news.

From six o'clock in the morning onwards, without interruption until the funeral in the early afternoon, the inmates of the hospital, the people of the leper village and those who had come from the surrounding countryside filed past the coffin in the room in which he had lived and died, to take leave in reverent dignity of their beloved dead.

The grief of these African men and women as they expressed it in their songs was deeply touching—an audible witness of their gratitude, their devotion, and most of all their love for their "Grand Docteur" who had helped them and had understood their actions, their joys and their sorrows…

In spite of the short time between the announcement of Doctor Schweitzer's death and burial, a great grieving multitude gathered. There were members of the Government, the Minister of the Interior, the Minister of Defence, and the Minister of Public Health; the Director of the Cabinet of the President of the Republic of Gabon…Representatives of Catholic and Protestant Missions and presidents of many different organizations had come, and Ambassadors or those representing them from France, Germany, England, America and Israel…Uncountable people from near and far filled the big compound of the hospital.(10)

The Legacy Lives On

Dr. Schweitzer's positive effect on the world did not come to an end with his death, however. Thanks to the efforts of countless people who have been touched by his ideas, Schweitzer's legacy lives on. There are numerous organizations worldwide committed to perpetuating the Doctor's legacy, and even a network of collaborative international organizations, AISL (Association Internationale pour l'oeuvre du Dr. Albert Schweitzer de Lambarene), working together to see that Schweitzer's ideas remain a vibrant part of our modern world.

For example, The Albert Schweitzer Fellowship of Boston, MA, U.S.A., keeps Schweitzer's legacy alive by sending medical students from the U.S. to work at the Schweitzer Hospital at Lambarene, and also runs a Schweitzer Fellows Program in the U.S., sending students in health professions and related fields into underserved communities to carry out direct service projects.

Lambarene Today

In particular, Schweitzer's legacy lives on at the hospital that was the centerpiece of his personal dream. The Schweitzer Hospital in Lambarene is much more modern today, but is still serving the needs of the African natives it was created for. According to The Albert Schweitzer Fellowship's website (**www.schweitzerfellowship.org**) over 35,000 people take advantage of the services offered by the hospital every year. Two surgeons and their staff carry out over 2,200 operations, and over 6,000 people are cared for in the beds of the hospital's wards annually. Just as they did when Schweitzer ran the hospital, the patients' families stay with their sick loved ones and help with their feeding and care. The hospital also has a dental facility that treats over 3,200 patients per year, and the hospital houses Gabon's only psychiatric ward. Without a doubt, Dr. Schweitzer's life project is alive and well and stands as a living legacy of *Le Grande Docteur* and his ethic of Reverence for Life.

Your Own Lambarene

When Albert Schweitzer's granddaughter Christiane informed him that she wanted to go to Lambarene to lend her hand to the hospital's efforts, Dr. Schweitzer dissuaded her, telling her: "You can have your Lambarene anywhere."(11) As Brabazon points out in *A Biography*, what Schweitzer was saying is that in order to practice Reverence for Life, you do not have to undertake such lofty ambitions as building a hospital in the jungle. What is important is to do everything in your power to promote the spirit of Schweitzer's ideas wherever you are. Brabazon put it this way:

> The criterion is not that others should try to preserve what Schweitzer made nor even to imitate it but that they should try to find a true and valid expression, in action, of their own most humane, and human impulses.
>
> For the hospital, as Schweitzer said himself, was really only 'an improvisation.' He made it up as he went along. The theme on which he was improvising was a certain attitude that, once the name had come to him, was called Reverence for Life. Other people's improvisations on the theme could be, and should be, quite different. What mattered was the theme.(12)

In other words, if we can come to view our world with great reverence and act accordingly, we can create our own personal Lambarenes wherever we are. Christiane Engel took her grandfather's advice to a tee. She became a licensed medical doctor and has continued to share her passion for music, particularly the music of Wolfgang Amadeuas Mozart. Ms. Engel performs piano concerts around the world, and has used the healing power of music in her medical pursuits. On her website, **www.christianeengel.com**, she explains her love of Mozart and the power of his music: [His] music "reflects my ideals of harmony, peace, love, compassion and human understanding and it embraces hope and a belief in a higher truth and divine spirit."(13)

And, we too, can follow Dr. Schweitzer's advice. If we can incorporate Reverence for Life into our day-to-day existence— doing all we can whenever we can to promote the well-being, and limit the harming, of as many life forms as possible—we will be doing our own part to advance civilization. We don't have to travel halfway around the world to try to make the world a better place. We can work right in our own little corners of the world, doing whatever we can to honor the life of Dr. Schweitzer by sharing our own dreams with the world.

This book is a part of the authors' own personal Lambarenes, and in the following pages we will share a few of our ideas on how all people can work together to attempt to bring about a world full of people with greater Reverence for All Life.

Notes

1.) James Brabazon; *Albert Schweitzer: A Biography* (2000); p. 501.
2.) Dr. Louise Jilek-Aall; *Working With Dr. Schweitzer*; 138-39.
3.) Ibid. p. 73.
4.) "Reverence For Life;" *Time*; July 11, 1949; p. 73-4.
5.) Erica Anderson; *Albert Schweitzer's Gift of Friendship*; p.64.
6.) Dr. Albert Schweitzer; "The Problem of Peace in the World Today;" Nobel Peace Prize address, delivered in Oslo, Norway, November 4, 1954.
7.) Brabazon; p. 457.
8.) Ibid. p. 472.
9.) "The White Wizard's 90th: An Inquiring Visit to Dr. Schweitzer;" Hugh Moffet; *Life*; Feb. 19, 1915; p. 88.
10.) Brabazon; p. 497-98.
11.) Ibid.; p. 500.
12.) Ibid.
13.) Christiane Engel; www.christianeengel.com/biography .html

4

Some of My Favorite Schweitzer Stories

By John Webster

In this chapter I will share several anecdotes from the lore of Dr. Albert Schweitzer. Albert's daughter, Rhena Schweitzer Miller, approved the use of the anecdotes, and in several cases added some clarification. All are stories that I am particularly fond of, as I feel that they illustrate Schweitzer's greatness and uniqueness. Here is a man who had a deep concern for human and non-human life and who lived his life as a direct example of his enlightened way of thought. Each of the following stories portrays a glimpse of his spirit of Reverence for Life. I hope you enjoy them as much as I do.

On Doctor Schweitzer's first trip to Africa, he and Helene made a stop at the port of Dakar. As he was walking through the city, he happened upon two natives who were perched on a cart heavily loaded with wood. The cart was stuck in a newly mended street, and the two men were shouting at the poor animal that was laboring to pull the cart free. Schweitzer stopped and persuaded the two fellows to get off the cart. The three men then pushed the cart from behind until it was freed and could move on.

When Schweitzer traveled across Europe, he usually traveled via train. When asked why he always traveled third class, he would reply: "Because there is no fourth class any more." His main reason for traveling third or fourth class was to save money. Another was that he felt at home with the common folks and could visit with them about their work and perhaps learn something that he could use at his hospital in Africa.

On an October day in 1955, Dr. Schweitzer was one of many passengers on a third-class car of a train traveling from the

English Channel to London. Schweitzer was arriving in London to receive the Order of Merit, Britain's highest honor, which was to be bestowed upon him by Queen Elizabeth II. When Albert got off the train, he was immediately surrounded by reporters and photographers who had rushed down the platform from where the first-class coaches had stopped. His fellow third-class travelers may well have wondered who was this revered man who had ridden with them in the third-class compartment and appeared to be so much like them?

When Dr. Schweitzer and his wife were held as prisoners of war in 1918, both suffered from the confinement and from various illnesses. When they were released in July of that year, they were so weak they were unable to carry their own luggage. A crippled man, who had no belongings of his own, offered to help the Schweitzers with their luggage. They gratefully accepted the offer. Throughout the rest of his life, Albert vowed that he would always remember to help others with their luggage, even at the risk, as sometimes happened, of being mistaken for a thief.

Thirty-one years later, in 1949, Albert and Helene were visiting the United States. On a hot summer day in Chicago, Albert was standing on a Union Station platform visiting with friends and stretching his legs after a long train ride. Albert noticed a woman carrying two heavy suitcases. He immediately broke off the conversation with his friends, cautiously approached the lady, picked up her suitcases and took them onto the train for her. Several bystanders, feeling guilty after watching the 74-year-old gentleman's display of good-will, located other heavily-laden travelers and imitated Schweitzer's example. Union Station looked on in amazement.

When Albert was a young man, he liked to dance. He and a group of his friends would sometimes take off and spend the night dancing. Schweitzer sometimes said, "The only reason they invite me to come, is so I can play the piano all night".

Throughout his life, Schweitzer encouraged other people to

dance. He thought that if young folks did not learn to dance, they were idiots. He also encouraged people to be sure to dance with the "wall flowers" (the girls sitting around the side who did not have partners). I would imagine that he, himself, helped a few "wall flowers" to enjoy a dance or two.

Albert was not one to spend a lot of money on clothes. He preferred to use what money he had for his hospital. In fact, he was known to have worn the same felt hat for over forty years. He would wear the hat during the evening hours in Africa and most of the time when he was traveling about in Europe. So, as you can imagine after all those years it began to look a bit worn. One day later in his life, when Albert was at his home in Günsbach, his secretary (without his knowledge) bought him a new hat that was exactly the same as his old one and replaced the old with the new on the hat rack. As Dr. Schweitzer was on his way out to visit a bereaved friend and pre-occupied with thoughts of what he might say that would be helpful, he grabbed the new hat and put it on. His secretary was sure that she had won the battle and gotten him into a new hat. However, when Dr. Schweitzer returned, he said: "This is not my hat. What have you done with my hat? I want it back." And he had it back.

In 1905, when Schweitzer was scheduled to play the organ for the King of Spain, he went to his tailor in Günsbach and had a frock coat made for the occasion. Albert was very proud of the beautiful coat. It was very strongly built, and he wore it at all the great events that he participated in during the many years of his life, including the presentation of his Nobel Peace Prize speech. In 1958, when someone asked Schweitzer if he was still wearing that same frock coat, he glared at him and said, "Of course; that thing is still good for two hundred years".

Albert was noted for having hair that was hard to control. Even as a child he had trouble keeping it combed. On one occasion as an adult, Schweitzer was asked how he would like to be introduced at an event where he was to give a speech. He replied: "Oh, tell them that the fellow over there who looks like a shaggy dog is Albert Schweitzer."

While walking with a friend through a park, Schweitzer insisted that they walk on the extremely rough path rather than on the grass where the walking was much easier. When the companion asked why, Albert explained that on the grass they would crush the blades and also any insects or worms that might be there.

When a companion noticed an ant crawling on Schweitzer's shirt, he reached to brush it off. "Don't do that," the Doctor said and then asked: "Do you know how to pick up or brush off an ant without breaking one of its legs?" In a similar situation on another day, a different companion slapped a mosquito that had landed on Albert's arm. Schweitzer vehemently said: "You shouldn't have done that; that was my mosquito."

Schweitzer's work ethic often seemed super-human. He would work long hours without much sleep. Once, after he had been working until four in the morning, a friend said to him: "You can't go on burning your candle at both ends like this." Answered Schweitzer: "Oh, yes you can, if the candle is long enough".

In her delightful book, *Working With Dr. Schweitzer*, Dr. Louise Jilek-Aall tells of her time at Lambarene. In Chapter 14, "Reverence for Life" (page 194), she shares another idea from Dr. Schweitzer. A doctor should have the courage to share a patient's pain. As the patient suffers with his or her body, the doctor should suffer in his or her heart. If the doctor can stand the pain, then the patient can too. I feel this message should be not only for doctors, but for all of us as we relate to those who experience pain of any kind. "To suffer with" is the meaning of compassion.

While Dr. Schweitzer was building his hospital village, he would take time to check the holes that had been dug before the poles were put in to make sure that no creatures such as frogs and lizards that would be crushed were hiding there.

After becoming well known, the Schweitzer hospital village received many visitors from all over the world. On one occasion some thirty French sailors made the journey inland from Port Gentil to visit. As Dr. Schweitzer was showing them around the grounds, one sailor asked him, "But where is the temple?" To which came the prompt reply, "Did Jesus have a temple?"

Visitors to the Schweitzer hospital village were often invited to stay for lunch. On one occasion a very dignified fellow, perhaps a chaplain, did what was seldom done at the dining room table: he got up and made a solemn speech in which he beseeched the Lord to spare Dr. Schweitzer for many more years in health and strength. Schweitzer listened politely and made a very short reply. "Let us hope the Lord is listening." On such occasions Albert often had a twinkle in his eyes that was usually followed by a special wink, which no one will ever be able to duplicate.

When Schweitzer was a boy of school age, one of the guests at a wedding his father conducted was a crippled girl. Albert, in his innocence, asked whether this was the bride. The people there laughed at him and their response was: "Who would want to marry a girl with deformities?" Albert decided then that if this was the way the world was, someday he would marry a crippled girl. In the years to come, Schweitzer did not marry a crippled girl; however, he did marry a crippled world and worked all his life to make it well.

Albert never learned to drive a car, as he always traveled by train or boat. In later years when he was in Europe, he would sometimes have people chauffeur him to places he needed to visit. Often he would ask the driver to stop and give lifts to people walking along the road to shorten their journey and so that he could visit with them. One young man happened to be quite depressed and was not sure where he was headed in life or what he would do next. For the next few miles, Schweitzer did all he could to give the fellow a vision of hope for his life. When the fellow got out, he said, "I will think about what you said." Although we do not know the outcome, perhaps because they stopped and gave this fellow a ride, his life was changed for the better.

Dr. Schweitzer took pride in having played some of the finest organs and pianos in existence throughout all of Europe. In the dining room at his hospital in Lambarene stood an old piano that had been there for many years. It is impossible to keep a piano tuned in the midst of a tropical climate. Some of the keys had ceased to function for various reasons. Most musicians would not even attempt to play such an instrument. However, after supper each night, Dr. Schweitzer would announce the number of the hymn to be sung and then walk over and sit down at the old piano. He would play his prelude to the evening's choice and then everyone would join in singing. Obviously, the Doctor knew which keys had died and could improvise his way around them. The old piano was a special part of Dr. Schweitzer's life, and he was not about to give it up for a newer one. Many of those who had the pleasure to hear these performances in Africa were amazed and inspired by the Doctor's ability to bring forth music from the old, out-of-tune piano. From the majesty of the great churches and concert halls of Europe to the small, dimly lit dining room in equatorial Africa, we learn again and again of something special happening because of one special person and his "Reverence for Life," even for the life of an old piano.

At his hospital village at Lambarene, Dr. Schweitzer would carry in his pocket a small bag filled with rice and often would stop to feed some of the chickens or other birds. On his way from the dining room, he would share crumbs with the many animals that would follow him. Two of the items buried with him at the time of his death were his old hat and a small bag of rice. It was indeed fitting that during the Doctor's outdoor memorial service, several of the goats munched on the flowers around the coffin and a mother hen with her four chicks remained for the duration of the service.

The Man's Friend

The following event was reported by Dr. Edgar Berman in his book, In Africa With Schweitzer. *Dr. Berman recorded the story while working as a temporary replacement for the chief surgeon at the Schweitzer community clinic at Lambarene during the fall of 1960. This is of one of my all-time favorite stories about Schweitzer, one that I feel clearly shows the depth of feeling he had for all life, human and non-human. It is another prime example of Reverence for Life demonstrated in the life and work of Dr. Albert Schweitzer.*

On Saturdays work around the hospital at Lambarene was usually scheduled only until noon. On this particular Saturday the operating room was to be more busy than usual. As the hospital staff were about to leave the breakfast table to begin work, a raggedly dressed, shriveled old native man of about seventy entered the dining room porch, desperately wanting to see Dr. Schweitzer. A hospital helper at the door refused entry to the man, and the ensuing commotion prompted Dr. Schweitzer, Dr. Berman, and the others to investigate.

The old man was barefoot, his hair was matted, and tears trickled down his sweaty face. He looked totally worn out, as if he had been laboring strenuously for a long time. The man seemed relieved and thankful when he recognized Dr. Schweitzer. Joseph, an African native who had been Dr. Schweitzer's helper for many years, interpreted the man's story. He told those present that the man lived about forty miles downstream and had spent most of the last two days rowing his pirogue (small canoe) upstream to the hospital.

With a choked voice, the man said, "I've brought my oldest friend up to see you, Dr. Schweitzer, because I feared my friend would die. Everyone in my village told me that only the white doctor's magic could make my friend well, that Dr. Schweitzer was my only hope."

Dr. Schweitzer was silent until the man had finished and then asked, "Where is your friend?" The old man pointed to a large, woven-reed mat lying near the door. Somewhat surprised, Schweitzer and his co-workers turned to look at the mat. Looking closely, they saw the nose of a dog protruding from one end. The straw mat was the means by which the old man had carried his pet and protected it from the hot sun. The man gently opened the mat, revealing a large dog, which weighed sixty or seventy pounds and was cushioned by a worn blanket. The dog was gravely ill. His dry tongue hung from the side of his mouth, his eyes were glazed, and he was gasping for breath. The old man knelt beside his friend and lovingly wet the dog's parched tongue with a damp cloth that he dipped into a bottle of water he carried, meanwhile saying that some hunters had accidentally shot the dog. "They didn't mean to," he murmured.

Dr. Schweitzer tenderly turned the dog on its back to examine it. The dog was obviously near death. There was a large gaping wound in the upper abdomen that glistened with the sheen of busy flies, but the terrible odor did not seem to bother Schweitzer as he carefully examined the dog. He ordered some paper napkins from the dining room to keep the flies from the wound. Dr. Schweitzer then told two helpers to transfer the dog to a stretcher and take him immediately to the operating room. He put his hand on the man's shoulder and said, "Your friend is very sick, but we'll try to save him." The man threw himself at Schweitzer's feet, held onto his legs, and tried to kiss his hands.

Dr. Schweitzer was visibly moved by the whole affair, as were Dr. Berman and the others. This old man had used all of his waning strength to paddle two days against the rushing current and had borne his sick "friend" off the boat and carried the heavy load up the steep hill to the dining room.

Dr. Schweitzer helped the old man up, keeping a hand on his shoulder. Dr. Berman reported that Dr. Schweitzer seemed to want to clasp the man to him. Then, almost as if to hide his feelings, he quickly turned to one of the younger doctors who was scheduled to go to the operating room and ordered him to get things ready and prepare to operate on the dog. "I'll be down," he said.

The young doctor replied that it would be an hour or two, as he first needed to operate on a woman patient. Dr. Schweitzer remained silent for a moment, trying to control his obvious anger. Giving the young doctor an ice-cold glare, he asked how long the woman had been afflicted by the problem to be corrected in the operation. "Two years," the doctor replied.

Dr. Schweitzer exploded, "She can wait another two hours; this man's friend can't!"

As they walked down the hill toward the operating room, Dr. Schweitzer said to Dr. Berman, "We've done so many operations on animals here, but they usually die of pneumonia."

Together the two doctors walked into the operating room where the young doctor was preparing for the surgery. The dog had lost a lot of blood from the wound and was also very dehydrated. As they watched the young doctor begin to clean the wound in preparation for the operation, the dog gave his last gasp.

When the dog stopped breathing, Dr. Schweitzer turned and went outside. His brow furrowed and shoulders hunched in sadness, he went over to the waiting native and took him to a bench. Sitting with him he sadly explained, through Joseph's translation, that they had done everything possible but had failed. His friend had died.

Schweitzer spent the next twenty minutes consoling the old man. He told him how much he admired the man's love for his friend, but also advised him that he must now begin a new relationship with another friend. "I understand your grief," Dr. Schweitzer said. "But go home to your village. We will give your friend a proper burial." With his arm around the sobbing man's shoulder, Schweitzer led the way to the man's pirogue. After giving him food and water, he wished him well and sent him toward his own village.

Dr. Berman followed Dr. Schweitzer back into the operating room, as Schweitzer wanted to tell the helpers where to bury the remains. Everything was about cleaned up, and the young surgeon was getting ready for the next patient. "Where is the man's friend?" Schweitzer asked. One of the helpers pointed to a trashcan containing all of the post-operative soiled sheets and empty bottles.

Again the old Doctor's temper burst forth: "How could you degrade that body? Haven't you learned yet that there is as much dignity of the spirit in death as in the spirit of life—in any life—even this poor animal's? Do you have so little feeling even for the spirit of the friendship between this dead animal and that old man?"

Trying to calm himself, Dr. Schweitzer added, "Give him a decent burial." He mentioned a place on a hill where other pets were buried, then slowly turned and left.

Weary to the point of exhaustion, the eighty-five year old doctor slowly walked toward a favorite place on a stone wall next to the river. He could often be seen there in the early evening, petting one of his many animal friends—a deer, a pelican, a chimp. On this day he sat alone. Perhaps he was contemplating the importance of all life and why sometimes people failed to respond with reverence. Would his example of Reverence for Life ever become a vital ethic in our world when it was even lacking, at times, in the midst of his own community clinic at Lambarene? When Dr. Berman came out of the operating room an hour or so later, Dr. Schweitzer was still sitting on the wall, now fondling a fawn which had come over and was nuzzling him.

Reflecting on the incident, Dr. Berman had this to say: "That meeting between an ordinary primitive tribesman with his sick dog and this sophisticated philosopher, musician, and physician reflected a melding of Schweitzer's deep spirit of life, his religious beliefs and his concern for his fellow man." Dr. Berman also noted that throughout the morning's events with the

50

old man and his dog, Dr. Schweitzer had not mentioned the animal as anything other than "the man's friend".

May we all come to have the same level of Reverence for All Life that Dr. Schweitzer exhibited so often throughout his life!

Let Them Come!

Erica Anderson related this incident. Dr. Schweitzer, in his 80's, was at his European home in Gunsbach. Those at the house tried to protect him from the steady stream of visitors. If the Doctor caught them telling someone that he was overrun and had no time, he would become sad and angry. "Let them come," he would always say. "You never know whether there is not something I can do for them."

One Sunday morning Erica was telling a caller that unless his reasons were urgent it would be kinder not to burden the Doctor with more visitors. But just then Dr. Schweitzer entered the room and said: "Who is it? Does he want to come?" Informed that it was a young man phoning from a few miles away, Dr. Schweitzer said, "Of course, yes."

Fifteen minutes later the young man arrived with his wife and baby. Dr. Schweitzer greeted them. The father, an American, spoke: "I am stationed in Wiesbaden. I work on airplanes, but I read some of your books and I wanted so much to meet you and I have a few questions, if you could give me the time." Dr. Schweitzer replied that he had to go to the church, but informed the young man that he was welcome to come and after the service he would be glad to try to answer his questions.

Upon returning to the house, Schweitzer asked Erica to translate: "Ask him how he liked the tone of the organ?" "Tell the Doctor," the young man answered, "that I am a mechanic: the sound of an airplane engine sounds just as beautiful to me. I don't understand much of music, but I was happy to see and listen to the Doctor." Schweitzer smiled. When Erica turned back to the young man, he had burst into tears. "Forgive me, I am so ashamed, this is silly; I don't know what's the matter with me. It is just that to really see him and meet him is such a strong experience." He continued, "I had so many questions I wanted to ask him. Now being with him, I need not ask anything. That he is as he is, that he does what he does, is the answer to everything. I have asked my father what the meaning of life is. I have asked my minister. I have discussed such problems with friends. None gave me a satisfactory answer—but he does."

Dr. Schweitzer put his hand on the young man's shoulder. "Tell him that I am just as moved as he is. It is good to show a true and real emotion; there is no need for him to feel ashamed." Dr. Schweitzer spoke softly and his eyes were misty.

"I don't have to ask you anything," the man said. "It is as if I feel the meaning of life clearly now; I sense now what I have to strive for. Your philosophy expresses it perfectly; I begin to understand. It became clear when I met you – reverence for life, concern about all living creatures – not in theory, but in reality."

Dr. Schweitzer insisted the young family must stay for lunch. The young man did not talk much, but his eyes were shining and he seemed happy. Several times the Doctor exchanged glances with him. Once Dr. Schweitzer, leaning toward him, asked, "No questions?"

After lunch, Dr. Schweitzer noted the name and address of the young man carefully in his address book. "I want you to write to me. I want to know how things turn out for you," he said. When they left, the Doctor stood waving until the car turned and disappeared from sight.

"You see, Erica" the Doctor said, "one must never turn anyone away. This meeting meant something to that young man. One can never judge beforehand who really needs help of some kind or other."

5

A Memorial Sermon for the War Dead

By Dr. Albert Schweitzer

Italicized text by John Webster

In this chapter I share portions of a sermon preached by Dr. Albert Schweitzer on Sunday, December 1, 1918, at St. Nicholas Church in Strasbourg, during a memorial service for the dead of World War I. In the autumn of 1917 Dr. and Mrs. Schweitzer had been forced to return to France from Africa as prisoners of war, and had been released in July of 1918.

Had the people of the world heeded Dr. Schweitzer's post-War message and responded in a positive way to it, all the wars since then could have been avoided. Yet the wars of the world continue on and on. As we experience selected parts of the memorial message of December 1, 1918, let us remember also the war dead of more recent years.

"How shall we celebrate their memory? Have you ever followed the coffin of one who was part of your life and made a sudden resolution to unite yourself with the departed one by vowing that from that moment on you would do something or give up something in memory of him? I believe that is what we men of all nations must do now. We must promise to vow for those who fell in the war.

"Let us first make the simplest and most natural resolution—that we will not forget them or what their death means. . . . What else shall we vow for the dead? That they have not died in vain. . . . Now that we can look back at the war as a thing of the past, those who made the supreme sacrifice appear as a single army. Differences in uniform or nationality have disappeared. They are men united in pain and suffering. They all present us with a challenge.

"For our sins they were delivered up. It was too easy in all nations to think of individual well-being or pain. Human life, that mysterious, irreplaceable treasure, was rated too low. People too glibly spoke of war and the misery it brings. We got used to risking a certain number of human lives, and we glorified our inhumanity in song. When the inevitable came, it was a thousand times more cruel than any of us had imagined. It was so ugly and horrible that we can no longer glorify it. Only suffering and terror remain.

"Disregarding all barriers of nationality we remember today those human beings who were sacrificed to the spirit of heartless cruelty. We humiliate ourselves before these dead, and we promise that the heartless spirit in which they were sacrificed shall be destroyed. The frame of mind in which this generation grew up must be destroyed, for the enormity of its sinfulness caused the suffering of the world. We shall teach our children what we have learned and leave to them, as our legacy, the commandment 'Thou shalt not kill,' for we now know its meaning has far deeper relevance than our teachers and we ourselves ever dreamed of. Those millions who were made to kill, forced to do it in self-defense or under military orders, must impress the horror of what they had to endure on all future generations so that none will ever expose itself to such fate again.

"Reverence for human suffering and human life, for the smallest and most insignificant, must be the inviolable law to rule the world from now on. In so doing, we do not replace old slogans with new ones and imagine that some good may come out of high-sounding speeches and pronouncements. We must recognize that only a deep-seated change of heart, spreading from one man to another, can achieve such a thing in this world. The fallen were sacrificed because of a frame of mind that had not yet understood the meaning of the commandment 'Thou shalt not kill,' the dead have made atonement for our guilt. Their suffering has taken our guilt from us, so that a new age may come and we may work for it.

. . .

54

"If you listen you will hear the sound of the kingdom of God in the air as no generation ever could before. We are called upon to take the step which until now has never been possible for man. We have no alternative: the dead are helping us and forcing us to take it. There will be no more sorrow, or crying, or pain, for the former things are passed away. The 'former things' is the world without reverence for human life, a world which has excluded itself from the love of God and placed itself under the yoke of misery that man can bring upon fellow man. The present thing is the kingdom of God, for which Jesus died. Millions in the past few months have also died for the new kingdom. They will have died in vain if we remain a generation that hears yet does not hear, sees yet does not see."

These words spoken by Dr. Albert Schweitzer in 1918 are appropriate and worthy of our attention in any year when wars and the preparation for wars are occurring. Can we, today, still hear the sound of the Kingdom of God, or have we become deaf and blind to the still more excellent way of Reverence for All Life? It is now up to those of us who are living in these moments to listen to the sounds of the Kingdom and to respond with deep respect and love for all that lives. We must share the message of relatedness and oneness with all the peoples of the world. We all are partners and it is time to stop killing one another in the name of war or any other name. It is time to put aside our nationalities and other differences and unite in the name of Reverence for All Life. May we do this as a memorial to all who have lost their lives due to the ways of war and violence. In the spirit of Jesus, we can vow to do our part to bring into being the Kingdom of God in a greater way than ever before.

6

He Had a Dream!
A Pictorial Biography

By John and Ty F. Webster

Higher, ever higher,
With your dreams and your desires
Higher, ever higher,
The ideal you long to serve.

Higher, ever higher,
When the clouds begin to gather,
Higher, ever higher,
By the starlight of your faith.(1)

These words inspired Albert Schweitzer for many years. He kept them in a frame beside his desk in his house at Gunsbach, France, where they can be seen to this day. They serve as testament to the wonderful dream that Dr. Schweitzer lived out during his incredible life.

From boyhood, Schweitzer was quite a dreamer. As a young schoolboy, instead of concentrating on the lessons of his teacher, Albert often sat in class daydreaming about outdoor activities or what he might become when he grew up. In his teenage years, Schweitzer learned not to waste class time dreaming, and he subsequently became an excellent student. He did not, however, stop dreaming. He continued to dream great dreams: the kind of dreams one has when wide-awake, thinking and exploring possibilities for the future.

One of Albert's favorite places to think and dream was "the rocks," located on a hillside above Gunsbach, from where he had a panoramic view of the surrounding countryside of the Münster Valley with the Vosges Mountains looming in the distance. What a great place for dreams to be born and nurtured! He returned to this favored spot as often as possible throughout his life.

Dr. Schweitzer on "the rocks," his favorite spot in the hills above Günsbach.

At the age of 21, at his parents' home in Gunsbach while on holiday from his studies at Strasbourg University, Schweitzer created a dream that would guide him for the rest of his life. He determined that he would aim for great personal achievements in scholarship and the arts for several more years, but when he turned 30, he would devote his life to the direct service of humanity.

Portrait of Schweitzer at about age 21.

After attaining much success in the fields of philosophy, theology, and music, Schweitzer kept his promise to assist those less fortunate than he. In his thirties, Albert became a medical doctor and in 1913 moved to Africa. He built a hospital near the village of Lambarene in the heart of the jungle in what is now the Republic of Gabon, bringing much-needed modern medical care to the natives there.

At his hospital on the banks of the Ogowe River, Dr. Schweitzer not only eased the suffering of countless people, he continued to think and dream about a better, more civilized world.

4)

Dr. Schweitzer overlooking the Ogowe River during the first years at his jungle hospital.

As he thought and dreamed, Schweitzer concluded that in order for humankind to continue to progress as a civilization, it must come to a new realization: it is not only human life that is sacred; *all* things that live are equally sacred. In September of 1915, from the depths of his wide-awake dream nurtured by reason, knowledge, and thought, and with a little help from an African sunset, came the profound message and ethic of "Reverence for Life."

Dr. Schweitzer spent the rest of his life living out his dream and demonstrating its message to the world. The dream involved helping, being kind to, and having great compassion for people.

5)
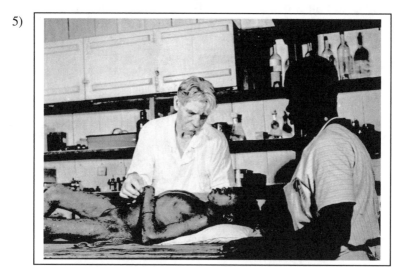
The Doctor tending to a patient at his hospital.

The dream involved being kind to everything that lives. The Schweitzer village clinic at Lambarene became a safe haven not only for people, but also for many plants and animals. In fact, Schweitzer was famous for his many pets.

6)

Sizi the cat.

7)

Parsifal the pelican.

Albert's dream was nurtured by music, especially that of Johann Sebastian Bach. He was a noted organist and raised money for his hospital by performing concerts throughout Europe. While in Africa, he could often be found at the end of the day playing a special piano presented to him by the Paris Bach Society.

8)

The musician at his piano in the heart of the jungle.

The dream was shared through worship, from the pulpit of St. Nicholas Church in Strasbourg—where he first presented his ideas of Reverence for Life to the world—and also at Lambarene.

9)

Sermonizing to humans and animals alike during a
Christmas celebration at Lambarene.

The dream was shared with the world. Dr. Schweitzer was awarded the 1952 Nobel Peace Prize, and he used his growing fame to influence world opinion on critical matters such as the dangers of nuclear proliferation and weapons testing. He spoke eloquently about the ongoing conflicts between people and nations, urging all of humankind to begin to behave with greater reverence toward one another and the world. Indeed, from his jungle outpost, Dr. Schweitzer kept a watchful, caring eye on the world.

10)

A watchful eye from the African jungle.

Over the years, Schweitzer personally shared his dream with many people by a smile and a special twinkle in the eyes and, if one was lucky, by his unique wink.

11)

Dr. Albert Schweitzer died on September 4, 1965, at the age of 90, but his great dream lives on today. In particular, it lives on at his hospital at Lambarene. Schweitzer's African living quarters have been preserved as a museum, which serves as a memorial to the great man who once lived there.

12)

Dr. Schweitzer's living quarters at Lambarene.

And the modern Albert Schweitzer Hospital at Lambarene carries on the good work of its founder. The doctors and staff provide health care to thousands of people every year at the hospital and in the surrounding area.

13)
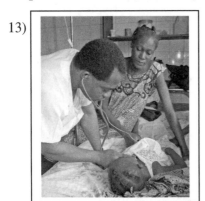
Dr. Kokou tends to a young patient.

14)

Georges leads an outreach program.

The dream also lives on in Schweitzer's European hometown. Today at Günsbach, atop the rock on the hill where he so frequently returned to celebrate, re-examine, and nurture his dream, there is a sculpted stone statue of Dr. Schweitzer. It serves as a monument to the great man, his great life, his great dream. And it serves as a reminder that Dr. Albert Schweitzer's dream is now **our** dream. The dream of **Reverence for Life** lives on with us. It is a powerful dream with the potential to transform the world. If we can grasp the dream of Reverence for Life, the dream will grasp us and enable us to reach out in service to all that lives. Let us all dream great dreams and have the courage to share our Dreams of Reverence with one another and the world.

15)    16)

The Schweitzer monument at "the rocks," overlooking Günsbach.

Note

1.) Words taken from page 23 of *Albert Schweitzer: an Introduction* by Jacques Feschotte; Beacon Press. Boston. 1955.

About the Photos

Photos 3,4,5,7,8, and 9 are from the Albert Schweitzer Papers of the Special Collections Research Center at the Syracuse University Library. 1,3,4,5,6,7,8,9,10,12,13, and 14 are used with the permission of The Albert Schweitzer Fellowship in Boston, MA. 11 is courtesy of Rhena Schweitzer Miller. 2,15, and 16 are from the authors' personal collection. For more info, see p. 305 in the back of the book.

7

Dr. Schweitzer's Ethic: A Second Look

By John Webster with Ty F. Webster

Throughout the remainder of this book, the authors will continue to explore the ethic of Reverence for Life and related topics. We will share what Dr. Schweitzer's ideas have meant to us personally and how we interpret their meaning in relation to today's world. We begin by re-examining Schweitzer's ethic.

The ethic of Reverence for Life offers a powerful, profound message. Yet, in spite of its power, the ethic is not difficult to grasp when we truly think about it. Human beings are thinking beings, and it is important to remember that "thought" lies at the core of Dr. Schweitzer's ethical system. As we think, one of the most basic conclusions we can reach is that we possess a will-to-live. We can easily recognize that we do everything in our power to assure our own survival. And we recognize, too, that we do not strive merely to continue to live, but to live as well as possible. We naturally strive to maximize pleasure and comfort and to minimize pain and discomfort.

We can also easily realize that we are not alone in the world. We are surrounded by a vast array of life. Billions of other people and countless plants and animals share our home here on earth. If we examine any of these other life forms, we can come to understand that all of them share our desire for survival. From the largest mammal to the smallest microorganism, every single life form does everything in its power to continue to live and thrive. To use Schweitzer's terminology, we can know that we are "life which wills to live, in the midst of life which wills to live."

As we look out into the world, we can see the will-to-live all around us. We perceive that all life forms—people, trees, dogs, bugs, flowers, birds, ad infinitum—possess it. We look at the many as having the same will-to-live as we do, and we realize that all events of creation are related. In order to be true to our own will-to-live, we must extend the concept of will-to-live to include every living being. Thus, we become aware of the "universal will-to-live" that unites us with one another. We are at one with the many. In other words, we come to have what Schweitzer termed "reverence for life," for *all* life.

That is what makes Schweitzer's ethical system unique. It provides for the well-being not only of humans, but of everything that lives. Reverence for Life establishes no division between higher and lower, between more valuable and less valuable life. This is also what makes the ethic so challenging. We are not allowed to separate ourselves from the rest of creation and put ourselves on a pedestal. As Dr. Edwin Schick aptly points out:

Reverence for Life is easy so long as we can choose which life or whose life we should respect. This is not what Schweitzer meant. The call to love and not to hate has little substance so long as we can choose who to love and who to hate. The upsetting feature of "Ehrfurcht vor dem Leben" is that we no longer have the choice. Reverence for Life embraces all life, no exceptions. From the one at the center, the circle expands outward to family and extended family, to clan and tribe, to nation and world, all of humanity. The expansion however does not stop with humanity. It enfolds all of life, animals and insects, plants and the smallest entities known.(1)

When a person becomes compelled to approach all life with the same degree of reverence he or she has for his or her own, all life becomes part of his or her own experience. From such a point of view, "good" means to maintain life, to further life, to bring developing life to its highest value. "Evil" means to destroy life, to injure life, to keep life from developing. If we have been touched by the ethic of Reverence for Life, we will do all we can to maximize good and minimize evil in the world. We will work to help all life whenever possible. We will come to realize that *every* encounter with *each* life form is an "event relationship."

One important result of adopting Schweitzer's ethic is that we come to each event relationship with no pre-conceived thoughts about who or what is more or less valuable. This means that when we encounter a bug, for instance, we think it is no more or less valuable than we are. The bug is no more or less important than a bird or a dog or a person. We recognize the bug's will-to-live as part and parcel of our own and that of birds and dogs and people. We see it as a part of the universal-will-to-live. And we do all we can to avoid harming the creature and to sustain its existence.

Dr. Schweitzer once said, "The ethic of Reverence for Life is the ethic of Love widened into universality."(2) In other words, our will-to-live can become a "will-to-love." It is easy and natural to love those who are near and dear to us: family, close friends, pets, etc. By adopting the ethic of Reverence for Life, we can come to view all life throughout creation as a part of our own family. We perceive our inter-relatedness to all events in the universe, and so we come to have a deep love for all life.

However, with this love comes a great amount of responsibility. No longer can we sit in a proverbial ivory tower, separated from reality, and declare: cats are more important than mice, birds are more important than bugs, eagles are more important than fish, people are more important than whales, white people are more important than black people, Christians are more important than non-Christians, people who live on one side of the tracks are more important than those who live on the other side, our nation is more important than other nations.

We are all equal, and our actions in every instance should reflect this fact. In each situation, as we come in contact with another life form, we can start by thinking "this life is no more or less valuable than mine." We can then continue with reverence for the other life and for ourselves, behaving in a manner that is beneficial for both of us, and for all of creation.

The ability to know that all of life has the will to live just as we do is what separates humans from all non-human life. The lower life forms are not capable of this realization. They are limited to an ignorant existence based purely on self-survival. An eagle does not realize that a fish has the will to live nor does a cat know that a mouse has the will to live. The eagle and the cat look at the fish and the mouse only as another meal and so are indifferent to the sacredness of those lives.

Human beings, however, *can* overcome indifference. We have the opportunity to evolve beyond this ignorant approach to life. We can make the enlightened decision to attempt to assist all forms of life in their varied attempts to survive. We can celebrate the sacredness of the fish and the mouse, as we realize that they experience the joy and pain of life just as we do, and we can subsequently do all that we can to help them survive and thrive.

As Schweitzer pointed out, however, it is impossible to preserve life in every case at all times. It is a fact of life that in order for some life forms to survive, others must die. It is impossible to live our lives without directly confronting this reality. When we find ourselves in a situation where it is up to us to decide what will live and what will die, we should never make the decision lightly. We should always use Reverence as our guide to make whatever choice we determine is best.

We may decide, for example, that a plant in a particular place is an invasive weed and will have to be destroyed so that more desirable plants may propagate. We may decide that we cannot catch a mosquito in our house and put it outside, so it becomes absolutely necessary to kill it. We may decide that it is necessary to sacrifice a worm in order to feed a bird.

It is up to each individual person to decide what is necessary in each situation when it comes to destroying or injuring life. If for some unavoidable reason we find it necessary to kill a weed, mosquito, worm, fish, mouse, etc., we should shoulder the responsibility for the demise of that life. The resulting guilt we experience should cause us to reach out and help some other life within our circle of influence at another time. Above all, we should always remember it is good to maintain and encourage life, and it is bad to destroy life or to obstruct it; and although it may be *necessary* to destroy non-human life, it is never *right* to do so.

It is important that we make the effort to help non-human

life at every opportunity so that we are more willing to help human life whenever we can. By taking time to be kind to any non-human life forms that might cross or be on our path, we can sensitize our inner being so that when we encounter fellow humans along the path, we can always respond with kindness and non-violence. If we can be sensitive to the well-being of all the many forms of non-human life we encounter, we surely can be super sensitive to the well-being of all members of the human community.

It is here, in our relations with fellow humans, that we find the ultimate challenge. We are challenged to allow Reverence for All Life to push negatives such as hatred, greed, revenge, racism, and violence out of our lives. We are challenged to treat our fellow human beings at all times, in every encounter, with the respect and compassion that we desire for ourselves.

This calls us to continue to struggle with an ongoing question: "Should it ever be necessary to kill another human being?" There may be room for argument on the topics of euthanasia and abortion. But generally speaking, I submit that the ethic of Reverence for Life says "NO!" It should never be necessary to kill another human being. It certainly is not right and should never be necessary.

Therefore, I come to the conclusion I will make a number of times in this book: all war is evil and must become obsolete. In a world based on the concept of Reverence for All Life, there is no place for the concept of war. It is impossible to wage war without killing. To wage war is to regress to an ignorant, indifferent, and inhuman way of life. If we are to continue to progress, or even exist, as a species, we must come to resolve our conflicts through the compassionate routes of dialogue and cooperation. Although this seems a daunting task given the course of human history, it is a task that we are capable of doing.

Dr. Schweitzer said as much himself. During his Nobel Peace Prize lecture in 1954, he proclaimed: "All men...are, as beings capable of compassion, able to develop a humanitarian spirit. It abides within them like tinder ready to be lit, waiting only for a spark."(3)

It is up to all of us, working together, to provide that spark. It is up to us to bring about what Schweitzer, in the same address, called "the reign of peace:" a time when "the spirit becomes a living force within us and leads us to a civilization based on the humanitarian ideal." And we must work diligently toward this end in all due haste. For another of Schweitzer's statements is as true now as it was when he presented the lecture: "the situation today is such that [the reign of peace] must become reality in one way or another; otherwise mankind will perish."(4)

It is true that the ethic of Reverence for Life puts a tremendous responsibility on each of us as members of the human family. Where there are wars, we must bring peace. Where there is hatred, we must bring love and understanding. Where there is racism, we must bring equality. Where there is injustice, we must bring fairness. Where there is ignorance, we must bring enlightenment. We must continue at all times to do everything we can to bring about a more human, humane world.

Our very survival is dependent upon developing a way of life more in tune with the concept of Reverence for All Life. Fortunately, the personal rewards of doing so are great. Remember the words of Dr. Schweitzer, who told us that if we allow our life to become filled with Reverence for Life, it will become, "richer, more beautiful, and happier. It will become, instead of mere living, a genuine experience of life."

May we all experience the power that Reverence for All Life can have upon our hearts and minds!

Notes

1.) Dr. Edwin A. Schick; *Albert Schweitzer: A Voice For The Twenty-First Century* (2005); p. 41-2. (Used by permission.)
2.) Schweitzer; *Out of My Life and Thought* (1998); p. 235.
3.) Schweitzer; "The Problem of Peace in the World Today;" Nobel Peace Prize address, delivered in Oslo, Norway, November 4, 1954.
4.) Ibid.

8

My Courtroom

By John Webster and Ty F. Webster

"Man makes distinctions only as each case comes before him, and under the pressure of necessity, as for example, when it falls to him to decide which of two lives he must sacrifice in order to preserve the other. But all through this series of decisions he is conscious of acting on subjective grounds and arbitrarily, and knows that he bears the responsibility for the life that is sacrificed."
--Albert Schweitzer; Out of My Life and Thought.

There is a little courtroom located somewhere in the midst of my mind. Whenever I am faced with an ethical decision, I dart into the room, close the door, don my judicial robe, and pound the gavel. The court is in session, and I am challenged to be both judge and jury.

My courtroom does not house volumes of law books filled with strict codes or telling of past decisions and precedents. These resources would not be very useful because every situation involves different partners and different events and is different from every other case that has come before me. I must consider and evaluate each situation on its own and never assume that it is just like one that happened yesterday or last week.

On a wall of my courtroom hangs a poster that declares, "Reverence for All Life." Another sign proclaims, "We are life which wills to live, in the midst of life which wills to live." Still others read, "Good is to promote and help life; Evil is to harm and destroy life;" "Everything that lives is my partner;" "Do not harm or kill any partner unless it is absolutely necessary;" and "It should never be necessary to intentionally harm or kill a human partner."

These words are constant reminders of concepts that must become a vital part of my thinking and my being. If I am to make creative decisions and live according to the principles of Reverence for All Life, I must remember to act with all of these crucial concepts in mind.

It almost seems as if Albert Schweitzer had visited my courtroom. I often wish that he were here, especially whenever I am called to make difficult decisions about right and wrong. But then I remember that in fact Schweitzer is here. He is very much alive in my courtroom and my life, providing much needed guidance. And the same is true of all my partners from the past and present, including Jesus, who constantly brings his message of love and compassion. Often, when I have to make particularly difficult decisions, and if I have time, I consult other human partners (fellow judges) and get their perspective on the case.

I am glad to have these references, because my courtroom needs to be filled with all the knowledge that is available to me. It is of utmost importance that my decisions are based on sincere thought. I must think about my decisions and take great care that they are not quick, thoughtless, or haphazard reactions to the situation at hand. The more resources I have, the more likely I am to make the correct judgment. Yet in the end, I know it is I who must decide what will be done. All of the final verdicts in all of the cases in my court are left up to me, and it is I alone who must take responsibility for them.

Unfortunately, there are still many times when I end up making the wrong decision. This happens most often when I forget to open the door to my courtroom and consult the many resources available there. Most often when I am wrong, I have forgotten to think. My reaction comes from a preconceived notion or prejudice. Other times, in spite of my best intentions, I later realize that the decision was incorrect. In these circumstances, all I can do is admit my error and hope that the partner or partners I have wronged will forgive me. This should also remind me to forgive whomever may have said or done something to harm me.

In other cases, I sometimes find the situation cannot be resolved without harming or possibly even killing another living being. These cases always make me sad, but I know we are unavoidably faced with conflicting wills-to-live. As Dr. Schweitzer put it, "One existence holds its own at the cost of another." In these cases, all I can do is use my best judgment and make the decision I feel serves the greatest good for all of creation.

When I do make a decision to harm some life form(s) I must be sure that I am doing so only out of necessity. And after doing so, I must be certain to be diligent in my reverence and not harm any further life out of carelessness. I must take the advice Dr. Schweitzer gave in *Civilization and Ethics* (1987; p. 318):

Whenever I injure life of any sort, I must be quite clear whether it is necessary. Beyond the unavoidable, I must never go, not even with what seems insignificant. The farmer, who has mown down a thousand flowers in his meadow as fodder for his cows, must be careful on his way home not to strike off in wanton pastime the head of a single flower by the roadside, for he thereby commits a wrong against life without being under the pressure of necessity.

And once I have decided that it is absolutely necessary to harm a living thing, I should then feel the full weight of my decision and experience the guilt of knowing that my decision has caused another living creature to come to harm. It is most important to realize the consequences of our actions and experience guilt for whatever life we may have been responsible for injuring or destroying. At all times, however, I must bear in mind the key precept: "It should never be necessary to harm or kill a human partner."

Any guilt, however, should serve a beneficial purpose. It should not be a negative guilt that turns me against myself and causes me to dwell only on my shortcomings. Rather, it should be a constructive guilt that makes me aware of my challenges and calls me to a more excellent way of behaving. My guilt should cause me to reach out to help other living creatures in other instances, whenever the opportunity comes along, in an effort to atone for the wrong that I have committed because I deemed it necessary. Good guilt should bring me a greater sensitivity and feeling of Reverence for All Life.

Sample Cases

To illustrate how things work in the courtroom of my mind, I will share some recent cases. The first case took place one morning last summer. It was a lovely morning: bright, clear, calm, and cool. The birds were singing their morning songs, and the greenery of the woods behind our house seemed to be beckoning me. As such, I decided I would like to go for a hike and enjoy the sights, sounds, and smells of nature. I quickly entered my courtroom. Thinking about it, I realized that I would unintentionally but inevitably step on and very possibly kill or injure a number of creatures living in the woods, such as ants, worms, or other small creatures. This, I thought, contradicted one of the main tenets of my courtroom: "It is good to maintain and to encourage life; it is bad to destroy life or to obstruct it."

Some people might find this a bit silly, fussing over insignificant insects. But I knew that Dr. Schweitzer would agree with me. In order to develop our Reverence for All Life, we need to remember that no partner is more important or less important than any other. No partner is more valuable or less valuable than any other. This means that we need to consult the judge in our courtroom when the decision that we need to make involves a bug just as much as when the situation involves a person. The bug deserves our respect just as much as a human partner. When we think about what our actions might do to another creature, instead of asking, "Can it talk? Can it think?" we should ask, "Can it suffer? Does it have a will to live?" and then act accordingly.

I gave the dilemma some consideration and decided that in spite of the inherent risk to my various insect partners in the woods, my spirit would benefit from a hike. I felt that my time in the woods, appreciating the beauty and mystery of the natural world, would increase my feeling of reverence for life. In this case, I decided to rule in favor of myself. I promised to be as careful as possible and to watch my step as often as possible. And I vowed to do whatever I can to help other creatures in other situations to make up for any harm occurring during the hike.

As fate would have it, an opportunity to atone for any damage done on the hike presented itself almost immediately upon my return to the house. I decided to check the birdbath in our front yard to see if it needed more water. It did not, but I noticed a large beetle in the water, struggling to get out. I grabbed a stick and let the creature crawl onto it, then set the stick down in some tall grass nearby. I knew that my action would not make up for the fact that I may have harmed some insects on my hike, but I was happy to know that I had used my feelings of guilt in a positive manner in this instance and saved this insect's life.

Another case in the courtroom of my mind is never-ending. It involves my relation to the earth's environment. I am faced with this case frequently. For instance, I open my courtroom every time I think about driving my car somewhere. When I do so, I am immediately faced with the knowledge that driving my car will inevitably pollute the environment.

I use this knowledge to assist me in deciding whether it is really necessary to make the trip I am planning to make. Sometimes I determine that the place I am planning to drive to is not so far away, and it would be healthier for me and the environment if I would walk. Other times, I realize the trip I am planning to make is not that important at the moment and can wait until I have other business to combine with it.

Often, however, I conclude that the trip is necessary. There would be no way to accomplish the tasks I need to get done if I did not drive the car. In these cases I get in the car and pollute my way to wherever it is that I am going. But in doing so, I experience the guilt of causing harm to the environment, and I do my best to use this guilt in a positive manner. I think of things I can do to atone for this damage. For instance, I buy cars within my price range that are as fuel efficient as possible. And I do my best to support politicians who share my view of the environment and let them know my feelings about the environment, hoping that they will be able to assist in bringing about a national energy policy that is more environmentally friendly.

Another ongoing case in the courtroom of my mind relates to the world political situation. Unfortunately, this case is taking up a lot of my time right now, much of it late at night when I should be sleeping. That is because at the moment I write these words, my country is waging war in Iraq. I know the war is causing much suffering and loss of life to people in the armed forces on both sides, to many innocent civilians, and to much non-human life, as well. As a result, my feelings of guilt weigh very heavily upon me.

Although I am entirely opposed to the war, I know that the elected officials of my government are responsible for this evil campaign, and my tax dollars are helping to finance it. So I cannot deny that to a certain extent I am guilty for it. I cannot deny responsibility for every life that is lost in this war.

As a result, I am using my guilt to help me do all I can to atone for these tragic losses. I am doing everything in my power to stop this horrible violence. I have written my Congressmen to be sure they know my feelings about the matter. I have attended many peace rallies and even organized some myself. I put up signs around my town that say such things as "Let there be peace on earth" and "Give peace a chance," so that other people who oppose the war will know that they are not alone. And most of all, I hope. I add my hopes and prayers to the millions of others from peace loving people around the world who desire and work for an end to the violence in Iraq and to all violence everywhere. In this manner I buoy up my feelings of Reverence for All Life, so that they do not get swept away in the flood of violence and irreverence that is washing over the world now.

I could go on and on with examples of recent cases from the courtroom of my mind. When a courtroom is always open, it hears many, many cases! But I will end here by urging the readers of these pages to keep their own courtrooms open at all times. Remember to open the courtroom of your mind whenever you are confronted with an ethical dilemma, no matter how big or small. And always remember to use the principles of Reverence for All Life as the basis for every verdict.

9

Who Is My Partner?

By John Webster

"Let man begin to think about the mystery of his life and the links which connect him with life that fills the world, and he cannot but bring to bear upon his own life and all other life that comes within his reach the principle of reverence for life."
--Dr. Albert Schweitzer; For All That Lives; *Ann Atwood and Erica Anderson.*

In considering will-to-live, another way to look at life is in terms of partners. I suggest that everything with the will-to-live is my partner. This means that I am part of a great network of partnership that includes people, cats, flowers, dogs, pigs, rabbits, bears, trees, snakes, rats, bugs, fish, birds, grasses, et cetera, et cetera. Who is my partner? You are my partner. Everyone who lives, everything that lives is my partner.

As a network of partners, we form the great process of creation. In this process, the many become one, time and time again. All events throughout all of history become one in the creation of me and of you and of all things. We may envision the many separate wills-to-live becoming one again and again as the process of creation continues. All are united as our individual will-to-live becomes one with all other wills-to-live. When any one in this network of partners hurts, we all hurt. When one is poor, we all are poor. We are one. We are all partners, intricately related to one another. We are mutual caretakers of all that lives.

Because each partner is related to every other partner, we must all continually work together to help each other along our separate life paths. The "universal will-to-live" is the reality that binds us together and urges all partners to do their best in working for the betterment of all life. Life is dependent upon a fragile balance, and our survival is dependent upon working together to maintain this balance. We must all behave as partners. When we fail to respect the will-to-live of any of our partners, we upset the balance and lessen the quality of all life.

As humans we have a special obligation to respect the balance within our network of partners. It is, for the most part, only humans who can understand this balance. Only humans can experience and demonstrate the reality of Reverence for Life. This is what separates us from non-human life. Non-human life is mostly indifferent to the well-being of other life. However, as humans we can overcome this indifference. We can think and know that it is good to maintain and encourage life and that it is bad to destroy life or obstruct it. We can realize that when we harm or hinder any of our partners, we also injure ourselves.

Being a partner is always unconditional. In being a partner there are no preset conditions to be negotiated. We need to realize that every partner has the will-to-live just as we do. We also need to realize that no partner is more important or valuable, or less important or valuable than any other partner. This means that the smallest bug is as important as the largest tree. A beaver is as important as a person. A mouse is as important as a cat. A fish is as important as an eagle. All are important parts of the greater whole. Therefore, we should not harm or destroy any of our partners unless it becomes absolutely necessary.

We must understand that we are partners with all living things. We are never far away from one or more of our partners. When we realize this, our senses of belonging and purpose are greatly enhanced. If you look around, you will probably realize that you are close to a plant of some kind, an insect, a pet, or another person. With partners all around us, it should be easy to find one or more that need some support. The plant may need water. The pet may need some food or just a kind word. A human partner may need the support of a hug and a kind word or just someone to listen to their concerns. We must remember these partnerships when we begin to feel lonely. For then we will remember that in fact we are not alone. We are in the midst of a vast world full of partners.

I submit that we have a special obligation to help all of our human partners. We must come to realize that all people are our partners, regardless of their color, religious beliefs, or the language they speak. There is only one world, and all people must work together to care for it. It should never be necessary to harm or kill another human being. Perhaps a new approach to our "enemies" is in order, one that is based on forgiveness and understanding. We can say: "That person is my partner, not my enemy. That person has feelings just as I do. That person has hopes and dreams and fears and worries just like me. Although I feel that he or she has hindered me in some way, it was probably done unintentionally. Or if it was intentional, it possibly is because he or she does not understand me. I will do my best to raise the level of understanding between us."

The nature of partnership is to help one another. However, it is unfortunate that not all human partners have discovered this essential idea and are not always ready to help take the proverbial rocks off another partner's path. In fact, they sometimes may even intentionally put more rocks on the path of a fellow sojourner. When this happens to us, instead of responding with retaliation and revenge, we need to forgive the partners who have hindered us and continue our journey as best we can. There is no benefit in saying, "They have harmed me, now they will get what is coming to them." Instead we can say, "I will not hold this against them."

Also, we must take inventory of our own actions to see if we might have done something in the past or might presently be doing something that may have caused the other partner(s) to want to hinder our journey. If we find this to be true, we might ask to be forgiven. And we should then alter our behavior in order to avoid repeating the same problem. We should attempt to use dialogue and respectful communication in order to work with our fellow sojourner(s) to find a solution to the problem suitable to both or all of us. In this way, we can invoke the spirit of Reverence for All

Life and bring about a world with more peace and cooperation and less conflict and ill will.

By invoking the spirit of Reverence for All Life at all times, we can make the lives of our partners—human and non-human alike—more enjoyable. And at the same time, we can increase the joy in our own lives. We can take pride in knowing we are helping to maintain the fragile balance within the great network of partners, which encompasses all of life.

"Peace on Earth" by Jo Meyer

10

Partners From the Past

By John Webster

"When I look back on my early days, I am stirred by the thought of the number of people whom I have to thank for what they gave me or for what they were to me."
--*Dr. Albert Schweitzer;* Memoirs of Childhood and Youth.

I have suggested that everything that lives is our partner. This means that I am your partner, you are my partner, and everything that is alive right now is our partner. All living creations possess the will-to-live and are therefore related.

I now suggest that all forms of life, human and non-human, throughout all of history, are also our partners. Every life form that has ever lived has helped to make us what we are today. Although this is perhaps a difficult concept to comprehend, it is an important realization to make in order to foster a feeling of Reverence for All Life.

It is easier to accept this idea when we think about the close human partners in our own personal histories who have influenced us. We all have special partners from the past who have touched our lives and given us unique gifts that will always be with us. A few examples from my childhood on a farm in southwestern Wisconsin, may help to highlight this important concept.

I owe a special "thank you" to my parents. Because I was an only child, my parents could concentrate all of their parental love upon me, and they did. My mother, Helen Robinson Webster was a schoolteacher for many years before she was married. After my birth, she no longer taught professionally, and I became her only student. She had been a first grade teacher, so during those early years of my life I truly received professional instruction. She remained a great teacher to me throughout her life, and I am continually indebted to her for the lessons she taught me.

My father, Orville, was a farmer. Like most farmers, he worked long hours and seldom had a day off, yet he could always seem to find time to attend my sporting events, and once a year would take me to watch our favorite professional baseball team, the Chicago Cubs, at Wrigley Field in Chicago. He enjoyed his family and his neighbors, and he was my best friend through the years. He was very knowledgeable on a wide variety of subjects and always seemed to have good advice, which he not only spoke, but demonstrated as well. For instance, he often told me, "Be kind to old people; you will be old yourself someday." And I have always remembered his advice for winter driving: "Whenever you have to drive through deep snow, remember to give it the gas and hit the deep snow going fast, because if you ever stop you are done." Sometimes when I drive in snow I wish that Dad could be with me, and then I realize that, of course, he is.

I also owe a thank you to the hired man on our farm, Paul Doescher. Paul was as much a part of our family as he was an employee. He was a special partner who could always seem to find time to play with me after his long day of work was done. Paul had a very good way of relating to animals. He would take time to love and enjoy all of the animals around the farm, treating them as his friends, and not merely as dumb animals or livestock. I can still see him petting the cows and cats while calling them "Ol' Boss Cow" or "Ol' Mouser." As I think of it now, I realize that he radiated a true sense of Reverence for All Life, which continues to affect my thinking and the theme of this book probably even more than I realize.

My list of special partners from the past could go on and on. However, I will stop here and suggest that you, the reader, take a few moments to think about those people from your past who are special to you, or who have had a positive influence on you in some way. Pause for a moment and offer them a special thank you for the gifts that they have given to you.

Doescher and ol' Mouser

The point I want to make here is that every partner and every event is interrelated, and that is true not only with regard to the present, but also the past. Events that happen now are directly affected by those that happened in the past, and they have a direct effect on those that will happen in the future. Similarly, people from our past directly affect us in the present. One more memory from my childhood can serve as an illustration.

While teaching first grade at a school in Madison, Wisconsin, my mother sometimes served as a demonstration teacher. This meant that from time to time other teachers would come into her classroom to observe her teaching style. A number of years later, Mom took me into the one-room Elk Grove country school near our farm to register me for the third grade. The teacher, Mrs. Doyle, spoke to my mother with an obvious feeling of intimidation. "I think that I remember you," she said. "I observed your teaching in a Madison demonstration class a number of years ago. You made a very big impression on me."

I imagine that it would have been easy for my mother to take advantage of Mrs. Doyle's obvious discomfort. She could have made Mrs. Doyle feel inferior or inadequate, or criticized her teaching methods. Instead my mother did everything she could to make Mrs. Doyle feel comfortable. As a result, this relationship between teacher and parent was not one of intimidation. In fact, it developed into a warm, professional friendship.

Mrs. Doyle was my teacher from grades three through eight. In those years, it was not uncommon to see her coming up our driveway at the end of the school day, but I was never too worried I had done something wrong. I knew she was only coming to chat with my mother and seek her advice. She was a talented teacher who taught her students well, and after six enjoyable years in her classroom, I was well prepared for high school.

So, not only did my mother have a profound effect on me, she had a profound effect on my elementary school teacher through an event from my teacher's past. And my elementary school teacher also had a profound effect on me. Plus, I know that my own interactions throughout my life have influenced others' lives, as well. And so it goes. All of the partners in our past have provided influences that combine to contribute to who we are in the present. Likewise, the way that we influence all of our partners now, in the present, will have an effect on whom or what they become in the future.

Thus, it is crucially important that we are careful to be only positive influences on all of our partners. We must remember always to help and never to hinder them. By always treating all of our partners with full respect, we allow the spirit of Reverence for All Life to be passed on from generation to generation.

11

Finding Partners

By John Webster with Ty F. Webster

"We cannot let ourselves get frozen into regarding everyone we do not know as an absolute stranger. No man is ever completely a stranger to his fellow man."
--Albert Schweitzer; Albert Schweitzer, *documentary movie filmed by Erica Anderson, produced and directed by Jerome Hill.*

We can find partners wherever we come in contact with life. However, finding that very special partner with whom you might intimately share much of your life is not always easy or predictable. In many cases, special partnerships come about as a result of interesting coincidences. Such was the case for my wife—Liz—and me.

Elizabeth Clarson and I lived only thirty miles apart in the southwestern corner of Wisconsin for the first seventeen years of our lives. During that time, however, our paths never crossed. In fact, neither of us knew that the other existed. Not until a few years later, when we were living thousands of miles apart, did circumstances allow us to meet one another. As often happens, our meeting came about with the help of mutual friends. In this case, those friends were named Martha and Albert Splitgerber.

After graduating from the University of Wisconsin at Madison, Liz was teaching Home Economics at Plymouth, Wisconsin, and renting a room in Martha and Albert's home. Meanwhile, I had graduated from Arizona State University and was attending The Iliff School of Theology in Denver, Colorado. At both schools I was fortunate to have a number of great partnerships—developing some meaningful friendships and cultivating a number of more professional relationships with my teachers and professors. However, I had not managed to find the extra-special, personal partnership that I desired.

During these years Martha and Albert spent their winters in Mesa, Arizona, where they rented an apartment from my parents. When I was home in Arizona during vacations from school, they would tell me about this attractive, young schoolteacher who was living in their home back in Wisconsin. I listened interestedly, and Liz and I began corresponding.

We spent a fair amount of postage money and decided we would like to get to know one another better. So one summer day in 1964, I set off on the long journey from Colorado to eastern Wisconsin. We had decided it was time to find out for ourselves who it was we actually were writing to. It was a very worthwhile journey, for as a result, Liz and I decided we would like to pursue a special partnership together.

During the next year, Liz and I spent more money on postage and a lot more for airplane tickets as we both continued to move around the country. Liz moved to Tallahassee, Florida, where she attended graduate school at Florida State University. I served as a student minister at the Methodist church at Englewood, in western Kansas, and completed my third year of studies at Iliff.

Although I have many fond memories from the early days of our relationship, there are several that stand out. I particularly remember the Christmas season of 1964. On Friday of the weekend before Christmas, I was in Englewood preparing for the Sunday church service. Liz was flying into Oklahoma City on Saturday morning, and I planned to drive to the airport to meet her. As I tried to sleep that night, I heard the clatter of freezing rain on the roof of the house where I was staying.

The next morning the ground was so slick with ice, I could hardly walk to my car. But I had to get started early as it was about 200 miles to Oklahoma City, and of course I didn't want to be late getting there. When I reached the main highway, I decided to test the road conditions by tapping the brakes very lightly. I immediately found myself in the ditch. I managed to drive back onto the road but continued with great care, as I now knew it was extremely slippery. Before long, though, I headed up a hill and suddenly found myself in the ditch on the opposite side of the road, facing in the wrong direction.

I managed to drive out of the ditch once again, but had to give serious consideration as to whether I could justify going on. I thought about Liz arriving in a strange city with no one to meet her, and my mind was immediately made up. I decided the risk was worth it and headed on down the road. Soon, the sun came out, the ice melted, and I was at the airport in Oklahoma City in plenty of time to meet Liz's plane.

When we returned to Englewood, we were greeted by Houston Little, the farmer in whose home I was staying. He said that when he saw me starting out on the icy roads that morning, he thought I was crazy. But now that he saw the reason for my journey, he had changed his mind and declared he would have done the same thing.

After the Sunday worship services, Liz and I drove to Mesa to spend the holidays with my parents and those mutual friends, Martha and Albert. I had decided our partnership was indeed extra special, and on New Year's Eve I asked Liz to marry me. I am sure it was a difficult decision for her, as it is not an easy task to be a minister's wife; but to my eternal pleasure, she also felt that ours was an extra special relationship and said the word every man proposing marriage wants to hear: "Yes!" Elizabeth Clarson said she would be happy to become Elizabeth Webster and share her life with mine.

We planned a September wedding, which proved to be one of several milestones for us in 1965. That same year, Liz received a Master's Degree from Florida State, and I received a Master of Divinity Degree from Iliff. After graduation I accepted an appointment in the Kansas West Conference of the Methodist Church as the minister of the Pleasant Hill Church in rural Ash Valley in central Kansas and associate minister of the Methodist Church in nearby Larned. I soon developed many new partnerships with the parishioners of both churches. Everyone did all they could to make me feel at home and to make my entry into the realm of professional ministry as easy and comfortable as possible, and for this I am forever thankful.

Plans progressed for our September 5 wedding at the Pleasant Hill Church. Liz arrived several weeks before and busied herself with making preparations for the event. Soon our special day was at hand. The wedding was exciting and meaningful for a number of reasons. Members of the Pleasant Hill Church were very gracious in helping with the wedding plans—working to make the event extra special—and a wonderful surprise came when a number of friends from the Englewood Church arrived for the ceremony.

Coincidentally, I find it interesting to note that although we did not realize it at the time, as our ministry and life together were just getting started, Albert Schweitzer's life and active ministry in Africa was coming to an end. The day Liz and I were married was the same day Albert Schweitzer was memorialized and buried at his hospital in Africa. It was not until many years later that Dr. Schweitzer's life and message of Reverence for Life would become a vital part of my life and the focal point of this book.

During the four years we lived in Larned, two more very special partnership events occurred for Liz and me. On July 21, 1967, we welcomed a very special will-to-live into the world. After much discussion, we named our first son Jay Brian. On November 25, 1968, a second will-to-live brought his unique cry into the world, and we named him Ty Franklin. What great gifts these two partners have been to their parents over the years!

From Pleasant Hill and Larned, we moved on to serve churches in the communities of Munden, Haddam, and Morrowville, in north central Kansas. In our three years there, we had the great pleasure of meeting a number of new partners in ministry. Then we relocated to western Kansas for a six-year stay at Hoxie, where both Jay and Ty started school while I served as minister to congregations in the United Methodist churches in Hoxie, Menlo, and McGraw. We continued to meet more partners in ministry while there, as well as during our one-year stay in Marion, Kansas. In 1979, Liz and I decided to return to our home state and moved to Melrose, a small town in western Wisconsin. We celebrated partnerships with many parishioners at the Melrose, Cataract, and Shamrock United Methodist Churches for eight years until my retirement from the active ministry in 1987.

The special partner I found and married continues to be a meaningful part of my life and was an important part of all the churches where we served, as she was especially talented at being a minister's wife. In fact, it would be much more accurate to say that she was my co-minister. Although now retired from her profession, Liz was a teacher and also the Gifted and Talented Coordinator for many years in the Melrose-Mindoro School District.

I feel very fortunate to have been blessed with such an incredible partner. How wonderful it has been to have such a special person by my side all of these years! How wonderful to have someone I could count on to always be there for me in my hour of need, someone to share my joys and happiness with, and someone to ease the pain of the sorrows and losses that I have experienced over the years. Although, as with most relationships, ours has not always been smooth, I am blessed to be in a partnership with someone who has always been willing to approach problems with an attitude of forgiveness and cooperation and a willingness to work things out. What a beautiful thing it is to be in a partnership of unconditional love.

The Moral of This Love Story

One of the many things I particularly cherish about my relationship with Liz is that it helps me to better understand the importance of my relationship to all people. I realize that, in all reality, Liz and I have been together all of these years because of a happy coincidence. Without the introduction by Martha and Albert all those years ago, our lives would not have become intertwined in such a meaningful way. In fact, I likely would have never met Elizabeth Clarson.

This, however, would not make Liz any less of a special person. Even if the coincidences that brought us together had never occurred, she would still be a special person, no less deserving of my respect and my love. Had she remained unknown to me, she would still be one of my human partners, and she would still be extra special to many people. She would still be her parents' daughter, her brothers' sister, and her friends' friend.

I feel much the same way about all of the partners I have had in my professional life: all of the partners from all of my years of study and preparation to become a minister; all of the partners I had the privilege to interact with at all of my churches and in all of the communities we lived in over the years; and all of the partners I have met since my retirement. Everywhere we have gone, Liz and I have made new friends—met new partners who have enriched our lives immeasurably. I greatly cherish all of these partnerships and the effect they have had on my life.

Yet I realize that, in a sense, it was coincidence that brought me into contact with each and every one of these partners along the way. And I find it interesting to think that all of these people, had we never encountered them, would be unknown to us. This, though, would not make them any less important, any less valuable. They still would be important partners to all of the special people in their lives.

And so, too, do I realize that all of the people I have *not* had the good fortune of meeting in my lifetime are special partners in their own right. All of the people in all of the United Methodist churches I never served, plus all of the people of all faiths and religions all around the world, and all people who do not belong to a particular religion or faith—in short, all people everywhere—are my partners. Though they may not be special partners to me, they surely are to somebody; and given the right circumstances, they could become so to me, as well. If I only had the time or the ability to meet all of them, then they all could become my special partners. All people deserve to be treated with my love, honor, and respect.

We should always remember this and make every effort to treat all people—extra special loved ones, close friends, acquaintances, and people unknown to us alike—with the same level of love, honor, and respect: with the same amount of reverence. We should view all of our partners all around the world in the same loving light as we do those human partners we have had the good fortune to befriend or to be partners with on a deeper level. There are no strangers in this world. There are only partners we have not yet had the opportunity to become friends with.

Every encounter with a person we do not know is an opportunity to make a new friend. Every situation is a partnership possibility. When we realize this and begin to treat *all* of our partners—known and unknown, human and non-human alike—with the full reverence they deserve, we open up greater possibilities for meaningful interaction with all life. Subsequently, our lives become richer and more full of meaning, and the world becomes more peaceful and full of reverence. We must always remember: Every encounter with every life form every day is an opportunity to bring love to life, an opportunity to act with Reverence for All Life.

12

The Wedding: a Special Day of Reverence

By John Webster

Weddings are events of special reverence. They represent in concrete form the abstract love that "makes the world go 'round" and is the essence of Reverence for All Life. Here, I present the story of a very special day in my life and the life of my family. The occasion was the wedding of my eldest son Jay and daughter-in-love Steffi.

When I came home from work on Mother's Day in May of 2001, Liz informed me that our son, Jay, had phoned and wanted me to call him back. This seemed strange. Why would he want to talk to me on Mother's Day? With much curiosity, I touched a "memory" button on our telephone and was connected to Jay's apartment in Düsseldorf, Germany. Jay soon divulged the reason for his call. He had a very important question to ask me: Would I be willing to officiate at a wedding ceremony for him and his German fiancé, Steffi, in Wisconsin in September?

The request did not come as a complete surprise, as Jay and Steffi had been "seeing each other" for six years. Steffi was the reason Jay was living and working in Germany, and they were engaged the previous Christmas. The September date, however, was news. With no hesitation and great enthusiasm, I made my reply: Of course I would be happy to officiate at the ceremony! I would have been disappointed had they not asked me.

In Germany, weddings are normally divided into two parts, the legal ceremony and a church ceremony, at separate times and places. Jay and Steffi decided it would be advantageous for several reasons to have the legal ceremony in Wisconsin, with the more formal church ceremony in Germany at a later date. My hope for the event on this side of the ocean was that it would be unique, meaningful, and full of reverence.

Jay and Steffi arrived in early September to prepare for the September 16 wedding, which was to be held in Perrot State Park, a mile down the road from our home in Trempealeau. The plan was to hold the ceremony, weather permitting, on the observation deck overlooking the Trempealeau River and Trempealeau Mountain in this very scenic corner of the world. In the event of rain, we would move to a room in the park's nearby Nature Center.

As I prepared for the ceremony, I asked Jay and Steffi to make a list of gifts they felt were important in the continuing development of a marriage partnership. Several days later they came with a long list. We decided they would choose ten gifts from their list to focus on. Each would be printed on its own poster and displayed at the ceremony. The words would be written in both English and German to signify the unification of two cultural backgrounds into one relationship and to make Steffi's mother, Irmgard—who was making her first trip to the U.S. for the ceremony—feel more at home (although she could understand much more English than we could German).

On the day of the wedding we all kept a close eye on the weather reports as the ceremony time approached. The last one before we headed into the park looked questionably promising. The rain on the radar screen appeared to be 40 or 50 miles away but moving in our direction. Perhaps we could get the ceremony in before it arrived. Such was not the case, however. Just as the caravan of cars bringing the wedding party and its 30-some guests—all very dear friends and family members—arrived at the parking lot near the deck, sprinkles began to fall.

So, it was on to Plan B and the Nature Center. Changing the setting did not pose a problem, but something else did. The room was a haven for flies looking for shelter from the cool September day, and there was a literal swarm of the pesky critters. We knew this beforehand, and in fact, Jay's brother, Ty, and his friend, Matt, had checked out the room earlier in the day and considered spraying the flies with an insecticide. Although they opted not to do so, their decision was made not so much out of reverence for the lives of the flies as it was for the children who were playing in the building at the time. The flies had come very close to becoming a "necessary kill of the moment." Instead, they became uninvited guests at the wedding, which really was much more appropriate, given the theme of my wedding message.

Hurriedly, the room was rearranged to provide an organized setting for the wedding. Two posters with messages printed in both English and German were placed on the fireplace mantle to highlight the unifying theme. One said, "Will to Live – Reverence for Life / Lebenswille – Ehrfucht vor dem Leben." The second: "Love is a Circle / Liebe ist ein Kreis."

We had chosen the song "Love is a Circle" to use as a unifying theme for this marriage, which was bringing together two families from two countries on two continents, along with a host of friends and relatives, into an ever-widening circle of love. I have always felt that the words affirm a basic truth, and we thought the song especially appropriate for this ceremony. It was used to celebrate not only this special union but also the continuing relationships of our family and friends. The ceremony began and ended with everyone singing together the refrain:

Love is a circle; it knows no bounds
The more you give the more comes around
Love is ours alone to give – it lives in us, it's beautiful.

The individual verses were sung at appropriate points throughout the ceremony, with the refrain affirming each one's message.

Love is a circle round and round
Love is up, Love is down
Love is inside trying to get out
Love is whirling and twirling about.

Love is a circle trying to bend
Love is pieces trying to mend
Love is darkness waiting for light
Love is power and love is might.

Love is a laugh, Love is a look
Love is the chance somebody took
Love will hide, Love will show
The more you give the more it grows.

Love is a circle round and round
Love in the corners of squares can be found
Love is reaching spreading its wings
Love will dance and love will sing.(1)

When it came time for my special message, I shared the ideas I felt were so central to this blessed occasion:

"Marriage is a special partnership: a partnership involving the giving and receiving of many important gifts. The first gift that we celebrate is the will-to-live. The will-to-live is a special gift that relates each of us to God, to one another, and to all that lives. We are life which wills to live, in the midst of life which wills to live. We might ponder for a moment what we are in the midst of here in the park. The first thing that comes to mind probably are the flies. But there also are the birds, the flowers, and the trees. When it comes to the will-to-live there is often conflict, but the amazing thing is that our will-to-live often aims at becoming one with other life and this is what we celebrate. Today, Jay's will-to-live and Steffi's will-to-live unite in ways that will allow many meaningful events to take place. In many ways their lives become one.

"The second gift we celebrate is Reverence for Life. Reverence for All Life. This reverence can often turn the conflict between wills-to-live into harmony. We can thank Albert Schweitzer for the phrase 'Reverence for Life.' This idea first flashed into Schweitzer's mind 81 years ago this month as he journeyed up the Ogowe River in Africa. Thereafter, Schweitzer often suggested that Reverence for all that lives is the key to becoming human and the key to becoming civilized.

"Today, as we stand beside the Trempealeau River in Wisconsin, we affirm that Reverence for All Life is still important and perhaps is our only hope for becoming fully human. The will-to-live filled with Reverence for Life brings us to the sacredness of these moments."

Then it was time for Jay and Steffi to share the list of gifts they had selected as most important in the molding of a meaningful partnership. Jay turned to Steffi and began: "I vow to give you the gift of Compromise." Speaking in German, Steffi returned the same vow to Jay: "Ich gebe das Geschenk der Kompromissbereitschaft." The pattern continued as Jay vowed in English and Steffi echoed in German the remaining nine gifts: Love/Liebe; Sharing/Teilen; Togetherness/Zusammen stehen; Trust/Vertrauen; Understanding/Verständnis; Patience/Geduld; Passion/Hingabe; Friendship/Freundschaft; and Happiness/ Fröhlichkeit.

The bride and groom then exchanged the wedding vows they had written together, and sealed their union with the same golden rings Liz and I had used in our own wedding ceremony 36 years earlier. Then I made their union official:

"For as much as Jay and Steffi have known each other for over six years, and during those years have traveled some 100,000 miles to be together as much as possible, and for as much as they have written their vows together and shared them with us today and have exchanged rings, I pronounce that they are husband and wife together in the name of God, and of Jesus, and of the Holy Spirit. Amen.

"May we, with love and friendship, support Jay and Steffi as they strive toward an ever more meaningful partnership. May they not only reach inward to each other with love but also reach out to the world with love and service. In the name of Jesus we pray. Amen."

The bride and groom turned to face the congregation, and, with great pride and much love, I made the announcement: "I present to you Jay and Stefanie Webster!"

As the newlyweds shared a short embrace, there was a brief moment of silence broken by Matthew, the two-year-old son of Jay's cousin Cathy and her husband Gary, when he exclaimed what we all were thinking: "I like that!"

With a sense of joy and a sigh of relief, I felt that my original hope had been fulfilled: that the service might be somewhat unique yet meaningful and filled with the attitude of Reverence for All Life. How great it felt for the first time to have a daughter in the family, a daughter who would call me "Dad."

Note

1.) Phyllis Hiller; "Love is a Circle;" Words and music copyright 1971 by Oak Hill Music Publishing Company. Used by permission of Ms. Hiller.

13

Beyond Borders

By Jay Webster

When my father asked me to contribute a chapter to his book, I was initially a bit overwhelmed. Where should I even begin? This is his book, and I was not sure I had anything to say that would enhance the ideas he was presenting. After much thought, though, I realized that my experience as an American expatriate has given me a broader perspective on life both inside and outside U.S. borders, and this perspective might provide the foundation for a chapter that would be "book-worthy."

My personal circumstances have lead me down a path that has taken me far from my native shores for an extended period and brought a wonderful woman into my life, my wife and eternal love, Steffi. Because Steffi is German, I have had the chance, if not been forced (gently, most of the time), to look at the United States from a perspective that I could never have otherwise had, the perspective of an outsider. I claim no superiority or uniqueness in my set of circumstances, only a perspective that is my own, gained from the journey along my own specific life path. I have endeavored, therefore, to contribute to the book something of value based on my particular accumulation of experience.

In many ways my journey began as I watched my younger brother, Ty, walk up the passengers' boarding ramp onto a waiting 747 at Chicago's O'Hare Airport in 1990. He was bound for London Heathrow, off to spend his junior year of college studying abroad at the University of Nottingham in Great Britain. I clearly remember a twinge of jealousy. I was wishing it was me walking up that ramp. It was my first inkling, the first planting of the seed of an idea, that maybe I should consider expanding my horizons—get out and see the world for myself. I grew up in small towns in rural Kansas and Wisconsin, and went through my early adult years without expanding my personal universe much beyond the Chicago metropolitan area. I studied at North Central College in Naperville, Illinois, and moved into the heart of the Windy City after obtaining my degree.

I was perfectly happy living in Chicago. But at some point in that first year after Ty left, the seed sprouted. I became determined to see a bit more of the world. Maybe it was simply his going that did it, the realization that if my little brother could strike off to see the world, so could I. Maybe it had to do with the things I started reading around that time. Maybe I just developed some hint of disaffection with where I was. Whatever the case, I remember being captivated by the letters written on that flimsy, crinkly, exotic, light blue airmail paper with the foreign stamps that Ty sent me from England. There was something out there beyond my limited boundaries—some mysterious, wonderful things, my knowledge of which was confined to books and TV shows. And my kid brother was there, experiencing them, and reporting back to me. Why couldn't I go there, too? What was stopping me? Nothing!

So finally it was my turn to walk up that ramp at O'Hare. Okay, I was only going for six weeks. But what an experience! The whole trip, to this day, is still so ingrained in my memory. My brother, his friend Mark, and I backpacked around Europe for a month, and I was instantly hooked. Medieval castles, classic art, Italian pasta, Greek gyros, French wine, the wide, azure expanse of the Aegean Sea, Swiss chocolate, German bier, cultured French cheeses, snow-capped Alpine mountain peaks, the Coliseum in Rome before my very eyes like a page from a history book come to life. And I was experiencing all of it first hand.

I went back to Chicago without much thought of an immediate return, but my imagination continued to be fired by my favorite writers. The likes of Henry Miller, Ernest Hemmingway, and James Joyce—my holy triumvirate—seemingly called me back for further European experiences. After two more years in Chicago, the urge became too great to resist. I packed my bags and headed to Dublin, Ireland, where my brother was then living. I had very little money and even fewer plans or ideas of what I was going to do. I knew only that I wanted to stay on European soil for as long as possible. It didn't work out completely the way I wanted, but I had some great experiences, met some great people, lived in Paris and Spain for a bit, and was back in Wisconsin with hardly a dollar to my name after six months.

The experience only enhanced my affinity for life in Europe, and I was determined to return. So a year and a half later, there I was, back in Dublin. I lived there for six months and then spent a month in Prague before my funds ran short again. I re-stocked my coffers in Wisconsin for a further six months and headed back to Ireland. My roommate was a musician, and I signed on as his band's "roadie," lugging around gear and helping out with the sound system. He was tired of "the scene" in Dublin and wanted to give Germany a shot. I was game for pretty much anything. As it turned out, fate was smiling on me.

In Germany I met Steffi. I felt that she was a great girl: the one I had been waiting for. And to my immense gratitude, Steffi felt the same way about me. We began to spend as much time together as possible.

Before long, it came time for that unavoidable day: the one where you get introduced to "the family." The situation can be anxiety-inducing in the best of circumstances, but I was especially nervous. What would her family think of me, a wayward American who could speak only a few words of their native language? I'm happy to say that all of my fears were unfounded. I think her family could sense the powerful bond that was starting to grow between Steffi and me. At any rate, they welcomed me with open arms, as if I were already a part of the family, from the day that I met them.

Unfortunately, work was not always steady for the band. Gigs were hard to come by, and we were living so literally hand-to-mouth that we didn't know from week-to-week if we were going to be able to stay in Germany. The threat of having to pack it in cast a shadow over the early days of my relationship with Steffi.

If things did not work out, I would have to return to the States. We knew we couldn't justify maintaining such a long-distance relationship after being together for only a few months. But somehow the band hung on. The gigs kept coming just often enough, and we were able to stay in Germany for a full year. My relationship with Steffi continued to progress, and when I finally booked a ticket back to America, she already had a ticket to come and visit.

We had a wonderful six weeks in the U.S., highlighted by a memorable road trip with brother, Ty, in a little 1984 Honda Civic wagon. We traveled from Wisconsin, via New York City and Washington D.C., to visit our Aunt Gerry in Orlando, Florida. I introduced Steffi to my American friends and family, and I'm happy to say that she was as welcome in my circle of love as I was in hers. One of the saddest moments in my life was when she boarded the plane back to Germany, as I did not know for sure when I would see her again. Thinking back on it, the faith she put in me to come back to her was monumental, considering the circumstances. But by that time, there was no doubt in my mind that I would do just that. "If" had nothing to do with it. It was only a matter of "When."

I toiled the fall away, picking apples in a small, family-run orchard in Wisconsin, and by Christmas I had saved enough money to fly back to Europe. Steffi was now in Paris, France, living with a family and working as their au pair, or nanny. Paris was the city of my dreams. The fact that it had been home to fellow American expatriates such as Miller and Hemingway (two-thirds of the aforementioned triumvirate) had endeared it to me, and my two previous visits had done nothing to lessen my affinity for "the City of Light."

I found a tiny room (and I do mean tiny) on the top floor of a very nice building in Paris' 17th arrondissement and enjoyed a wonderful five months of bohemian wanderings throughout that magical city. Steffi and I curled up in our little nest on the 3 days that she had off each week, and our love continued to flower amidst the blooming boulevards of the Parisian springtime. I must say that I wouldn't trade those five months for much of anything. But our time, and my money, eventually ran out, and it was back to America for me. Alone.

By then we knew that if we were going to continue our relationship over the long-term, we needed to be in the same location for more than a few months at a time. Steffi was preparing to start her university studies in Germany, so if we were going to be together, I needed to find a way to relocate there. I endeavored to find truth in the old cliché: "Where there's a will, there's a way." After another stint in the apple orchard, I flew back to Europe in November. Before long, I found an apartment in Düsseldorf, Germany, and landed a job teaching English. That was 1997. Steffi and I married in 2001, and I am still here. Well, in Europe, anyway. In the spring of 2003 we moved to Dublin. I am back home, at the roots of my European life, so to speak.

So here I am, an expatriate: a word that had so much meatiness for me in the "dreaming days" of my early adulthood. It's what I so desired to be, something that suggested being and not being at the same time, belonging and not belonging, here and not here. In a way, it's something that I still enjoy: the sense of strangeness, foreignness, even, that washes over me when I fly back to the U.S. It is a feeling of disorientation pervaded with familiarity. Home and, yet, not-home.

I love having more than one "home" country: getting an understanding of countries that are not America. But I have not refuted my American-ness. I don't deny it and, to a great degree, relish it. However, I cannot say that I am always proud to be an American. In some ways I am more vulnerable than most Americans to feeling the shame that America as a nation sometimes brings upon itself through its actions. Because the press and the people in the countries where I have lived are so open in expressing their displeasure of the more-than-occasional blunder in U.S. foreign policy or madness on the national scene in America, I am often faced—as my countrymen back home are generally not—with the awareness that my home country is far less than perfect. (I find it interesting to note that these same people, who readily criticize America's mistakes, are generally more able to understand the things that make America great, as well.)

That is one thing that strikes me, from this overseas seat, about America as a nation: its inability to question itself, or even to acknowledge or grasp the ways in which its policies affect the daily lives of people around the world. When our bombs fall on people in other lands, we cannot feel the pain and suffering that falls with them. When an embargo clamps down in another region of the globe, we cannot fathom what it is like to face empty store shelves or to take a sick child to the hospital and find no medicine. When the U.S. government coddles dictators or topples regimes, bullies or ignores the international community—all according to its whims and the political winds of the day—the plight of the people in those countries is far from our minds. We tend to believe what we're told, take it on faith that our government is acting in the best interests of the people in those areas. We don't want to believe that our government acts primarily in its own interests and the interests of the big corporations who profit from our government's actions.

I understand this shortsightedness, for I had it, too, when I lived in the U.S. But now I realize that many Americans have trouble seeing that there are other ways of doing things, of going about their business in the world. It is a blind spot that is the result, I suppose, of living in such a vast and unvaried land: a land that is the lone undisputed superpower in the world. It is an ignorance I have found myself trying to explain to people in the countries I have lived in, after they have encountered some of my countrymen who are stricken with Ugly American Syndrome: acting like the world is made for them alone and wondering, often at the top of their lungs, why things are not going the way they want them to.

I will, to a certain extent, defend my countrymen's behavior. Because while Americans are often good at displaying their lack of grasp of the world that is Not America, the majority of the time their actions are not mean spirited. They are simply being confronted with things outside of their realm of experience. So when fellow Americans ask my wife or me if we have TV in Germany, or when they think Austria is part of Germany, or make off-color jokes about Hitler or Nazis, it is usually not the result of willful ignorance. Generally, these are nice people of at least average intelligence. They are curious and, in their own way, attempting to reach out and understand the rest of the world. They simply haven't been exposed to other cultures or points of view that would enable them to understand how ridiculous they are making themselves seem.

And although I do not blame these people for their ignorance, I am aware that it is problematic. This inability to comprehend the rest of the world ultimately leads to the U.S. being cut off from the world community. What many Americans fail to realize is that too often the definitions we use to make ourselves feel that we belong to a group or community—whether it be national, ethnic, religious or otherwise—also serve to exclude the "others" that don't belong to our group. It is one of the most basic human urges, this need to belong, and it is one of the most important. It makes us social creatures striving for connections. This is a noble, honorable, creative, and rewarding endeavor. But it can also become an obstacle to understanding those outside of our own groups.

The challenge for America, and the rest of the world, too, in this divided, fractured age, is not only to nurture our existing connections but to overcome them, in order not to be constrained by them. We must look beyond our borders, personal as well as national. And we must strive to reach out to those who are outside of those boundaries and make new connections with them. In so doing, we must not only respect those people's differences but also work to understand them and, ultimately, be enriched by them. We must first do this on an individual basis: each of us striving in our own way, seeking to make our own connections. For then, eventually, a time will come when nations as a whole will be able to make these same connections.

I will use a hypothetical example: If I am an American and I am told that the nation of Ham doesn't support our President, and the members of Congress are re-naming hamburgers in the Capitol cafeteria "Freedom burgers," should I hate this Ham place and its people because they are different and don't agree with the leaders of my group? Should I try to get as far away from this Ham and its people and its culture and its products as I can? Should I vilify and ridicule it? Should I sow seeds of division and discontent? Should I make my circle smaller and smaller?

Or should I take a different approach? Should I view my leaders' commands as only one possible option and then listen for myself to what the people of Ham have to say? Should I perhaps visit their country, meet their people, sit at their tables...in other words, reach out, form connections and make my circle larger?

And what if it is not another country? What if it's my own neighbor who comes from another country or another ethnic group or another religion, or any of the other boundaries we use to define our groups? Rather than chastise each other because of our obvious differences, shouldn't we sit down and break bread together, seek to understand each other? We don't always have to agree; how can everyone everywhere agree on everything? But on the other hand, how can this world survive if we are forever dividing it and fighting those who are on the other side of our divisions? So many walls and divisions and prejudices are erected between people and groups that have never had the opportunity or made the effort to connect with and understand one another. I feel fortunate to know first hand that these walls are merely illusions.

I know how blessed I am to have found Steffi: someone to connect with and share my life with on a personal level. But I also feel another dimension of blessing through the connections I have made because Steffi is from Germany. My whole circle of love has been infinitely enriched by my connections with Steffi's family, her friends, and their culture. From the very beginning, I have been welcomed in the warmest regard in her country. This is a fact I do not take lightly, for I am well aware that our path could have been much more difficult had that not been the case.

I now feel as equally at home in Germany as I do in America. Steffi's friends have become my friends and her family my own. And I believe that it is the same with Steffi. How rich we have both become through our union. We were lucky enough to be able to have wedding ceremonies in both America and Germany. These were wonderful celebrations that brought many people from our different circles together to sit at the same table, to rejoice not just in our union, but in the coming together of disparate circles, in the dissolution of boundaries. People from many separate nations coming together in our widening circle of love.

It makes me infinitely happy that Steffi's mother, Irmgard, was able to visit my family in Wisconsin for our wedding ceremony there. And how wonderful it was to have my mom and dad meet all of Steffi's family when they came over for our German wedding. They were welcomed, as I knew they would be, with open arms. Spoken language difficulties were overcome, time and time and again, by the language of love. As Irmgard put it, "We speak to each other with our hearts."

So now we are one family spanning two continents, two countries, two ways of life. While Steffi and I still have to cross international borders in our frequent journeys to visit our families, the human boundaries between them have been made meaningless.

I have seen the same thing happen again and again with friends of ours who are together with partners from other countries. And it's not something that happens only with partners. I know so many people who have visited foreign countries and made connections with the people there. I have had this experience countless times. Everywhere I have gone, in every country I have traveled to or lived in, I have made close connections with at least a few people in those places.

There is no doubt in my mind or my heart that every one of us needs to be working to break down borders. I've seen and experienced first hand how rich it makes the people who strive to accomplish it. Our enemies should not be the people who live on the other side of borders, but the borders themselves. The borders must be removed. I love being American, and Steffi is proud to be German; but our union, by superseding our individual borders, has brought so much to both of us. So by way of wrapping up my chapter, I would like to make a wish. My wish for the world is that we make borders nothing more than lines on maps or definitions that describe us, that our boundaries and borders become tools to help us expand our circles by encouraging us to reach out beyond them, rather than confinements that divide and separate us from one another.

14

Our Journey to Germany and France

By John Webster

In September of 2002, Liz and I traveled to Germany for the second wedding of our son, Jay, and daughter-in-law, Steffi. (As I mentioned in Chapter 12, it is common for Germans to have two wedding ceremonies: a legal ceremony and a more formal church ceremony.) This was our first journey to Germany, and so our first opportunity to meet Steffi's brother, Roland, and sister, Alexandra, and their families. It was great to see Steffi's mother, Irmgard, again. And our other son, Ty, also joined the extended family celebration in Düsseldorf (where Jay and Steffi were living) and Wegberg (Steffi's home town). How nice it was to have our families together for this special occasion!

The German wedding was a beautiful ceremony in a picturesque church in Wegberg. Alexandra and her daughters, Karolin, Annika, and Julia, made the occasion extra special by providing lovely music. Over seventy friends and family members from no less than five different countries were in attendance at the wedding. What a wonderful, international gathering: more proof that we live in a small and interconnected world!

Our journey lasted two weeks, so we had plenty of time to take in some of the sights in the region. One day, Jay and Steffi took us on a short train ride to the nearby city of Cologne, where we took a tour through the massive Kölner Dom (Cologne Cathedral), a masterwork of the High Gothic period and one of the largest cathedrals in Europe. The building is one of the few in Cologne's business district that was not destroyed during the Allied bombardment of WWII, largely because it was used as a landmark by pilots. In my mind, it stands as yet another reminder of the evils of war. It would have been a great tragedy had this incredible stone structure been destroyed.

On the following Wednesday morning, Liz, Ty, Jay, Steffi, and I climbed into a BMW rental car in Düsseldorf and headed off on what I suppose could be termed a pilgrimage of sorts.

Our destination was the Münster Valley, snuggled in the midst of the Vosges Mountains in the Alsace region of France. We were headed for Schweitzer territory. A highlight of the day was a drive through the renowned Mittelrhein (Middle Rhine) river valley, where picturesque, centuries-old towns nestle on both riverbanks below steep bluffs topped by many medieval castles. Inevitably, we compared the Rhine valley to the Mississippi River valley, our home in the United States. Both valleys are spectacular in their own way.

In the evening we drove across the border between Germany and France, passing buildings that only a few years ago served as border patrol checkpoints. For many years, all travelers were stopped here and questioned when they crossed the border from one country to the other. This is no longer the case. Although at times during their history they have disliked each other intensely and even been on opposing sides of bloody wars, both countries are now members of the European Union. You can now pass as freely between these countries as you can between states in the U.S. Maybe it really is possible for people to learn to trust one another and for nations to give up a bit of their own nationalism for the sake of the greater good.

Dusk was falling as we drove into the Münster Valley. I remember it vividly, as I was especially excited that evening. After all, this was the valley where Albert Schweitzer grew up, and where he returned so often throughout his adult life. With great anticipation I looked forward to the following day, when we could visit some of the places that were so special to this man who has become such an important part of my life and thought these last several years.

One of the places we visited the next day was Schweitzer's birthplace. In *Memoirs of Childhood and Youth,* Schweitzer reminisced, "I was born on January 14, 1875, in little Kaysersberg in Upper Alsace in the house with the turret, on the left side as you leave town." At the time of Schweitzer's birth, Kaysersberg was a part of Germany; after the First World War Alsace once more became a part of France. The ground floor of the turreted house where Albert was born, as well as the building next door, is now a museum that honors the one who was born there. Only persons who have accomplished something extra special with their lives have their birthplaces turned into museums. So it is with Albert Schweitzer.

The turreted house in Kaysersberg, France,
where Albert Schweitzer was born in 1875.

Half a year after Albert's birth, his family moved to Günsbach, in the Münster Valley, where his Father served as pastor for the next fifty years. With much interest, the five of us spent that September day enjoying the spirit and beauty of the small village nestled in the Münster Valley where Schweitzer spent so much of his life, and where the spirit of his being lives on today. (We mono-lingual Americans were extremely fortunate to have Steffi with us, as she is very proficient in translating German and French spoken words and signs into English.)

Our first stop was Schweitzer's house. He had the house built in 1928, and it was his European home for the remainder of his life. Schweitzer chose to locate the house close to the street, rather than toward the back of the lot, so he could be closer to the townspeople, whom he loved so dearly. It was common for the locals to bring gifts of eggs or vegetables and place them on the windowsill of his study when he was there. Today, several rooms on the first floor of the house are open to the public as a museum. Our guide told us that about 5,000 people visit the museum each year.

Dr. Schweitzer's European home in Günsbach, France,
now houses The Albert Schweitzer museum.

Schweitzer's study has been kept just as it was when he left it for the last time in 1959. The room doubled as his bedroom, with his desk at one end and his bed at the other. This was a convenient arrangement because Schweitzer often worked late into the night, writing letters and studying, and did not want to disturb others staying in the house. In another room of the museum, a piano occupies one wall. The piano, which has foot pedals so that Schweitzer could play it like an organ, is the very same one he used for so many years in Lambarene, Africa. It was shipped back to Günsbach several years before Schweitzer's death. Other rooms of the museum are used to display archives, including many of the letters Schweitzer wrote and received throughout the years. With tremendous interest and a great sense of awe, I stood in this historic place and tried to soak up as much of the atmosphere and information as possible. How exhilarating it was to be in the same place that Schweitzer spent so much time during his life.

Dr. Schweitzer (on right) in the doorway of his Günsbach home in the early 1930's.

The Webster family on the same doorstep some 70 years later.

We then set out on our walking tour of the quiet streets of Günsbach. We stopped off at the two houses where the Schweitzer family had lived while Albert's father was pastor of the local church. It was in the second house that Albert had awakened that quiet morning of his 21st year and decided that at age 30 he would devote his life in some capacity to full-time service to humanity. Schweitzer spent a good portion of his youth in this old presbytery, and until 1925 always came back to visit his father there. As I walked past the house and looked toward the upstairs windows, I had the awesome feeling that I was indeed retracing the footsteps of a very special and important person, a person who, at the age of 21, had already spent a good deal of time thinking about the man Jesus as He was portrayed in the Bible and the Jesus who was portrayed by the music of Bach. The house, which now belongs to the Albert Schweitzer Foundation, has been renovated and adapted as a place for meetings and contemplation. Bedrooms are available for people who wish to spend their holidays there.

We walked past the building where, as a boy, Albert had started school and on to the church—its tall steeple rising above the village—that had meant so much to the young Schweitzer. It was here on the church's organ, which Schweitzer later helped to redesign, that young Albert began his musical endeavors.

We then left the village and strolled along the path up a nearby hill, the same hill where the young Schweitzer and his friend had set out to hunt birds that morning long ago. I was filled with deep emotion as I looked back down to the church from which the bells rang forth the Commandment which so influenced Schweitzer. May that concept, "Thou shalt not kill," ring into each of our hearts every day that we live, just as it did for Schweitzer on that memorable childhood day.

A View of the Günsbach Church from the hill above town.

Farther up the hill we came to one of Schweitzer's favorite spots. He called it, "the rock," or "the rocks," and would often retreat there to write or just to think and enjoy being so close to nature. From this serene spot in a clearing of the woods on the hillside above town, Albert could see the church, the village, the Münster Valley, and the Vosges Mountains in the distance. Schweitzer spent many meaningful moments here throughout the years.

A view of Günsbach from the hill above the town.

Today at this spot, there is a large, stone statue of Schweitzer, reminding all who retrace Schweitzer's footsteps up the hill to remember that "Reverence for Life" and the spirit that urges people to do great things and achieve excellence are not passing fantasies, but are ongoing foundations of hope in our lives.

As we consider the Münster Valley and Albert Schweitzer's European hometown, Günsbach, let us remind ourselves that Schweitzer also had a home in Africa that was very special to him. And let us also realize that today the entire world is his home as he lives on in all the lives which continue to radiate the very special message and ethic of Reverence for Life. Some of us may never be able to visit Günsbach or Lambarene, but each of us can experience the Schweitzer message right here in our lives and in any part of the world that is special to us.

Back in Wegberg after our exhilarating journey, we prepared to leave Germany and return home. While saying goodbye to Alexandra, I said without really thinking, "Thanks for sharing your family with us." Alexandra's immediate response was, "No, now it is *our* family!" So I quickly replied, with a slight feeling of embarrassment and a wonderful feeling of celebration, "Thanks for sharing *our* family with *us*."

Imagine the entire world as our family and that we can now say, "We are one!" We can share *our* family—the family of the world—with *us*. We all are partners. If all the world's people were inspired by the ethic of Reverence for Life, we could go anywhere in the world and feel secure, as there would be a great union of our "wills-to-live." This feeling of the many becoming one in support and friendship is awesome and comforting. Would that this oneness and support could be a reality more often! Indeed, it can be when we experience and demonstrate oneness and "strangerlessness" in the corner of the world where we happen to be at any given moment: when we make the concepts of Reverence for All Life an integral part of our lives.

114

15

A Summer Day Filled with Partners

By John Webster

"Reverence for life affords me my fundamental principle of morality, namely, that good consists in maintaining, assisting and enhancing life..."
--Albert Schweitzer; Civilization and Ethics.

Today was a beautiful, comfortable summer day in my little corner of the world. It was 75 degrees Fahrenheit, sunny, and clear along the banks of the Mississippi River in Trempealeau, Wisconsin: a perfect day to appreciate and feel reverence for all of the various living partners—human and non-human—that I encountered throughout the day. As it turned out, most of the partners that came into my sphere of awareness on this fine day were of the non-human variety. The only human contacts were with Liz—my partner in marriage—and our son, Ty, who paid us a brief visit.

During the morning hours, Liz was busy doing some house cleaning. In 38 years of marriage I have learned that things go much more smoothly in our partnership if I lend a hand on cleaning day. So I did not protest too much when Liz requested that I get rid of the various spiders, which had been busy with their web building around the house. I grabbed my "bug cup"—a large plastic cup and lid that I keep handy for the relocation of any insect-type partners that find their way into the house—and captured several large "daddy-longlegs" spiders.

I took the spiders one-by-one out to find new homes in the back yard. I don't know if the spiders were pleased with the move, but figured that any future human visitors to our home might not like spiders and would not miss them at all. I also captured several flying ants in my cup and ushered them out of the house. Although

I am happy to have ants and spiders as partners, I don't always feel the need to share our house with them.

About mid-morning, I heard an excited call from Liz, who was dusting in the dining room. She had noticed Tipper, one of our two housecats, looking very intently out the window. When Liz investigated to see what was so intriguing to the cat, she noticed something dangling from the overhang of the roof just outside the back door. Upon closer examination we discovered that the creature was a bat, and it seemed to be trapped. Both of its wing tips were stuck, and the bat was struggling to get loose. I could sense the creature's pain and anguish. Its will-to-live was obvious as it desperately tried to free itself.

I suffered along with the creature for what seemed like a long time, hoping it would manage to free itself; but then I realized this would not happen. We began to wonder what might be the best way to help. After a frantic search, I found a long, narrow mop handle and stepped outside. Cautiously and as carefully as possible I pushed one of the bat's wing tips loose.

With one wing free, the bat resumed its struggle. To my great relief, the creature soon managed to free its other wing and flew to a new, safer resting place around the corner by the chimney. I felt very good that I had been able to assist a fellow partner in its moment of need. The experience once again reminded me that it is always rewarding to assist any partner that can use some help.

Later in the day, after Liz had gone to work, I was watching my favorite baseball team, the Chicago Cubs, on TV. I heard a noise outside the back door and got up to investigate. I discovered a young woodchuck making the ruckus as it attempted to get a drink from a pail of water on the back step. What a treat: we don't get to see "chucks" very often.

However, my celebration soon turned to concern as the creature was also hungry and began to chomp on a nearby houseplant that Liz had set outside. I suddenly found myself in the middle of conflicting wills-to-live. Should it be reverence for the life of the hungry animal or for Liz and her plant? I decided it would be best for all partners involved in this little drama if the plant were not eaten, so tapped on the window and urged the woodchuck to move on to other vegetation out in the yard.

A little later I noticed a few squirrels in the back yard. As Liz was not yet home, I decided to put some sunflower seeds out for them. Liz is not a big fan of feeding squirrels and raccoons. She says (rightfully so, perhaps) that they should fend for themselves and not be so lazy. I, however, get quite a kick out of watching them eat. But I soon realized I had made a mistake by putting all the seeds into one pile. This meant that only one squirrel could eat at a time. Squirrels, it seems, have no reverence for life except as it relates to themselves. Would one let a second squirrel eat at the same pile at the same time? No! One greedy squirrel even chased a nearby rabbit away, although the bunny was not remotely interested in the seeds. So my reverence for life urged me to put some more seeds out in different spots so that more than one squirrel could eat at the same time.

In the evening, I had another opportunity to act with a sense of reverence. I noticed that the hummingbird feeder outside our window was full of ants. Although it is possible that the ants were happy swimming around in the sugar water, I knew this was dangerous for them and figured the hummingbirds probably didn't like drinking from a feeder infested with ants. So I fished all of the ants out of the feeder. I think the hummers and the ants were all better off after my actions.

Just before dark, I took one more reverential action. I removed the bird feeder from its stand in our front yard and hid it in a garbage can. I have learned to do this in order to protect the raccoons that tend to visit our yard at night. If we leave the bird feeder out, they climb up and hang on it. This not only puts a sizeable dent in our birdseed supply, it also strikes me as a danger to the raccoons. I fear they might get hung up on the feeder or knock it off and hurt themselves.

Last night the raccoons knocked the hummingbird feeder down and dismantled it, so tonight I brought that feeder in the house and put it where I hoped the in-house ants wouldn't find it.

The only non-human partners who are supposed to be in our house are Tipper and our other longhaired cat, Moonbeam. However, ants are allowed to stay unless they become too numerous. Then some of them are ushered—in the bug cup—from the confines of the house to a new home outside (which is probably only a back door to their regular home under the house somewhere). A world filled with partners is such fun and at times a real challenge!

Now, as dusk settles over our two acres of wondrous woods and weeds that look out across the Mississippi River toward Minnesota, I reflect on what a special day this was. I cannot recall having to intentionally harm or kill any of my partners. Many days involve will-to-live divided against will-to-live, and we must make choices about what we will allow to live and that which we must kill. But no such choices were necessary for me today. However, I am sure that as I walked about the yard I unintentionally stepped on a few ants or other bugs and for that I am sorry. Mostly, though, I am happy I had so many opportunities to experience Reverence for All Life.

As I glance out the back door, I see that our family of five raccoons has arrived, and they are eating the sunflower seeds left by the squirrels. (Don't tell Liz, Tipper and Moonbeam, but I threw out a little bit of cat food for them. Boy, do raccoons ever like cat food!) What a great way to end a day involving many partners. At this moment I celebrate the will-to-live of five raccoons, some fireflies flickering in the yard beyond my window, two cats, and one human. And also—I hope—flitting somewhere through the night air, one bat with a slightly sore wingtip.

<u>16</u>

Moonbeam the Cat: A Story about Trust

By John Webster

I am a cat, the hero of this story. I was born on a farm in the rural township of Farmington, near Mindoro, Wisconsin, USA. I am not sure exactly where on the farm I was born, as our mother moved us around frequently. The first place I remember living with my brothers and sisters was under a granary located beside a busy highway that ran right through the middle of the farm.

One day Mom carried us one-by-one across the highway and up the drive between the two farmhouses to a new home behind the garage. As I look back, I sure feel fortunate I didn't get run over by a car or truck on that road where so many of my kin met their demise. I guess Mom must have been very careful with her precious packages.

When I was old enough to venture out on my own, I would sneak over to the houses hoping that one of the humans who lived there might have left something good to eat lying around. But I didn't trust those humans. They looked so big, and I was not about to let any of them get close to me. I was also scared of the dog that lived on that farm.

There was a fellow who lived in the bigger of the two houses who must have liked me. He would often come out of the house, sit on the back step, and talk to me. I later found out that one reason he liked me was because I closely resembled a cat of his killed on the highway just a few months before I was born. We both had long yellow fur, and if the other one looked anything like me, he must have been quite handsome!

This man started leaving bits of food on the back step, and, when no one was there, I would sneak over and eat it. I soon started to look forward to those handouts. Before long, when I would see that man sitting on the step, I would slink—keeping my body very close to the ground—over to where he was and position myself just out of his reach. I still did not trust him, even though he talked real nice to me and gave me good stuff to eat. After many days of this, I finally inched close enough for this man to touch me. I was awfully scared, but he seemed very nice. He did not hurt me, and in fact his petting felt good. Even so, I would not let him pet me for very long.

Little by little I continued to develop more trust in my human acquaintance. Then one day he left the back porch door of his house open a crack and put some food just inside. Little did I know it was a trap. As soon as I was inside, he shut the door and never let me go outside again! Looking back, I have to admit it is probably the best thing that ever happened to me.

At first I was very scared, but I soon came to like my new home and my new human friend. He was kind to me and fed me well. The house was huge, with big rooms upstairs and down. The spot I claimed for my very own was under the bed in the master bedroom. I felt safe there, and it was a good hiding place when there was any commotion or strange people were around. I found that I shared the house with another cat, named Wiederman. However, lucky ol' Wiederman was allowed to go outside and come back in whenever someone would open the door for him.

My friend began to call me "Moonbeam" because it seems I was born about the same time some guy with that nickname was running for President of the U.S. The name seemed strange, but I liked it and slowly became accustomed to it. I grew accustomed to my new home, too, as it was really very cozy. As for my human friend, I grew to trust him more and more.

Several days after I was "captured," the lady of the house arrived home from a trip to England. I was not happy with a strange person around and spent a lot of time under the bed again. But she seemed very nice, and little by little I learned to trust her, too. Eventually, I even let her touch me, and now I very much enjoy her petting and caresses. However, the guy who coaxed me into that house remains my best friend and companion. I have always enjoyed riding around on his shoulders and sleeping next to him at night.

At first I got to eat tuna fish and other good stuff, like chicken and turkey, very often. Then, much to my dismay, after I had lived there for several years, my friend decided to become a vegetarian. When asked why, he would say: "It is better for me; it is better for the animals; and it is better for the world that I don't eat meat." He didn't mention that it was not better for me. I really miss the tuna and other good stuff. However, I suppose my friend has a good point. After all, I'm an animal, and I sure wouldn't want someone to eat me for dinner. And besides, I soon discovered that I really like baked potatoes, sweet potatoes, squash, sweetcorn, and especially, mushrooms. So I still get to eat lots of yummy human food.

One night our next-door neighbor, the farmer, came to our door and told us that Wiederman had been hit and killed on the road. We were all sad and missed Wiederman very much. But I have to admit I liked having all of the attention focused on me. However, I wasn't the only cat for very long. The humans soon invited a lady kitten in, and she was a keeper because right away she knew enough to use the litter box. Her name is Tipper because the tip of her tail is white and the rest of her is darker. She has become a good friend of mine, but we do not have a romantic relationship, as we both had to make visits to see the vet early in our adult lives. However, that is another story—one I don't like to think about if I can help it. They did let me keep my claws, thank goodness!

As I said, Tipper and I are friends, but I don't even trust her all of the time. Sometimes she gets a funny look in her eyes and I know she is about to chase me under the bed. However, when Tipper is sitting on my partner's lap and I come along, she quickly gets down so I can have my favorite spot. I have let her know in no uncertain terms what she had better do in that situation.

For me, trust is so very important. I trust my friend because he is always nice to me. He lets me come and sit on his lap or snuggle against his shoulder when I wake up from my naps or almost any other time. It is nice to know that he is there when I need him. When I come begging at mealtime, he tries to find something for me even if it is only a cat treat.

If my friend weren't kind to me, I would not trust him. Once in a while he accidentally steps on my tail or kicks me. Even though I know his actions are unintentional, I run under the bed. It then takes some time to build back the usual level of trust I have for him. It takes time and effort to develop trust, and it can be lost so quickly. I'd like to trust all humans, but I usually say, "the heck with it" and run under the bed when strangers come into my house. If they want to see me, they can get down and look under the bed.

After several years of living in that farmhouse, my human friends decided to buy a house in Trempealeau, a town 30 miles away from the farm. They took all the furniture and other stuff out of the house and I wondered what was going to happen to me, as even my hideout under the bed was gone. Before long, though, my friend put me in his mini-van and took me for a ride. I was scared and let him know I was very unhappy by making a loud howling noise the entire trip. He tried to comfort me, but it didn't help much.

Finally, after what seemed an awfully long time, we stopped and he took me into a house and told me it was my new home. I didn't really believe him until I found my safe hideout under that same old bed. I soon learned to like my new home. There is a large picture window looking out on a big river that is spelled with a lot of S's and I's. During the cold winter days the sun comes in the window, and I enjoy sleeping and relaxing in the warmth of the sunlight.

Often on these cold days, my friend pulls a chair up next to the fireplace and sits with his feet near the fire while he reads a book or writes something on a piece of paper. When I see him there, I like to mosey over and jump up on his lap and then his shoulder for a hug or two before settling back down on his lap. My friend always puts his book or writing materials down and makes room for me. He keeps telling me to jump up quick before my tail gets too hot from rubbing on the fireplace glass. My friend grumbles a little about having his reading or writing interrupted, but I bet he would miss me if I were not here. Because he always makes time for me, I continue to trust him and call him my friend.

I especially enjoy the days that are warm enough to have the windows open so I can sit in the window and smell the outside air. Sometimes that gives me the urge to go outside. Then I sit by the door and pull on it with my claws to see if by chance it might not be latched. It almost always is, so I cry loudly, hoping someone will let me out. But no one ever does. My friend says I will live longer if I stay inside away from the hawks and foxes. He tells me these other animals don't have the same reverence for my life that he and his wife do. Maybe he is right, as I have already celebrated my thirteenth birthday, and they say that outdoor cats usually don't live so long.

Recently, my friend has been calling me his partner. However, he also calls everything else that lives his partners, too. I have heard him call the lady of the house his partner and also the neighbors, Tipper, the ants, and even the bugs. (I still think I am more important than any bug.) My partner says we need to be kind to all creatures and have Reverence for All Life. He makes statements like this: "We should never kill or injure any living thing unless it is absolutely necessary."

Although I listen to my friend, I'm afraid I can't always follow his advice. I have been known to eat spiders whenever I can find them. And I have to say that mice had better stay out of the house or Tipper and I will get them. After all, we're cats; we're not like humans, who can learn to treat all life with great reverence.

But boy am I glad that humans can! I'm very happy that my best friend had reverence for my life and brought me into his house and his life thirteen years ago. I know that my life has been much happier and probably a lot longer as a result of his kindness. And that is why I have become such a good listener. You see, my friend spends a lot of time talking to me, and I lie there and listen. My friend says it means a lot to him just to have somebody around to talk to, and I agree with almost everything he says. So maybe even a cat can have a little reverence for life for someone other than himself. And I sure hope everyone who reads my story can learn to listen to my friend's message and develop a greater sense of Reverence for All that Lives!

17

A Sheep Named "Orph"

By John Webster

"Wherever any animal is forced into the service of man, the sufferings which it has to bear on that account are the concern of every one of us. No one ought to permit, insofar as he can prevent it, pain or suffering for which he will not take the responsibility."
--Albert Schweitzer; Civilization and Ethics.

Hello! My name is "Orph." I am a sheep, and I have an important story to tell. I was born on a farm in Lafayette County, southwestern Wisconsin, USA. For some reason my mother was unable to take care of me after I was born, and I became an orphan. That's how I got my name. Several days after I was born, a man and a boy came and put me into a big box. They took me for a ride to another farm about a mile down the road.

This was my new home. Because I didn't have a mother, I had to be fed milk from a bottle with a nipple on it. The boy who had brought me to the new farm with his father had the duty of feeding me several times a day, and we soon became good friends.

He would let me follow him around the pasture and even, sometimes, up around the house. I think this was a very big privilege for a farm animal. The boy was very affectionate and would often take time to pet my nose and talk to me. Over the years, we spent a lot of happy times together.

My life on that farm was most enjoyable. I had everything I wanted to eat and drink. The sheep pasture was in an apple orchard and during the late summer and fall, I would gorge myself with apples. I took pride in the fact that I could eat more apples than any of the other sheep.

Once I reached lamb-bearing age, I gave birth to little lambs every springtime for many years. What a miracle a new life is! More often than not I would give birth to twins. I thoroughly enjoyed raising my little ones, but I was always glad when it was time to wean them, because when they got too big, they would almost lift me right off the ground at mealtime.

As I was growing older, my human friend was growing up. I think he was a good baseball player, because often in the summer I would see him throwing a hard rubber ball against the garage door and catching the ball as it bounced back to him. Sometimes he would take his bat and ball to a level spot in the cow pasture, hit the ball, and then chase after it. I think he lost quite a few baseballs, as he spent a lot of time with an exasperated look on his face, tramping around in the weeds looking for something

As time went by, my friend seemed to get busier and busier. He was not around the farm quite as often, and I would see him driving back and forth to high school every school day during the school year. Even so, he remained a good friend and always managed to find time for me. He would often come out to the pasture, talk to me, pet my head, and give me something to eat and drink.

Then one year some strange things started to happen on the farm. Animals were being loaded up and hauled off in trucks much more than usual. Strange people were driving in and out, looking things over around the farm. I wondered what was happening to all of the other animals. As more of them were taken away, I began to wonder what was going to happen to me.

Eventually, I was the only sheep left in the pasture. I think all the other animals on that farm were sold. Then one day I was loaded into a truck and taken to the next farm up the road. I learned that this was to be my new home, as my friend and his parents were moving to some place called Arizona. My new friends are really nice people who say I can live here the rest of my life. They are neighbors that my human friend respects and trusts. He promised me the people would take good care of me, and they certainly have.

I enjoy my new home, and almost every summer my friend comes from Arizona to visit me. He has been a good friend for my entire life and has made my life much more enjoyable than it would otherwise have been.

I feel very fortunate, because I know that many farm animals are not treated as well as I. I have heard horrible stories about farm animals that are not seen as precious life forms with strong wills to live, but instead are treated only as numbers or looked at only in terms of how much money they are worth or can make for the farm.

I hear that many times when animals get sick on some farms, they are killed rather than cared for, because this is cheaper. It would sure be wonderful if more farm animals could live out their lives being loved and cared for as I have been. Maybe as the reality of Reverence for All Life becomes a more active part of human thinking, farms will become places where all animals are treated with respect for as long as they live, cared for when they get sick, and never sent off to be slaughtered. That is my wish for all of my fellow farm animals around the world!

<u>18</u>

Calliope the Tree

By Ty F. Webster

"In his daily life Schweitzer takes his own injunction to revere life so seriously that it sometimes astonishes those around him. He himself reports that the natives consider his views impractical and perverted when he tells them they must transplant young palm trees instead of cutting them down when a clearing is being made."
--"Reverence for Life;" Time *magazine; July 11, 1949.*

Hello. My name is Calliope, or "Cali" for short. I am a grapefruit tree. I have lived my entire life in Wisconsin. I know this is a strange place for a grapefruit tree, because we are semitropical trees and usually only grow in climates that do not get so cold in the winter. But you see, I am actually a houseplant. I have lived my entire life indoors, although when I was younger and smaller, my caretaker would sometimes put me outside to soak up the sunshine in the summer months. I say caretaker, because this fellow takes care of me; but I would rather call him my friend. So I will.

I was given to my friend as a gift almost twelve years ago, when I was just a little sapling, about one foot tall. I was a little worried at first, because it was pretty obvious he was not much of a gardener. I'm not sure exactly what color his thumb is, but it certainly is not green! He hardly ever has plants around, and when he does, they often don't fare nearly as well as I have. But in my friend's defense, I think he knows he is not much of a gardener. He usually only has plants when someone gives them to him (I was a gift from some friends of his college roommate), and he always seems sad when any of his plants die.

But I could tell right away this young man really liked me, and he did his best to take care of me. He made sure I got plenty of sunshine and enough, but not too much, water. And he always seemed to get a lot of pleasure out of seeing me grow. Whenever he noticed I had sprouted a new shoot or unfurled a new leaf on one of my branches, he would softly caress the new growth and compliment me for being such a fine tree. He still does this today.

Over the years I have grown and grown. One of the best days of my life was the day I realized I was actually taller than my friend. I was a little worried that he would be jealous of my height, but he seemed as happy as I was. "Just look how tall you have grown, Cali," he said, with a big smile on his face. "You are taller than me now. And although I have been done growing for years, you will continue to grow." And he was right. Now I'm over seven feet tall. In fact, now I'm so tall that sometimes my friend has to trim my top branches, because they grow right into the ceiling.

Now that I am so big, I live at my friend's parents' house. My friend tends to move around a lot, and I'm really too big to move easily. This actually works out pretty well for me, because my friend's mother has a very green thumb and keeps a lot of houseplants, so I have plenty of "green" company here.

My favorite time of the year is Christmas time, because for several years now, my friend and his family have decorated me as their Christmas tree. Just think of it: a grapefruit tree as a Christmas tree! You should see me with all of the lights and ornaments on. I look quite fabulous, if I do say so myself. And it always makes me feel good to know that none of my brethren from the evergreen family had to perish for a few weeks of Christmas tradition.

But what really shakes my branches are the things I hear about how so many other trees are being treated. As you may know, plants are very good listeners. We especially like music, and I particularly like classical music. Bach is my favorite. What I don't like to hear, though, are the stories about how so many trees are being chopped down around the world. Entire forests chopped right to the ground without a bit of regret in order to make a few men wealthier. Trees that have lived for hundreds and even thousands of years seen only in financial terms. How can anyone put a price on such a magnificent, beautiful thing as a tree? Don't these people realize that healthy forests are necessary for a healthy planet?

Lately, though, I've been hearing a lot of talk in the house that has seemed like music to my ears. My friend and his family have spent a lot of time discussing an idea called Reverence for All Life. According to this view, all living things should be viewed as important and treated well, including trees. I don't know about you, but I think that is a very good idea! I hope a lot more people around the world come to share this belief before all of the trees in all of the forests get chopped down.

19

It is Only a Fly!!!

By John Webster

"To the person who is truly ethical all life is sacred, including that which from the human point of view seems lower."
--Albert Schweitzer; Out of My Life and Thought.

Today is one of the "fly swatting" days of summer at the local Hotel dining room where I help with the morning cleaning. I dislike these days, because they mean that I will inevitably have to kill other living creatures. I understand the reasoning behind it. I realize that it is necessary to rid the dining room and kitchen of the pesky insects.

Flies don't eat much, but if it were your Walnut Burger they wanted to share and your nose they were using for a landing strip, the issue would be settled. The flies would have to go. Today it will not be my burger or my nose, as I will not be eating at the Hotel, but I must have reverence for those customers who will. No one wants to eat in a room full of pesky flies, and if we did not do something about the insects, the restaurant would surely begin to lose customers.

In the courtroom of my mind, where I am the judge and jury, the verdict is reached in favor of the human diners. However, I still feel sorry for the flies my co-workers and I have to kill, as the flies are our partners: fellow beings with wills-to-live just like our own. The killing may be necessary, but that does not make it right. I wish I could invent a fly trap that would allow us to capture the flies alive so I could take them outside and set them free far enough away that they would not come right back in. But I do not have such a trap. As such, I must bear the guilt of committing the kill.

I feel the full weight of the guilt for my actions, and sometimes I even find ways to save some of my winged partners. Yesterday, for instance, I saw a small one on the floor, unable to fly. I paused for a moment and thought, "I don't have to swat this one, I can pick it up in the soft cleaning cloth I carry in my pocket and take the fly outside." And so I did. Today, I trapped several flies in a corner before they warmed up and became super-active. Again, with the help of my trusty cleaning cloth, I ushered them outside and set them free. I was filled with a sense of joy and celebration as I watched them fly away.

I will never be convinced that the death of these creatures is not a big deal. I cannot justify my actions with the thought, "it is only a little fly," while I swat, swat, swat. It is so easy to say, "every fly must be killed!" when in fact a few can be saved. Our courtroom should always be open and the judge always alert enough to make decisions on an individual basis, even for things as seemingly insignificant as a fly or an ant or a worm.

We need to break the habit of saying: "It is just another fly." Swat! "It is just another ant." Stomp! "It is just another worm." Squish! For if we do not learn to be more sensitive and compassionate to all of our partners, we may very well find ourselves saying: "It is just another Iraqi," as one of our missiles blows up an Iraqi missile site and kills the people working there and any civilians living nearby. Or we may find ourselves saying, "It is just another African," as the fatality report comes in from another civil war being fought many miles away. Or we may find someone somewhere in the world saying, "It is just another American," as casualties from another terrorist attack are counted.

In our own private courtroom we may sometimes find it necessary to kill a fly or an ant, but *never* (I fervently hope) in any circumstance should we find it necessary to harm or kill another person. That brings us to the moral of this story: "It is extremely important to sensitize ourselves by saving some flies during the height of the fly season so that we can condition ourselves to act to save *all* persons in *all* seasons of the year."

20

The Thrill of the Hunt

By John Webster

"When we have a choice, we must avoid bringing torment and injury into the life of another, even the lowliest of creatures...
--Albert Schweitzer; The Animal World of Albert Schweitzer.

Although I now hold a reverence for all life, human and non-human alike, such was not always the case. As a boy growing up on a farm in southern Wisconsin, I was fascinated with guns. Where my "thrill of the hunt" came from I do not know for sure, but it was inside of me in its full force from a very early age.

My first memories of hunting come from my youth. I would sneak around the barns on our property with my BB gun trying to get a shot at the pigeons. Sometimes after dark I would talk our hired man, Paul Doescher, into accompanying me to the garage and holding a steady flashlight beam on the roosting sparrows so I could shoot them down with my gun. We would then take the dead birds into the barn for the cats to enjoy.

A few years later I became the proud owner of my first shotgun and soon thereafter, a rifle. During these years, I looked forward to the opening day of the pheasant, squirrel, or rabbit hunting seasons with great anticipation. When those special days arrived, I would literally head for the hills or wherever it was that I thought the chances were best to find the game I was after. I found a great thrill in being out-of-doors with the leaves crackling under my feet and the beauty of the fall colors all around, stalking the elusive game. When the hunt was successful (not all that often, as I was a rather poor shot) I felt very good knowing I had provided the main dish for our family's evening meal.

In my younger years, I was equally excited to head for the local stream to try to catch some fish for supper. My angling was not always successful, but I did manage to catch a few. And each time I did, I experienced the thrill of the hunt.

I remember, too, ordering several muskrat traps from a catalog and setting them along the stream that ran through our farm. One winter day while checking my traps, I discovered that I had caught a real live muskrat. At first I experienced the familiar thrill of success. But for some reason, this time was different. My thrill quickly turned to despair when I got a close-up view of the poor, trapped creature looking at me with fear and suffering from the grips of the trap. I killed the animal, as I felt I was supposed to. The despair was not great enough at that time to keep me from enjoying the hunt. But something had undoubtedly changed. I did not realize it then, but a seed had been planted deep within me: a seed that would one day germinate into the reverence I hold today for all creatures.

My conversion to the philosophy of Reverence for All Life was not a rapid process. I continued to hunt for many years, far into my adult life. In fact, I well remember that not so many years ago I got very excited to realize that Kansas, the state I was living in at the time, had a hunting season for mourning doves. I never found any doves to shoot, but I was more than ready if the opportunity had presented itself. And I continued to hunt in the fields and fish in the manmade lakes near my home.

My, what a change a few years and a few new ideas can make in the life of a person. Today, some 30 years later, I have spent considerable time and energy doing all within my ability to stop a mourning dove season from being established in Wisconsin, where I now live.

I'm not exactly sure when the change came about—when the seed planted in my youth sprouted and began to grow. But it has. Slowly but surely I have come to the realization that all life is sacred and has the will to live, just as I do. I understand that the muskrat I trapped and killed on that winter morning long ago, and all the other creatures I killed over the years while hunting and fishing, experienced unnecessary pain and suffering because of my actions. So my diet is now 100% vegetarian. I can no longer justify killing animals for the sake of food or pleasure. And although I continue to experience the thrill of the hunt, that, too, has changed for me. I continue to hunt, but now I use binoculars and cameras rather than guns. I enjoy hunting sandhill cranes, pelicans, bluebirds, eagles, doves, tundra swans, wild turkeys, fox, raccoons, muskrats, deer, and many other creatures.

Now, for me, the hunting season is always open. But no longer do I suffer from feelings of guilt and despair because my hunting is causing other living creatures—other beings with the will-to-live—to suffer. Now the thrill of the hunt is much more meaningful to me. I not only get to experience the beauty of the natural world, but I also have an awareness of a special relationship with the hunted that causes me to celebrate the sacredness of life. Upon coming into viewing distance of a wild creature, I celebrate an inner harmony that comes from knowing we both are a vital part of the world and that we are related in the great process called life. Rather than aiming a gun, I now aim my feeling of Reverence for All Life and the outcome is much better for all involved. I still get the thrill of the hunt, and the animal I am hunting gets to live to see another day, gets to return to its own home and its own family, gets to continue to be a part of the beautiful life process.

I am not trying to criticize those who hunt or fish. After all, I realize that even as I go into fields or forests with my binoculars and camera I may become guilty of harming some small creatures and plants with my footsteps. Yet I decide that the personal enjoyment I will receive from the hike outweighs the risks to these poor creatures. So who am I to criticize someone who decides that it is necessary to kill some wild game or fish? I realize these activities bring enjoyment to many people. Each of us must decide for ourselves what is necessary in each situation. But I hope that we all might accept the responsibility for every creature that we harm and allow the resulting guilt to urge us to help other creatures whenever an opportunity is presented to do so.

Perhaps for all those who hunt or fish there is at least a momentary feeling of remorse as they witness the suffering and death of the creature they shoot or catch, a remorse that is quickly overcome by the feeling of success and excitement. For me, though, the remorse has become too great to ignore. The feeling of guilt for having needlessly destroyed life during my days of hunting and fishing now motivates me to reach out to help all living creatures as a way of redeeming in a small way my actions in the past.

As such, I feel it my duty to present the idea of the sacredness of all life, so that those who hunt and those who choose not to, alike, can gain greater reverence for life in all of its precious, varied forms. For only in this manner can we ever hope to bring about a more sustainable world: a world filled less with hatred, anger and violence, and more with peace, love, and understanding. Only by fully understanding that all life is precious can we bring about a world more full of Reverence for All Life.

21

We Belong to Nature

By John Webster and Ty F. Webster

"The deeper we look into nature the more we recognize that it is full of life, and the more profoundly we know that all life is a secret, and we are all united to this life."

"What we seem to forget is that, yes, the sun will continue to rise and set and the moon will continue to move across the skies, but mankind can create a situation in which the sun and moon can look down upon an earth that has been stripped of all life."

--Dr. Albert Schweitzer; For All That Lives; Ann Atwood and Erica Anderson.

When the ethic of Reverence for Life takes hold of our lives, we tend to be drawn into the depths of nature. We realize more clearly that we have come from nature, that the natural world is ultimately our Home, and that we continue to have an ongoing relationship with our Home. We recognize that our survival is dependent upon how we behave here in our Home, and we come to understand that our position here is not that of mighty rulers, but of humble caretakers in the midst of a world full of partners.

All too often, though, we may find ourselves thinking that the earth and nature belong to us. When this is the case we tend to treat the natural world without the full reverence it is due. Naturalist author Aldo Leopold wrote in his classic book, *A Sand County Almanac:* "We abuse land because we regard it as a commodity belonging to us. When we see land as a community to which we belong, we may begin to use it with love and respect."(1)

If we are fortunate enough to own a few acres or a lot with a house, we may, at times, think that our real estate and whatever happens to be on or under it belongs to us. "We paid for it;" our thinking goes, "we can do anything we want with what is ours." As we drive or walk through a public park, we may have the feeling that the trees and animals are there for our benefit—that they, in fact, belong to us.

I see this as a flawed view. I feel it is more correct to say that we belong to the earth and all of nature. We come from nature, and our lives are in some way affected by all life since the beginning of creation. We humans are relative latecomers in the parade of life. Therefore, it might make more sense to say that the natural world owns us and that we exist only for the privilege of serving it faithfully as it continues to sustain us and provide us opportunities to enjoy its beauty.

As Leopold pointed out, all of nature is a community. When it comes to our relationship with the land and the natural world, we would do well to think in terms of a community of partnerships. We must realize that the air we breathe, the water we drink, the land we live on, every plant and all animals—especially all of humanity—make up a world community. When we damage or harm any single part of—any single partner in—this community, we degrade the well-being of the community as a whole. When we begin to damage too much of the community, we put the survival of the community at risk.

One of the greatest problems with humanity's view of the natural world is the tendency to look at everything in terms of economics. We place monetary value on everything and fail to see the intrinsic value of natural things. For instance, we look at a large tract of boggy wetlands and see the huge dollar signs that will result if we drain the land and put in an expansive parking lot and a strip mall with a cluster of retail shops. Money for the developers who oversee the project; money for the construction companies who build the shops and pave the parking lot; money for the store owners from the sale of products; money for the employees who work the jobs. Money, money, money!

But we fail to consider the true *cost* of all these things: the cost to the natural world. We fail to consider that the wetland is an important ecosystem for the maintenance of our environment. We forget that the wetland holds and purifies water that will otherwise run off into lakes, streams and rivers, carrying harmful pollutants and creating floods. We forget that the wetland is home to countless species of animals specialized to that environment, animals that become increasingly at risk of extinction as we continue to destroy their homes for our economic benefit. We forget, in short, that a tract of land in its natural state is often more "valuable" to the well-being of our world than any amount of revenue brought about through the destruction of that land.

In her book of essays, *Small Wonder*, author Barbara Kingsolver raised a very intriguing and pressing question about the tendency to look at nature in economic terms. She raised it in relation to the fate of a river near her home in Arizona—the San Pedro River, which is in great danger of being degraded as the result of development—but it applies to all natural places everywhere. She writes:

How can the San Pedro's case be argued in a human tongue whose every word for 'value' is tied to the gold standard of human prosperity? I feel frustrated in trying even to frame the question, for it occurs to me the question is this: If life must be a race to use up everything we have, who exactly will win that race?"(2)

It seems to me that at the present time the most important goal of our government is to "grow the economy." "The economy must continue to grow at all costs!" This too often seems to be the motto of the people we have elected (or that corporations have selected) to run our country. Indeed, U.S. President George W. Bush and his administration have enacted many new anti-environmental policies, overturned many long-standing environmental protections, and ignored world opinion on environmental hazards, all to the great benefit of big business and much to the detriment of our natural world.

Fortunately, their policies have not gone entirely unnoticed. A growing number of people are working to expose the administration's environmental atrocities and bring about a change to their policies. One such person is the dean of Yale University's School of Forestry, Gus Speth. A longtime environmental leader and an environmental advisor to U.S. President Jimmy Carter, Speth has authored a book titled *Red Sky at Morning*. As stated in a March 31, 2004, report by BushGreenwatch—an environmental watchdog organization that tracks the Bush administration's actions in relation to the environment (their website is **bushgreenwatch.org**)—the book offers eight approaches that can deter global environmental deterioration and an analysis of why most efforts thus far have failed.

In the report, Speth harshly criticizes the Bush administration's environmental record, describing "a pattern of obstructionist policies throughout the tenure that have impeded global efforts to address pressing environmental issues. . . ."

According to Speth, "Rather than join with European nations to forge agreements on how nations can reduce their reliance on fossil fuels, combat global warming, thwart further depletion of the ozone layer or reduce exposure to toxic chemicals, the Bush administration has chosen policies that curry favor with industry."

I submit that it is time for us and our elected officials to adopt a new motto in relation to the environment: *"Grow the sustainability of our environment!"* If, in the long run, our environment cannot sustain us, what difference does it make how much the economy grows? Who will be here to reap the profits when the environment that supports us has proven that we no longer belong because we fail to make creative contributions? To quote a nineteenth century Cree Indian prophesy: "Only when the last tree has died and the last river has been poisoned and the last fish has been caught will we realize that we cannot eat money."

There is a very real danger that we humans have already done so much damage to our world that it will be difficult, if not impossible, for a sustainable partnership to continue to exist. In other words, we may have already polluted ourselves and many other species out of existence.

But perhaps it is not too late. Perhaps our economy would do quite nicely if it did not always grow. Now is the time to improve our chances of survival by treating the environment with due respect, by protecting it rather than destroying it through the rampant use of limited resources to satisfy our greedy lifestyles. Now is the time for us to change our ways and realize that we belong to the earth and all that lives and that we must humble ourselves and become caretakers with reverence for *all* life and land.

Now is the time to realize the importance of preserving the few remaining natural areas in our world. As Kingsolver points out elsewhere in *Small Wonder,* we must realize our innate need for these special places:

> Oh, how can I say this: People *need* wild places. Whether or not we think we do, we *do.* We need to be able to taste grace and know once again that we desire it. We need to experience a landscape that is timeless, whose agenda moves at the pace of speciation and glaciers. To be surrounded by a singing, mating, howling commotion of other species, all of which love their lives as much as we do ours, and none of which could possibly care less about our economic status or our running day calendar. Wildness puts us in our place. It reminds us that our plans are small and somewhat absurd. It reminds us why, in those cases in which our plans might influence many future generations, we ought to choose carefully.(3)

An ideal partnership occurs when each partner contributes all that is possible to the well-being of the events that are in the process of becoming. As human partners, we have the unique ability to think and visualize what might be best for all involved. We have the ability to see and reach beyond ourselves. Therefore, let us think and see and act by reaching out to our natural community in ways that are in harmony with an attitude of Reverence for All Life.

Reverence for All Life calls us to a special relationship of love and respect for each event of non-human life and a still more profound relationship of love and respect for each event of human life. Let us remember always to have a special reverence for the entirety of our fragile ecosystem, which sustains us and of which we are all a part. With Reverence for All Life we must reach out to the smallest bit of creation as well as to the totality of the system that enables us to live. In other words we *must* take care of the world and *all* that dwells therein.

Notes
1.) Aldo Leopold; *A Sand County Almanac* (1949); p. viii.
2.) Barbara Kingsolver; *Small Wonder* (2002); p. 47.
3.) Ibid. p. 40.

22

Let's Get Them Before They Get Us

By John Webster with Ty F. Webster

"Today there is an absence of thinking which is characterized by a contempt for life. We waged war for questions which, through reason, might have been solved. No one won. The war killed millions of men, brought suffering and death to millions of innocent animals. Why? Because we did not possess the highest rationality of reverence for life. And because we do not yet possess this, every people is afraid of every other, and each causes fear to the others. We are mentally afflicted one for another because we are lacking in rationality. There is no other remedy than reverence for life, and at that we must arrive."
--Albert Schweitzer; *"Religion and Modern Civilization;"* Christian Century *magazine.*

One of the memories I have from my boyhood on a Wisconsin farm is of numerous bumblebees buzzing around the yard in springtime when the flowers began to bloom. For some reason I felt it my duty to kill as many of these big bees as I could. My weapon of choice was often a baseball bat, as I figured I could improve my batting eye while getting rid of the "pests." It was with no remorse at all, and even a sense of accomplishment, that I killed many a bumblebee during my youth.

My rationale for this killing was that I had to get them before they could get me. Whenever I encountered bees, I was always afraid of being stung. I had to kill the bees before they could sting me. I did not realize how ignorant this view was. I was a middle-aged man before I received my first bee sting, and I now know that bees do not go around stinging people just for the sake of stinging them. Stingers are bees' defense mechanisms, usually only employed when they feel threatened. I now know that the bumblebees I killed in my youth had no more desire to sting me than I had to be stung by them. It turns out I did not need to get them before they could get me.

Today, years later, I feel this view—let's get them before they get us—is employed far too often in humans' relations with fellow humans and other living things. I also feel it is a very distorted and misguided view that should be pushed surely and deliberately into the garbage can used for dumb and unethical ideas and replaced with a view more in line with Reverence for All Life.

I feel it is never right to knowingly harm another human being. With that said, it follows that it is not ethical to harm fellow humans merely because we think they may harm us sometime in the future. When our rationale for using violence is to "get them before they get us," we are not thinking with Reverence for All Life. We need to remind ourselves that those we are afraid of are people like ourselves in possession of wills-to-live like our own. In this manner, we can concentrate our efforts on responding to a perceived threat with love, compassion, kindliness, sympathy, empathy, peacefulness, and the power to forgive.

We also need to be realistic and aware enough to notice if another person or group of people might have reason to harm us. If they do, we should make haste to remove the reasons for that kind of hatred and anger. We must always be ready to ask ourselves "Why?" and "What?" Why might someone want to harm us? What have we done, or are we doing, to make them want to attack us? We must scrutinize our own actions to make sure that we are not, even inadvertently, posing a threat.

In general, people are like bumblebees, going about our own business. It is only when we feel threatened that we attempt to strike out. And if we feel it is very likely that someone might try to strike at us, then we may be very tempted to strike first.

Is there a risk factor involved in not striking first? Yes, there is the possibility the perceived attacker may try to harm us. However, I submit that the risk is many times greater when we strike out with violence to get the perceived attackers before they get us. Violence begets more violence. When the proverbial policy of "an eye for an eye and a tooth for a tooth" is put into motion, it tends to continue until everyone is blind and toothless. Unfortunately, meeting threats with threats and violence with violence is too often the way in our world today. As I write these words, ongoing violent conflicts rage amongst peoples and nations worldwide. Indeed, my own country, the United States of America, is deeply involved in several of them. And, unfortunately, these involvements provide sad examples of the points I am trying to make here.

Take the ongoing chapter in World History that has been termed the "War on Terror." This tragic chapter was initiated on the infamous day—September 11, 2001—when four passenger jetliners were hijacked and used as missiles of destruction. The World Trade Center in New York City was destroyed and the U.S.'s Department of Defense headquarters, The Pentagon, in Arlington, Virginia, was damaged during the attacks and thousands of people were killed. A terrorist network known as al-Quaida perpetrated this unconscionable act, an unspeakably horrible event that caused immeasurable suffering.

As utterly horrific as the events of that day were, I would argue that the ensuing events are equally unconscionable and serve as prime examples of the flawed human tendency to meet violence with violence. The Trade Center bombing could have been seen as a wake-up call. It could have provided the United States government with the opportunity to raise the questions: "What have we done to cause someone to hate us so much as to be able to do something this drastic, this horrible? What can we do to change this and work toward understanding and reconciliation?"

One reason for al-Qaida's terrorist activities was hinted at in an article published on June 23, 2002, by Agence France Presse: "So long as America persists in its unjust policy toward Muslims, we will go on hitting it everywhere." So, there is one clue. Evidently some people in Muslim nations feel threatened by U.S. foreign policy. Therefore, my government might need to re-evaluate its policy toward the Muslim world and take those feelings into consideration in the implementation of foreign policy.

It might need to create a clearer line of dialogue with the Muslim nations of the world in order to engender greater feelings of mutual respect and understanding between those nations and our own. As we know, however, this was not the U.S. government's response. Instead, the leaders of my country opted to go the way of revenge, meeting terror with terror. An attack against Afghanistan—seen as a host for al-Quaida operations—was summarily planned and carried out by U.S. led forces. Thousands upon thousands of human casualties, and plenty of destruction of non-human life, have been added to the September 11 body count as the conflict rages on.

And sadly, things have gotten even worse. Using the anti-terror mantra it continues to spoon-feed to its populace as its rallying cry, the U.S. government perpetrated what is perhaps the worst instance of an illegal, pre-emptive attack of all time. Claiming that Iraq had powerful weapons of mass destruction it was planning to use against us, and falsely linking Iraq with the terror of 9/11, the U.S. launched a massive military attack on that country. We, our government claimed, had to get Iraq before they could get us. As it turns out, though, the Iraqi's really didn't have the capability to get anybody anywhere. An exhaustive search for Iraq's weapons of mass destruction and the technology to produce them came up empty handed.

Meanwhile, destruction of life continued, and continues, unabated. As of August 2005, over two years after the "major hostilities" in Iraq ended, the casualty meter in the Iraqi conflict continues to rise. The U.S. soldier death toll since the beginning of hostilities on Iraqi soil has topped the 1850 mark, and an estimated further 14,000 U.S. soldiers have been injured.

Predictably, the toll has been much higher on the Iraqis. Iraq Body Count—a project developed by independent academics and researchers in the U.S. and Great Britain in order to establish a comprehensive data base of civilian deaths in Iraq resulting from military action by the USA and its allies—reports on its website (**iraqbodycount.net**) that as of August 2005, at least 23,500 and possibly as many as 26,700 Iraqi civilians have died since the hostilities began. According to the website, this tally includes "deaths that have resulted from military action during the 'major-combat' phase prior to May 1, 2003, and the current 'occupation' phase, including all deaths which the Occupying Authority has a binding responsibility to prevent under the Geneva Convention and Hague Regulations including civilian deaths resulting from the breakdown in law and order and deaths due to inadequate health care or sanitation." The numbers do not even take into account the thousands of Iraqi military casualties in the conflict. And it is to say nothing of the countless loss of non-human life resulting from the violence.

Surely there is another way: one filled with Reverence for All Life. It is my opinion that when we respond to the threat of violence *with* violence, we are using the mentality of bullies. It takes no thought or creativity to meet force with force. If we have reason to believe that something or someone is going to harm us, we must work extra hard to remove the conditions that might cause such an attack. And if we have been attacked, we must work toward forgiveness of and reconciliation with our attackers in order to bring about an end to violence.

We must follow the example of people such as those in the peace advocacy group, September Eleventh Families for Peaceful Tomorrows. Numerous family members who lost loved ones in the tragic events on September 11, 2001, created the organization out of a wish that terror and violence would be reduced, not increased, in the wake of the disaster. As stated on their website (**www.peacefultomorrows.org),** the group's mission is:

to seek effective nonviolent responses to terrorism, and identify a commonality with all people similarly affected by violence throughout the world. By conscientiously exploring peaceful options in our search for justice, we choose to spare additional innocent families the suffering that we have already experienced—as well as to break the endless cycle of violence and retaliation engendered by war.

While the U.S. military was dropping retaliatory bomb after bomb in Afghanistan, Peaceful Tomorrows was raising money to send to the families of Afghani casualties and working to educate and raise the consciousness of the public around the world on issues surrounding war and peace. And as the "War on Terror" continues, the organization continues to call for and work toward a more peaceful world. A statement posted on their website on the third anniversary of the 9/11 bombings stated:

Nearly three years ago, September Eleventh Families for Peaceful Tomorrows was born out of a shared belief that America's military response to the 9/11 attacks which took our loved ones' lives would result in the deaths of countless innocent civilians and increase recruitment for terrorist causes, making the United States, and the world, less safe and less free for generations to come. . . .

Our illegal, immoral and unjustified invasion of Iraq, a nation that had nothing to do with the September 11th attacks, has cost the lives of 1,000 American troops and an estimated 12,000 Iraqi civilians, while leaving tens of thousands of others physically and emotionally traumatized. Today, our continuing occupation, our failure to provide basic services like electricity and water, and our torture of prisoners at Abu Ghraib has turned Iraq into a focus of anti-American sentiment where a new generation of terrorists is being recruited from around the world. . . .

On September 11th, 2002, we urged America to participate fully in the global community, by honoring international treaties, endorsing and participating in the International Criminal Court, following the United Nations charter, and agreeing in word and action to the precepts of international law. Today, we redouble our call to return to full membership in the community of nations. . . .We draw hope from those around the globe whose historical experiences of terrorism and war have brought them not to a place of vengeance, but to a commitment to creating a peaceful world. . . .Through their witness and their efforts towards reconciliation, they have demonstrated that peace begins in the heart of every individual, and that people united have an unparalleled power to change the world.

Every day, we choose to create the world we want to live in, through our words and through our actions. Today, we reach out to others around the world who recognize that war is not the answer. Today, three years after September 11th, we continue to choose peace.

Clearly, this is a better way. If we feel that we are in danger of being attacked, or have already been attacked, we should not attack first or respond with more violence. Instead, we should employ our "People Power" to encourage those we are threatened by to join us in the "Partner Power" that can lead to "Peace Power." I feel that when we are fortified with a combination of People Power, Partner Power, and Peace Power, we need not fear the future. If people see that we are motivated by peace, love, and respect for them, they most likely will respond in kind.

The old way of thinking is "if someone hits you, hit him back." In the future we can choose to go in one of two very different directions. Our motto can be "hit them first and then hit them again and again so they can't hit back." Unfortunately, it seems that this approach is gaining in popularity, with very grave results. I submit a much better path to take is one in accordance with the principles of Reverence for All Life. Our motto can become "treat them with respect, for they are precious life, as are we." We can remember that all peoples in all places are just like us with wills-to-live just like our own. We can all work together to avoid giving anyone a reason to hit anyone else in the first place. We can keep our lines of communication open and listen to one another's grievances with a sense of compassion and understanding so that we can work out viable, peaceful solutions and avoid violence in all cases.

Let us remember to be people armed with "Peace Power" and "the Power of Forgiveness" rather than cowards hiding behind guns and bombs. Let us remember at all times to do all we can to let Reverence for All Life guide us in all of our thoughts and actions. In other words, let the bees be, and they will let us be, too.

23

People Power

By John Webster and Ty F. Webster

In President Eisenhower's speech of November 7, 1957, a few days after the launching of Sputnik II, he said, 'What the world needs more than a gigantic leap into space is a gigantic leap into peace.' This gigantic leap consists in finding the courage to hope that the spirit of good sense will arise in individuals and in peoples, a spirit sufficiently strong to overcome the insanity and the inhumanity.
--*Albert Schweitzer; "Negotiations at the Highest Level";* Peace or Atomic War.

One of the greatest powers in the world is "People Power." Due to our unique capacity to reason, humans have the ability to change the very world in creative ways. This great power can become even stronger when like-minded people join together in support of a common cause. When this happens, "People Power" becomes "Partner Power." And when we work together in a creative fashion using the principles of Reverence for All Life— including love, kindliness, sympathy, empathy, non-violence, and forgiveness—as our guide, "Partner Power" can evolve into "Peace Power," which can bring about a safer, gentler, more caring world.

It is a sad fact that in many cases, strength and power are equated with the possession of powerful weapons. As individuals, we may feel safer and more powerful when we have a gun, a knife, a baseball bat, or some other weapon for protection. Likewise, as a nation we may think we are safer with a great stockpile of powerful weaponry, including nuclear bombs and other weapons of mass destruction.

But is it not possible that we, as individuals, would actually be much safer if we did not have any weapons of violence and that we, as a nation, would actually be safer if we had no weapons of mass destruction? I think the answer to both of these questions is "Yes." It may be true that we *feel* safer and more powerful when we have strong weapons, but this feeling is merely an illusion. In reality physical weapons do not make us stronger. In fact, whenever people pick up a gun or a weapon of any kind, or whenever nations resort to the threat or actual use of military force in order to resolve a conflict, they lose their true creative power.

I have no patience with people or nations, including my own, who resort to force to solve their problems. I feel that the U.S. would command greater respect from other nations if people in those countries were not afraid that we would blow them to bits if they do not behave as we want them to. The only result possible when weapons are employed is destruction. Any time weapons of violence are used, somebody or something is bound to get hurt.

I feel that a much better approach to conflict resolution is to invoke the process through which People Power becomes Partner Power and is employed to bring about Peace Power. To develop People Power, we do not need bombs, guns, or weapons of any kind. All that we need is ourselves and an attitude of Reverence for All Life. People Power is non-violent power. It was a power used by Dr. Albert Schweitzer, Martin Luther King, Jr., Gandhi, and other wise people throughout history; and it is a power that we must learn to use more effectively in the 21st century. Peace Power is a weapon of mass creation, allowing us to resolve conflict in a constructive manner. When backed by enough Partner Power, Peace Power can actually be a stronger force than the most powerful bomb.

One of the greatest examples of this concept in action in modern history was the turn of events which brought a halt to the United States' nuclear test program in the 1950's. It came in the midst of the post-World War II Cold War nuclear arms race between the U.S. and Great Britain on one side and the Soviet Union on the other. Both sides wanted to establish the strongest arsenal of nuclear weapons, and tests were seen as an important tool in doing so. The problem, of course, is that the explosion of any nuclear weapon, be it in an act of warfare or during a test, is very detrimental to the health of the planet (and particularly to any life forms anywhere near the testing grounds).

Although the governmental leaders at the time were fully aware of how dangerous and harmful nuclear tests were, they did everything in their power to keep this knowledge hidden from the general public in order to stay a step ahead of "the opposition." Although many scientists knew of the inherent danger of nuclear weapons, they were under a virtual gag order and unable to speak out against the technology, at the risk of their very livelihood. In fact, Robert Oppenheimer, one of the leading minds in the development of nuclear technology and a central figure in the U.S. government's atomic energy program, was labeled a communist and stripped of his office in 1954 after voicing concerns about the ethics of continuing the nuclear arms race.(1) It was indeed a dire, dangerous time.

Enter People Power! Although most scientists were afraid to publicly question the safety of atomic technology, a number of them, including Oppenheimer and Albert Einstein, communicated their fears with Dr. Schweitzer—who, from his African jungle hospital and during his frequent trips to Europe, was keeping a close eye on international affairs. Schweitzer added his People Power to that of the concerned scientists who had contacted him. In essence, he called for greater Partner Power among the world scientific community to address the problem. The aim was to create the even greater Peace Power that would result from getting an informed world populace united in the effort. In a letter published in the London *Daily Herald* on April 14, 1954, Schweitzer called on scientists to rally together to alert the world to the dangers:

What the world should do is listen to the warnings of individual scientists who understand this terrible problem. That is what would impress people and give them understanding and make them realize the danger in which we find ourselves. Just look at the influence Einstein has, because of the anguish he shows in face of the atomic bomb. It must be the scientists, who comprehend thoroughly all the issues and the dangers involved, who speak to the world, as many as possible of them all telling humanity the truth in speeches and articles. If they all raised their voices, each one feeling himself impelled to tell the terrible truth, they would be listened to, for then humanity would understand that the issues were grave. If [they can] put before mankind the thoughts by which they themselves are obsessed, then there will be some hope of stopping these horrible explosions, and of bringing pressure to bear on the men who govern. (2)

Slowly but surely People Power began to take effect. By the end of 1957, 9,000 U.S. scientists had signed a petition calling for an end to the testing of nuclear weapons. Famed American scientist Linus Pauling, who headed the American petition effort, organized a similar petition for scientists from around the world. Dr. Schweitzer added his name to that petition, which eventually comprised the signatures of 9,235 international scientists, including thirty-six Nobel Peace Prize winners. Pauling handed the petition to the Secretary General of the United Nations on January 13, 1958.(3)

Schweitzer was encouraged by the turn of events but felt that more needed to be done. So in late April of 1958, he wrote a series of three speeches, which were broadcast via radio around the world. The speeches, *The Renunciation of Nuclear Tests, The Danger of Atomic War,* and *Negotiations at the Highest Level,* further alerted the world to the danger of nuclear weapons and elaborated the case for their ban and an end to testing.

In the last of the three addresses, Schweitzer called on the people of the world to join together as one to bring about a new spirit that would create an atmosphere of greater trust and cooperation between nations and allow all nations to work toward bringing about an end to the nuclear arms race:

We cannot continue in this paralyzing mistrust. If we want to work our way out of the desperate situation in which we find ourselves, another spirit must enter into the people…

The awareness that we are all human beings together has become lost in war and through politics. We have reached the point of regarding each other only as members of a people either allied with us or against us and our approach...Now we must rediscover the fact that we—all together—are human beings, and that we must strive to concede to each other what moral capacity we have. Only in this way can we begin to believe that in other peoples as well as in ourselves there will arise the need for a new spirit which can be the beginning of a feeling of mutual trustworthiness toward each other. The spirit is a mighty force for transforming things. We have seen it at work as the spirit of evil which virtually threw us back from striving toward a culture of the spirit, into barbarism. Now let us set our hopes on the spirit's bringing peoples and nations back to an awareness of culture.(4)

Fortunately, the people of the world were listening. Gallup polls showed a rapid change in the attitude of ordinary citizens, with approval for nuclear tests dropping from 64 percent to 27 percent worldwide. Even U.S. President Dwight D. Eisenhower and his hard-line, pro-nuclear administration could not ignore the numbers. In August of 1958 Eisenhower told his staff that "world opinion could be even more powerful than nuclear weapons," and later that month announced the suspension of U.S. nuclear tests as of October 31.(5)

Let's Do It Again

It is time once again for the people of the world to unite with a spirit of trust and mutual respect for life—to unite in an effort to turn People Power into the Partner Power that can become Peace Power. We live in a world that is yet full of fear and mistrust among the different peoples of the world. As Americans, we live in a nation whose leadership has declared an endless "War on Terror" that raises the levels of mistrust and animosity around the world to even higher levels, that pulls the world apart and recreates the "us versus them" mentality Schweitzer warned against.

In fact, U.S. President George W. Bush used very divisive language when speaking about the War on Terror shortly after the September 11 terrorist attacks in 2001. He went so far as to warn the nations of the world that if they did not support the U.S. in the War on Terror, they would find themselves in danger of becoming enemies of the U.S. In a joint news conference with French President Jacque Chirac on November 6, 2001, Bush stated: "Over time it's going to be important for nations to know they will be held accountable for inactivity. You're either with us or against us in the fight against terror."

The American leadership has even gone so far as to take the unimaginable step of making pre-emptive nuclear strikes a part of their stated policy. This sad fact was pointed out by U.S. Representative Dennis Kucinich in a speech titled "Peace and Nuclear Disarmament" (the full text of which can be read in chapter 28 of this book). Kucinich stated:

The recent disclosure that Russia, China, Iraq, Iran, Syria, North Korea and Libya are considered by the United States as possible targets for nuclear attack catalyzes potential conflicts everywhere...crucial political decisions promoting increased military actions, plus a new nuclear first-use policy, are occurring without the consent of the American people, without public debate, without public hearings, without public votes. The President is taking Congress' approval of responding to the September 11 terrorists as a license to flirt with nuclear war.

Another big problem with our "Endless War" is that it gives the powers-that-be license to continue their policy of spending more and more money on the military. In 2002 the United States allocated $343 billion for defense spending. Our allies spent another $205 billion dollars. In that same year, the U.S. spent only $39 billion on children's health; $34 billion for kindergarten - high school education; $6 billion on Head Start education programs for pre-school children; $2 billion to reduce our nation's reliance on oil; and a paltry $1 billion dollars to address the problem of world hunger.(6) And the current war effort in Iraq continues to drain the United States' coffers at a debilitating rate. As of August 2005, the bill for the U.S. operations in Iraq was a staggering $189 billion.(7) That is $189 billion not used to educate our children, provide access to affordable health care for all of us, create jobs for the increasing numbers of unemployed, develop sustainable, clean, and efficient sources of energy, and other such creative purposes.

It is often said that "money talks." I wish it were possible to designate my tax money for peaceful purposes. I wish that I could take the tax money that will be used on weapons of war and the fighting of wars and re-designate it for non-military use. I would want to pay my part in support of veterans' benefits and the support of the military establishment used in peaceful activities that benefit life in our own country and around the world. I would like to see our military's skill and might join with other countries to assist people around the world when they are afflicted by natural disasters such as earthquakes, famines, and floods. However, I do not want my money used for activities of war, which only kill and injure human and non-human life and sow the seeds of hatred and revenge that lead to further conflict in the future.

Unfortunately, it is not possible to pick and choose how we want our tax money to be allocated. So how in the world could we convince our government to get rid of our mighty weapons? That is where People Power comes into play. Imagine what would happen if people, many thousands of peace-minded people, would demonstrate by marching on Washington D.C. and all the State Capitals, demanding that all of our weapons of mass destruction be destroyed and that we not make any more of these weapons or sell them to other countries. If enough people marched in protest and continued to march in protest, our government (the people in charge) would have to make a decision. They could choose to put a number of us in jail; they could choose to shoot us down in the streets; or they could choose to do what we ask.

First, there are not enough jails for all of us. And second, if the government killed very many of us in the streets, there would be a strong outcry from our own people and people around the world. Therefore, people, many people, demonstrating to abolish all weapons of mass destruction could conceivably create a greater power than the weapons themselves.

Organizing a demonstration of such magnitude would take

an incredible amount of time and energy from many people. It is something to be hoped for and worked toward. But in the meantime, we should also do everything possible on our own to bring about a change in our nation's foreign policy so that it becomes more benevolent to all the people of the world. We must write our Congressional representatives, write letters to the editors of our local papers, and gather in groups of like-minded people to work out ways to bring about the change in spirit that Dr. Schweitzer spoke of. In short, we must cease to respond to the whims of our leaders and work together to begin to pressure our leaders to follow us, the people, to a more peaceful, caring place— to a world where conflicts are resolved in a constructive fashion, without resorting to force and the threat of violence.

When enough People Power becomes linked with sufficient Partner Power, there will come into being a great Peace Power that will bring about a renewed spirit of cooperation and unification and make our world a much better place for all that lives. There will come into being a world-wide Community of Reverence, where all people will work together to bring about a world based on the principles of Reverence for Life. People Power involves love. It involves courage. And it involves Reverence for All Life, which is the reality that brings us the power to change the world in creative ways.

Notes

1.) James Brabazon; *Albert Schweitzer: A Biography* (2000); p. 445.
2.) Ibid.; p. 444.
3.) Ibid.; p. 470.
4.) Albert Schweitzer; *Peace or Atomic War?* (1958) p. 44-45.
5.) Brabazon; p. 472.
6.) U.S. Budget 2002.
7.) National Priorities Projects' www.costofwar.com.

24

God Bless America?

By John Webster with Ty F. Webster

*"What is nationalism? It is an ignoble patriotism, exaggerated till
it has lost all meaning, which bears the same relation to the noble
and healthy kind [of patriotism] as the fixed idea of an imbecile
does to normal conviction."*
--*Albert Schweitzer;* The Decay and Restoration of Civilization.

"Nationalism of the worst sort was displayed in the last two
wars, and it may be regarded today as the greatest obstacle to
mutual understanding between peoples. Such nationalism can be
repulsed only through the rebirth of a humanitarian ideal among
men which will make their allegiance to their country a natural one
inspired by genuine ideals."

Albert Schweitzer spoke these words during his Nobel
Peace Prize address in 1954. To my mind, they are as pertinent
now as they were then. There has been an outpouring of
nationalism in the United States in recent years, particularly since
the tragic events of September 11, 2001. Although a certain
amount of nationalism can be a healthy form of national
camaraderie, the overbearing, "We're number 1," flag-worshipping
nationalism that has become an epidemic in the United States in
recent years is not healthy. It engenders a disregard for our
partners in the rest of the world and becomes the sort of obstacle to
mutual understanding of which Schweitzer spoke.

One manifestation of the rampant nationalism in this
country has been the repeated singing of the patriotic song, "God
Bless America." The original version of this beautiful song was
written by Irving Berlin during the summer of 1918, but he decided
it was too solemn for the revue he was then working on. Berlin
laid it aside until the fall of 1938, when he decided to rework it as a

"peace" song. Kate Smith sang the revised version on her radio show on Armistice Day of 1938, and it was an instant hit.

Since the events of 9/11, we have heard the singing of "God Bless America" many times. For weeks, the song was sung at every Major League Baseball game. Four years later it is still sung at many professional sporting events and other events, as well. As we continue to sing, I hope we all might ponder the song's message for us in this moment of history. Do we intend it as a self-centered, nationalistic demand, or rather—ideally—a prayer of hope?

I sometimes wonder if we are not singing "God Bless America" as a demand. This seems to me a horrible scenario, yet does it not sometimes sound that way? It's almost as if we are saying: "God, you had better bless us. God, bless America, or else…Bless America, and help us to get revenge on all those people who have threatened or attacked us. Bless America and do not let anyone else attack us, because we are the world's only superpower, and we could nuke your creation to smithereens."

God did not will the events of 9-11 to happen. But the dastardly events did happen. So maybe we did something wrong. Might it be that something we did in the past created the anger that caused certain people to plan and carry out the attacks? Is it possible that our response to the attacks—using violence and the threat of violence in Afghanistan, Iraq, and other places around the world—results in the continued build-up of anger and hatred, which might foster more terrorist attacks on our nation in the future?

I sometimes wonder when we sing "God Bless America" if we are asking God to forget about the well-being of all the other peoples of the world. One has to wonder if God (in human terms) is laughing or crying as we sing "God Bless America," while at the same time we are killing people in other parts of the world in the name of a "war on terrorism." After all, could it be that God will not truly bless America until we have eliminated all of our weapons of mass destruction? Could it be that God will not bless America until we allow all of our people to have access to

159

affordable health care? Could it be that God will not bless America until the vast disparity between the rich and the poor in our country is eliminated? Could it be that God will not bless America until we, his people, no longer resort to violence in our relationships with one another? Could it be that God will not bless America until we abolish the death penalty? Could it be that God will not bless America until we, the people, stop raping the world of its natural resources? Could it be that God will not bless America until we stop killing and injuring human and non-human life in other parts of the world? Could it be that God will not bless America until we learn to reach out to all the people of the world as our partners? Could it be that God will not bless America until America's prayer becomes a prayer for the well-being of the whole world rather than just for America?

We are living in a global community, more so today than ever before in history. Since we proclaim to be the world's only superpower, it seems to me that we should be more concerned about the well-being of all the world's people. Instead of singing "God Bless America, Land That I Love," perhaps we should be singing "God Bless All Peoples, World That I Love." That is wishful thinking, I suppose. Why should we be concerned about the entire world when we are the only superpower? But then again, what better time to show we care? If we are to develop an attitude of Reverence for All Life, we must come to understand that when we say, "all men are created equal," we are not limiting that statement to the people of our own nation. We are asserting that all people everywhere all around the world are created equal, that all people everywhere are our partners.

We sing, "Stand beside her and guide her." This would seem a logical request given the uncertainty of these times. But we must realize that the request is rather hollow unless by "her" we actually mean "us", as in "all of us: all people all around the world." We must realize the request is hollow unless we are willing to do our part and make some necessary changes so that we can become more receptive to the gentle persuasion of love with which God lures us toward a better way. We should be asking God to stand beside us and guide us to that still more excellent way of Reverence for All Life.

God won't stop the 9/11's from happening just because we faithfully sing. We can sing "God Bless America" until we are blue in the face, but unless we do our part and change our ways, God may not bless us. We need to continue to take inventory of what we, as a nation, have done and are doing, and be willing to admit our mistakes and ask for forgiveness. And, in the meantime, let us continue to affirm that God is with us.

Let's continue to sing "God Bless America." But let's sing it not with lots of "America is Number 1" nationalistic fervor, not as a declaration that we are justified in fighting our "righteous wars." Let's sing the song as Irving Berlin originally intended it: as a song of peace. Let us continue to sing "God Bless America," but let's use it as a tool that will, as Albert Schweitzer hoped, make our allegiance to our country a natural one inspired by genuine ideals. Let us sing it as an humble prayer of hope, realizing that we must do our part to make our nation an integral part of a more peaceful world community if the prayer is to be answered.

It would be our greatest blessing if the spirit of God were able to urge and lure us into living up to our full potential as a people of the world, leading the world by our example of Reverence for All Life. We could then truly be a superpower. So let us sing "God Bless America" as a prayer of affirmation that we will do our part to make our nation one which God can truly bless: a nation leading the world toward a time when there are no more wars. Will we still be the world's only superpower? Does it really matter, if we have helped to create a world where all people live together in peace?

<u>25</u>

Can We Stop the War?

By John Webster

This is not meant to be a real story (or is it?). However, the feelings that motivate the author's pen are very real. The names have been changed to protect the innocent (or guilty, as the case may be).

My name is Frank. It seems that in recent years my country, The United Kingdom of Oil, has become the world's only "superpower." That is to say, it has possession of more powerful weapons of mass destruction than any other nation in the world. A superpower with no opposition can choose to become a great example of humanitarianism or a big bully that loves to terrorize people of other countries as well as its own citizens while it goes about the task of building a huge empire. Unfortunately, it seems that the leaders of my country are choosing the latter course. As I write this, the drums of war are beating loud and clear.

Why must the world's only superpower go to war against anyone? As the only superpower we have the opportunity to lead the world into a wonderful new era when all nations live together in peace. We could lead the way to a time when nuclear, chemical, and biological weapons are abolished, and there is no more threat of war. We could set a great example for the entire world to follow: an example of peace and of Reverence for All Life. Well, you can scrap those ideas as long as this group of leaders is in office.

In recent months the Prime Minister of my country and his advisors have terrorized me (and others) by proclaiming that we are in the process of preparing to flex our military muscles and invade a much weaker country, The Hanging Gardens. This might well be a preemptive strike that would be in clear violation of

International Law. We claim that the leader of The Hanging Gardens possesses, or is in the process of building, weapons of mass destruction, and therefore we must remove him from power before he uses these weapons against us and other peoples. My own opinion is that the real motive is to gain control of the massive quantities of black gold known to exist beneath the sands of The Hanging Gardens. My Prime Minister and many of his friends, a number of whom he has appointed to positions of power in our government, are connected in various ways to the oil industry. These people would fleece their already bulging pockets with a lot more money if they could control the black gold located beneath the beauty of The Gardens. They seem utterly indifferent to the fact that a war would injure and kill many people on both sides. I guess money is more important than people.

Another sad but rather obvious reason for this foolish war would be the opportunity to use up some expensive weapons from our nation's vast stockpile of arms. It will also allow the armed forces to test some of their newly developed weapons on real, live targets. This, in turn, would give my government an excuse to purchase additional powerful weapons, bringing even more dollars into the pockets of the Prime Minister's circle of friends and relatives. Oddly enough, the people in charge of my country have great monetary interest not only in the oil industry, but also in our country's defense industry. If they are to make more money, the country must make and use more weapons. It seems incredible to me that the people who stand to make money from warfare are the same people who hold the power to declare war, but that's the way it works in my country.

Even though many of our citizens don't want war, my nation's Parliament has voted to give the Prime Minister the power to use force if negotiations and inspections should fail to rid the Hanging Gardens of the weapons they supposedly possess. Our Prime Minister has not been known to do much negotiating, so we will probably be going to war.

In fact, we are really at war with the Hanging Gardens already. Over a million of their people, mostly children, have died because our country, under the leadership of the previous Prime Minister from the other political party, did not allow The Gardens to import much-needed medications and materials to purify their water system. These activities are known as sanctions, but I tend to call it a holocaust. Somehow we need to wake up our nation before it is too late. What we really need to remove is not the leader of some other nation, but the lack of Reverence for All Life that exists right here at home. We must stop intentional and thoughtless acts of cruelty toward human beings and all other life.

It has become more and more evident that our Prime Minister is indeed intent on initiating war come hell or high water. It appears that the bombing will start sometime within the next few months. All the planes, warships, bombs, and troops are already in place and ready to go to war. Our government has made an announcement warning all United Kingdom of Oil citizens to get out of The Hanging Gardens, as war is imminent. Things do not look good.

It so happens that I would rather risk the possibility of death than be part of a nation that is injuring and killing life—both human and non-human—in a war in some far away country. With this feeling in my gut, I know that I must do something. So, I've called several people whom I trust, and we've talked about a possible plan of action. They've agreed that we must do something and do it as soon as possible. Little by little our plan has unfolded and grown. Concerned people have called other people who might be willing and able to help. Many of the people are not well known outside their own communities, yet some of those involved are well known throughout our nation and world.

Our plan for stopping the war involves a rendezvous of participating persons from The United Kingdom of Oil and other countries around the world *inside* The Hanging Gardens. Rather than heeding our government's warning for people to evacuate The Hanging Gardens, we will go there and put our lives on the line for peace. We will have to enter The Hanging Gardens by way of a third country as our nation has not allowed unauthorized persons to travel there for some time and even assesses a hefty fine on anyone who does. As groups of people arrive in nations bordering The Gardens, we plan to continue our journey to the country's capital and other major cities by car. Carload after carload of concerned citizens from around the world will pour into The Gardens even as the U.K.O.'s war machine is threatening to start dropping bombs. As war threatens to begin, news will surface that so many of our own citizens and civilians from around the world are in The Hanging Gardens. The leaders of the U.K.O. will be shocked to learn that so many innocent people have traveled to this place they want to bomb. Then the press releases will become public. And it will be a great benefit if some of the people risking their lives in The Hanging Gardens are quite well known. Hopefully, the list will include former Prime Ministers and members of Parliament, perhaps even a present member or two of Parliament, several famous athletes, actors and authors, a number of doctors, religious leaders, university professors, and many more people who are not as well known but are also willing to put their lives on the line for the people of The Hanging Gardens and for the sake of Reverence for All Life. Our nation's citizens and the people of the world will rally behind us. They will demand that our government stop its plans for war. Our government would not bomb its own people. Would it?!!

We know this is a risky plan, but it is very possibly the only way that we can live with ourselves as well as bring continued life to the people of The Hanging Gardens. We know that if we can stop the war from beginning, we can continue our presence in some regard until a plan of peaceful coexistence can be established. We are firm in our conviction that our example will not only bring peace to The Hanging Gardens, but also bring forth a greater spirit of peace and cooperation in all the peoples of the world.

Later

Well, the war did start. My nation's leaders authorized a preemptive strike that was in clear violation of International Law. The Hanging Gardens posed no threat to our nation. Our Prime

Minister's claim that they possessed weapons of mass destruction was a purposeful lie, as later proven by an official document termed The High Street Memo. Our armed forces managed to secure the oil fields, but only with a great cost in human lives. Yes, many people were killed, and the killing continues as the people of The Hanging Gardens are resisting our occupation of their country.

Why did the bombing begin? Why didn't my plan work? Sadly, I did not go to the Hanging Gardens. When the time came, I had twenty different reasons for not going, none of which make me feel any less guilty for shirking my responsibility to humanity.

Some people did go through with their plans and traveled to The Hanging Gardens to be human shields. However, not enough people went. More importantly, not enough famous persons joined the attempt to stop the war. If one very important person such as a great religious leader or great statesman had gone, perhaps the war could have been avoided. Although one great religious leader did speak out forcefully against the war, he was too elderly to travel to a foreign country. I commend him, but his voice was not enough.

It is obvious that it will take a great deal of "People Power" to persuade our Prime Minister and his cronies, to stop their "empire building" and not start or continue any more wars or make more nuclear weapons. However, I continue to believe that it is possible for "People Power" and an attitude of Reverence for All Life to bring about an end to all wars and to do away with all weapons of mass destruction. In the end, non-violent action is more powerful than violence.

As my country continues to kill, injure and terrorize persons in The Hanging Gardens, I realize that I am one of the many war criminals responsible for these atrocities and wonder what my punishment will be and from whence it will come. But for the time being, I wait for my government to end this current foolish and illegal war and wonder if it has already started the next one. Will I continue to turn my back on humanity or can I somehow find the courage to stand up and say with my life: **"STOP!!"**?

26

War is a Dirty Word

By John Webster

"Whereas the thoughtless modern world walks aimlessly about in ideals of knowledge, skills, and power, the goal of true and profound thought is the spiritual and ethical perfection of man. This requires a new ethical civilization that seeks peace and renounces war."
-- Albert Schweitzer, 1964 World Book Year Book.

"War" is one of the dirtiest words in the human language. It is a word that represents evil activity, and civilized people should not use it anymore. It is an immoral and dirty word whether it is used by the President or me or anyone else. "War" is a word that should be relegated to history books and not used in dialogue about the present or future. Using the word in such a context only indicates that the users are less than ethical or civilized.

By definition, war means killing and death. It means injuries and suffering. War means spending money and resources on something that is evil and destructive rather than on something that is creative and useful. War means violence used against our partners, both human and non-human. Life brings enough natural loss and suffering without the needless cruelties caused in wars.

Why is it that many people think that war is exciting and are not concerned about the consequences? War may be exciting if you are watching from a safe distance in the comfort of your own home and think your side is going to win. However, winning a war is an illusion. **No one ever wins a war!** When it comes to war everyone loses. When it comes to war, people die and are injured. When it comes to war, everyone involved is a murderer and a war criminal. That means you and me, if we are citizens of a nation that is waging war or selling weapons of war to other nations. One war only plants the seeds of hatred for the next war. It has been said that there will be wars and rumors of wars going on forever. Somehow we must get this evil and out-dated idea out of our thinking. Sadly, wars are very much a part of the world situation today. Indeed, my nation's leaders now tell us that we are involved in an endless "War on Terrorism." Why should we be stuck with an endless war, which is actually making the world less safe? For every person our huge and powerful military machine injures or kills in Iraq and elsewhere, the friends and loved ones of the casualties will vow to return the favor upon us. Instead of reducing terrorism with our attacks, we are in reality creating more terrorists with every person we injure and kill. Is this what we really want to do?

We must work quickly to make War obsolete. Small wars only lead to larger wars and larger wars can lead to the use of nuclear weapons. And as Dr. Schweitzer so aptly pointed out years ago, no one can possibly win a nuclear war: "Those who conduct an atomic war for freedom will die, or end their lives miserably," he warned. "Instead of freedom they will find destruction."(1) Indeed, nuclear war will mean the end of our world as we know and love it.

However, there is hope. For another of Schweitzer's statements also continues to ring true:

In the hearts of people today there is a deep longing for peace. When the true spirit of peace is thoroughly dominant, it becomes an inner experience with unlimited possibilities. It is only when this really happens, that the spirit of peace awakens and takes possession of men's hearts, that humanity can be saved from perishing.(2)

I truly believe that the attitude of human beings can change. All around the world, there are many, many of us who have a deep longing for peace. And working together, we *can* make the true spirit of peace become thoroughly dominant in the world. We can help humanity to decide not to have wars any more. One of my favorite songs says, "Last night I had the strangest dream...I dreamed the world had all agreed to put an end to war." The dream needs to become true. It can.

It is time that the leaders of our world lift us above what we are now to something greater. It is time that we insist that our leaders get on the "peace train" powered by non-violence and deep respect for all that lives. First, though, let us make sure that we are indeed on the peace train. Probably the only way to get some of our leaders on the path to peace is to make it the popular thing to do because so many of us are already there. Peace must start in the mind and heart of each individual person and then become a part of a national and international ethic as individual persons demonstrate the dynamics of peace and non-violence in their relationships with one another and with all the people of the world. It is our leaders' duty to represent the people, and we, the people, must insist that our national leaders demonstrate an ethic that is in harmony with our own.

Remember, war is a dirty word. When we use this word in the present and as we look to the future, we must remind one another to stop and substitute non-violent words such as forgiveness, compassion, compromise, peace, love, and reverence. When Reverence for All Life becomes an integral part of our thinking and of our day-to-day lives, war will truly become obsolete. We will always remember that it is good to promote life and evil to hinder and destroy life. We will know that we must never kill or injure life of any kind unless it is absolutely necessary and that it should never be necessary to harm another human life. There will be no way that we can justify the destruction of life. Let us quickly move toward becoming a new ethical civilization that seeks peace and renounces war. Let us quickly move toward a civilization that is founded on the concept of Reverence for All Life.

Notes

1.)   Albert Schweitzer; *The Words of Albert Schweitzer*; 1984; p. 88.
2.)   Ibid.; p. 91.

27

Garvey Blogs

By Ed Garvey

Ed Garvey is editor and publisher of the FightingBob.com website, an online opinion magazine that provides an educational forum for writers, viewpoints, and topics not welcome on the pages and airwaves of most mainstream media outlets in Wisconsin. This forum also has items of national interest. The forum's aim is to honor and revive the spirit and mission of its namesake, Robert "Fighting Bob" La Follette (1855-1925), the populist governor, U.S. Senator, and presidential candidate from Wisconsin. The Annual Fighting Bob Fest featuring progressive speakers, networking opportunities, and entertainment is held in September at the Sauk County Fairgrounds at Baraboo, Wisconsin. Check www.fightingbobfest.org for dates, speakers, and other information.

FightingBob.com features a daily GarveyBlog that we always look forward to reading. We thank Mr. Garvey for giving us permission to reprint a few of his blogs in our book.

Values Anyone?
(February 28, 2005)

Remember all the post-election talk about values? Read the news about Medicaid. The ranks of those depending on Medicaid are growing. Now 52 million of our fellow citizens depend on the program for health care. The numbers are up 40 percent since Bush became president, but he wants all of those folks to take a $40 billion cut. I'm not making this up. Add millions of pregnant women, children and minimum wage workers and cut the program by $40 billion. Values?

Lemme see. Spend a billion a week on Iraq, another six or seven billion on the defense department, cut taxes for the top 5 percent, urge privatization of Social Security, keep wages at pre-Bush levels while refusing to raise the minimum wage, and you wonder why people are feeling anxious about retirement?

Now is the time for the progressives, the liberals, indeed, all people of conscience to raise hell. The values we hear about are to put the 10 Commandments in the courthouse square, and to keep bad language off PBS while carefully checking out animated cartoon figures for gay tendencies. Have we lost our collective mind, our soul, or both?

$82 Billion, $82 Billion
(May 11, 2005)

Yes indeed, all 100 Senators voted yea for this latest installment to pay for the illegal invasion of Iraq. There must have been some celebrating at Halliburton as they will continue their profiteering with no-bid contracts to rebuild what we have destroyed. Amazing. Not one Senator voted no. Not one. I miss Paul Wellstone every day.

No demand for an exit strategy. No time line, no restrictions on the spending. Whoa Nelly! $82 billion taking the total well over $300 billion as we approach the 1600th combat death. Where is Gene McCarthy or Gaylord Nelson of today. Shame on the Senate.

Congress, White House, Supreme Court
(July 6, 2005)

The coup of 2000 came about when five members of the Supreme Court appointed George W. Bush president of the United States. Since then it has been like watching a disaster in slow motion; EPA, public education, the wall between church and state, CAFTA, outrageous debt, a breath-taking trade imbalance, an invasion without justification let alone a plan, the takeover of the Corporation for Public Broadcasting. And now we turn to the Supreme Court again. We have come full circle. This time the appointments will cement for decades the agenda of James Dobson, Tom DeLay and Newt Gingrich.

Scared? You had better be scared. We are looking to reversal of Brown v. Board of Education, Roe v. Wade, not to mention the end of affirmative action.

My old pal Howard Cosell used to say with disgust, "You deserve whatever you get." While not really true, in this case perhaps Howard is correct. We knew all the marbles were on the table in 2004 and yet the right out-hustled those who reject the rightwing agenda. So buckle your seat belt folks, we are in for a wild and crazy ride.

I'm not making this up. Reports are that the right will spend more than $50 million promoting their choice for the Supreme Court to replace Justice O'Connor, and then according to script, Justice Rhenquist will resign and we will start all over again. (Rove and Cheney wouldn't want two vacancies at one time. Too likely to create a deal—one moderate for one Scalia type.)

Our future is in the hands of 50 or so moderates in the Senate. Can they gather their guts to make this fight a winner? Don't bet the ranch, but don't sit idly by and watch either. Too much is at stake.

28

Dennis J. Kucinich
A Person Working for Peace

"If people can be found who revolt against the spirit of thoughtlessness and are sincere enough to spread the ideals of ethical progress, we will witness the emergence of a new spiritual force strong enough to evoke a new spirit in mankind."
--*Albert Schweitzer*; Out of My Life and Thought.

A True Statesman
By John Webster and Ty F. Webster

The ethic of Reverence for Life urges us to live peaceably and to work to bring about a more peaceful world. It calls us to speak out lovingly and convincingly for the reality of peace in a world torn apart by war, hatred, and selfishness. What the world needs now more than ever is people who are willing to make the goals of world peace and a sustainable way of life their own personal goals. One such person is Dennis J. Kucinich.

Kucinich is currently a U.S. Congressman. He was first elected to the United States House of Representatives in 1996 and is serving his fifth term representing Ohio's 10th Congressional District. On October 13, 2003, Kucinich officially announced his candidacy for the Democratic Party's nomination for the office of President of the United States of America in the 2004 Presidential election. Unlike most national politicians, though, Kucinich is a common person with an underprivileged upbringing. When he was growing up, his family never owned a house and lived in 21 different locations—including several cars—by the time he was 17 years old. In a recent year, Kucinich reported his personal net worth using five figures, while all of the other candidates for the 2004 Presidential election reported their net worth using six figures or multi-millionaire type numbers.

Although his campaign lacked sufficient funds to allow him to become well-known enough to make a big impact in the 2004 Democratic primaries, Kucinich did all he could to make his voice heard and to keep his favorite issues—an end to violent conflict in the world, universal health care for all Americans, a better national education system, sounder environmental policies, and more power to the working classes (to name a few)—on the national agenda. He was the only candidate besides eventual Democratic Presidential nominee Sen. John Kerry to stay in the race to the very end, taking his message to every state in the nation.

Rep. Kucinich is unlike most national politicians in other impressive ways, as well. In a world dominated more and more by corporations and special interest groups that act only for their own benefit and with total disregard for the greater good of all people, and in a nation where political agendas are increasingly controlled by these same groups and where it has been labeled "unpatriotic" to question these trends, Kucinich dares to challenge the status quo and do what he thinks is right. He is what we would call a present-day "Statesman:" a public servant who is concerned about the well-being of the whole world, not just his or her own country or political career.

Rep. Kucinich has been proving this for many years. In 1977, when Dennis was 32 years old, he was elected mayor of Cleveland. That made him, at the time, the youngest person ever to be elected mayor of any large city in the country. A foundation of his campaign was a promise to save Cleveland's municipal electric system, which the incumbent mayor had agreed to sell to private interests.

Kucinich proved to be a man of his word. After winning the election, his first act in office was to cancel the sale. This enraged the banks that had very close business relations with the private electric company. The banks let the upstart, new mayor know that if he did not agree to the sale, they would not renew the city's credit and the City of Cleveland would go into default. Kucinich knew when he refused the sale that he would be jeopardizing his political career. However, he listened to his conscience and made the decision to save the electric system.

The decision turned out to be a pivotal moment in his life. As feared, the decision cost him the mayor's office. The credit was cut, the City defaulted, and Kucinich lost his bid for re-election and was out of public life. For years, he could not even get a job in the city where he had once been mayor. Eventually, though, it became obvious that Kucinich's decision was the right one. The city's municipal electric system, which he managed to save, now provides savings of 25 to 30 percent for Cleveland's populace.

Kucinich has since said this about the episode: "I didn't realize it then, but I was really being asked to submit to a view of the world that holds that corporate values must triumph over the public good. That's the decision I had to take a stand on, and I tell you, it was a time in America when it was considered unseemly, in poor taste, to even raise the issue. People are now starting to look at the overwhelming influence of corporations in public life and how the public good can be undermined."(1)

Dennis has also stated: "Politics is not adequately responding to the needs of our times, nor to the requirements of the future. One reason is that money in the political process has become an end in itself, and when money equals policy, the public interest is shut out. Where money equals policy, you have an auction, you don't have a democracy. The democratic system has been high jacked by special interest groups."(2)

Fifteen years after losing his re-election bid for mayor of Cleveland in 1979, Kucinich made his first step toward a political comeback, winning election to the Ohio State Senate in 1994. In 1996 he was elected to the United States House of Representatives. He has been re-elected four times with a platform that includes working for a Department of Peace, nuclear disarmament, food safety, human rights, universal health care, educational opportunities for all, and new policies on global warming. Congressman Kucinich acts upon his belief that protection of the global environment is fundamental to preserving the life of all species. He has encouraged America to lead the way toward a sustainable, shared stewardship of the planet through measures such as reduction of carbon dioxide emissions and investment in alternative energy technologies. Dennis not only believes in sustainability, he practices it. He is one of the few vegans in Congress, a dietary decision he credits not only with improving his health, but also with deepening his belief in the sacredness of all species.

Kucinich has called for the labeling and safety testing of all genetically engineered foods. As a member of the Congressional Progressive Caucus, he has promoted a national health care system, preservation of Social Security, increased unemployment insurance benefits, and the establishment of wholesale, cost-based rates for electricity, natural gas, and home heating oil.

Working for world peace is a cornerstone of Congressman Kucinich's political agenda. He has taken many measures in his effort to bring about a more peaceful world. For instance, he has sponsored a bill in the House of Representatives that would create a cabinet-level Department of Peace with the goal of making non-violence an organizing principle in our society and to make war a thing of the past. While the United States continued its relentless march along the dastardly path to war and destruction in Iraq, Kucinich had the insight and courage to speak out on behalf of reason, common sense and peace. His was one of the woefully few voices that did not give in to popular opinion and instead spoke its conscience, relentlessly opposing military intervention in Iraq in 2003. And, throughout his presidential campaign, he continued his calls for an end to violence and the start of more responsible, peaceful, and humanitarian relations in Iraq.

Kucinich has become a constant voice for peace in a world that is becoming increasingly violent. On February 17, 2002, with a speech he entitled *A Prayer for America,* Dennis became one of the first of our nation's leaders after the tragedy of 9/11 to have the courage to speak out and declare that something is wrong with our violent response to the violence perpetrated against us and suggest that we are not heading in the right direction by answering violence with more violence.

On the floor of the House of Representatives on March 20, 2002, Kucinich delivered a speech, *Peace and Nuclear Disarmament,* which challenged his fellow representatives in the national government, as well as all of us in the public sector, to think about peace rather than war. We have received permission from Congressman Kucinich to include the speech in this book, and its text can be found later in this chapter.

On October 9, 2002, during the Congressional debate on the resolution that would give the President the authority to use force against Iraq, Kucinich used his five minutes of floor time to deliver a speech titled "Prepare for America's Future" that relayed a message from the youth of our nation to challenge and confront senseless violence, mindless war, and destruction. He has also given permission to use that speech; it, too, is printed later.

Congressman Kucinich's speeches and political record make it apparent that he bases much of his personal and political philosophy on the idea that all people and all nations are interconnected. We believe that Kucinich's ideas are very much in harmony with the theme of Reverence for All Life. That is why we have included them in this book. The Kucinich message incorporates peace, non-violence, and compassion. It calls all of us to work together to build a world based more on love, respect, and cooperation and less on hatred, fear, and intimidation. Congressman Dennis Kucinich represents not only the 10th District of Ohio but all of us who are looking for some changes that can bring about a world where all people can live together in a peaceful, sustainable manner as together we pursue that still more excellent way of Reverence for All Life. To find out more about Representative Kucinich, visit his website at **www.kucinich.us**.

Notes
1.) Sarah Ruth van Gelder; *Yes!*; online article: www.futurenet.org/22art/kucinich.htm; p. 3.
2.) Ibid.; p. 5.

Department of Peace
By John Webster

"Through working to create a Department of Peace, we take steps in a direction of really celebrating a higher purpose of nationhood. At looking at something much more fundamental which stands behind the principal of the United States. It is the principal of human unity: that we all are one, that we are all interconnected, that we are all interdependent. And when we come to that awareness, we realize that "I am you" and "you are me" and we share in this vast ocean of oneness. And when we come to that understanding, we begin to comprehend the beauty of peace."
--Dennis Kucinich at a Peace Alliance event on Feb. 20, 2005, in Ross, CA.

On April 8th 2003, Congressman Dennis Kucinich and co-sponsors introduced legislation in the U.S. House of Representatives that would create a Department of Peace. The possibility of this legislation being passed is real, and its time has come.

We need a Department of Peace. We already have a Department of Defense, which is really a Department of War, with a massive budget. In fact, a Department of Peace could be established for approximately 2% of the U.S.' yearly defense budget. Wars cost money and lives. If a Department of Peace could help defuse even one war, many dollars and many lives could be saved. A Department of Peace could promote cooperation between nations rather than confrontation and hostility that so often leads to violence. Plus, a DOP could promote non-violent conflict resolution within our own country.

Summary of Department of Peace Legislation

The Department of Peace would be a cabinet-level department in the executive branch of the U.S. Federal Government dedicated to peacemaking and the study of conditions that are conducive to peace both domestically and internationally. It would be headed by a Secretary of Peace, appointed by the President with the advice and consent of the Senate. The DOP's responsibilities would include:

- Establishing peace and nonviolence as organizing principles in our society both domestically and internationally.
- Expanding human rights around the world.
- Strengthening non-military means of peacemaking.
- Developing new programs that relate to the societal challenges of school violence, guns, racial or ethnic violence, domestic violence, and police-community relations disputes.
- Establishing a Peace Academy, modeled after the military service academies, which will provide a four-year program of peace education.

Within the U.S., the Department would develop policies which address issues such as domestic violence, child abuse, mistreatment of the elderly, and similar issues of cultural violence. Internationally, the DOP would make recommendations to the President on how to best address the root causes of war, proposing non-violent means of intervention before conflicts become violent. Just imagine how much more respect our nation would have in the world community if we could lead such an approach to worldwide conflict resolution.

What We can Do!

It is important that we contact our Congressional Representatives and ask them to co-sponsor the Department of Peace legislation that Congressman Kucinich and co-sponsors re-introduced in the United States House of Representatives on September 14, 2005. (The bill number in the last session was HR 1673; the new number is HR 3760.) It is important to get as many co-sponsors as possible. Congressman Kucinich will be working inside the House of Representatives to get co-sponsors. Let's do our best out in our own districts to convince our representatives to be co-sponsors.

We should also contact our U.S. Senators and ask them to please introduce the Department of Peace legislation in the Senate. When any of our Congresspersons visit our communities, we can personally urge them to support the Department of Peace. A visit to our Congresspersons' local district offices to put in a positive word about the DOP could really help this effort, as well.

To learn more about the DOP and new resources that are available, go to **http://www.thepeacealliance.org/main.htm**. online. Click on the "Take Action" section to become a Congressional District team leader or to participate in an active group in your district. If there is no one actively promoting the Department of Peace in your district, the task may just be waiting for you. When you visit the DOP website, find out if your representative was a co-sponsor of the bill in the last session. If he or she was, be sure to thank them and encourage them to do so again. If not, strongly urge them to support the legislation this time around. It is also essential to tell our friends and neighbors about the importance of having a DOP. For the Department of Peace to become a reality, it will take strong grassroots support from all around the country, with many people working to share the DOP message with others.

Why I Support Dennis Kucinich
By John Webster

On Saturday, May 31, 2003, I had the good fortune to be in the audience at the Orpheum Theater in Madison, Wisconsin, to hear a speech given by Congressman Dennis Kucinich. As I listened, I again realized why I feel that Rep. Kucinich is one of the only true statesmen in our government, and why I support him and the message that he brings to our nation and our world. It is impossible to talk about "Reverence for All Life" unless you are willing to consider the well-being of all people and the whole world. Dennis Kucinich was the only candidate for President of the United States in 2004 who spoke of our nation's relationship with the world not as enforcer of democracy or sovereign protector, but as an integral member in a worldwide community. Alleluia! In this chapter I will share edited parts of Kucinich's Madison speech. I have emboldened the word "world" every time it is used in the speech to emphasize how often Congressman Kucinich mentioned it. This is "Reverence for All Life" in action at its very best.

"We are here this evening to talk about how we can make America a nation among nations, a nation that is the light of the **world** instead of a nation that is threatening to the **world**. ...

...We are at a moment in our country's history where it is urgent that we reconnect with those finer sentiments; that we reconnect with those paths toward peace; that we reconnect with some deeper truths about America that lead us toward **world** cooperation, that lead us toward participating with the **world** community in creating peace, and that remind us how we can truly establish peace here at home. ...

...Our hope can create from its own wreck what we contemplate for this country, a dream of peace, a dream of brotherhood and sisterhood, a dream of cooperation with the **world**. ...

...Look at the distance we have come since 9/11, that great tragedy that struck our nation and the **world**... [Kucinich then talked about the unfortunate spell that 9/11 has cast upon our nation.]

...Let's talk about where that spell has taken us. It has taken us down a dark alley where the dreams for our country are suddenly disappearing. It has taken us and cut us off from the **world** community. After 9/11 the heart of the **world** was open to the United States. We could have worked with the **world** community in meeting the challenges of terrorism, in organizing **world**-wide to put together the experienced police work of a nation and nations to track down those who were responsible for any kind of acts of violence against people anywhere. We could have done that. But we chose to take another route. We chose to separate from the **world** community. We took a path consistent with the national security strategy which essentially says 'preemption, unilateralism, that's the way America, goes in the **world**.' But yet, we understand something else. We understand in our heart of hearts that the advancing tide in this **world** is towards human unity, not toward separation from the **world**. ...

...If you, as I, had the opportunity to watch city after city celebrating the bringing in of the new millennium, there really was a feeling of hope about it: a hope of the brotherhood and sisterhood of all people. I believe that really is where the **world** wants to go. I think that where the **world** wants to go is towards unity. We saw it again when people all over the **world** and all over the country joined in protesting the administration that was taking us into war. Now think about it. Despite the images that the media was putting out all the time, millions of Americans came forth and said 'No! This isn't the path we want to go,' because they had a sense of connecting with the rest of the **world**. This is a moment when we as individuals are called upon to assert a holistic **world** view, an understanding of the **world** as interdependent and interconnected. And as we insist on this connection to each other there is great power. We are affirming the power of our own

182

humanity, and we are confirming that expressive power which comes from understanding that we are all one.

What an important moment it is in human history for our nation, for our government, for those leaders who are working with mass consciousness every day to catch up on that tempo, to join with the course of history as it intends to confirm the purpose of our existence, which is to live out our lives in peace and prosperity. And so this is the moment for all of us to reconfirm our commitment to the people all over the **world**. This is the moment for all of us to insist that a government remember that its purpose is not to separate from its own people and separate from the rest of the **world,** but to rejoin the **world** community; and this is the moment that we can insist on specific measures that can be taken to reconnect America with the rest of the **world.**

As President of the United States, I will do the following things that will help America rejoin the **world** community. Number one, I'll lead the way to the United States reclaiming its obligation to push for total nuclear disarmament. It is time! [At this point there was a lengthy period of applause from the audience, including a rather loud shout of affirmation from yours truly.]

It is time! It is time for this nation to recognize that those 12 nations that have or are trying to get nuclear technology, that those 20 nations which have or are trying to get biological weapons, those 26 nations that have or are trying to get chemical weapons, those 20 nations that have or are trying to get missile technology, all represent a misdirection and all represent a threat to the common heritage that we have on this earth. And so it is time for the United States to once again take up the standard and to confirm the Biological Weapons Convention, the Chemical Weapons Convention, the Small Arms Treaty, the Land Mine Treaty, and to join the International Criminal Court. **Rejoin the WORLD America; it's a beautiful place!** [More applause!]

And maybe as we rejoin the **world**, the White House will not be such a lonely place. Maybe our leaders can relieve themselves of the burden of having to be policemen of the **world,** because that is not America's role. Our role is to work cooperatively with the **world** community and if we do that we can meet the challenge of international terrorism. That is the only way we can do it. …

…I think that it is time for America to start preparing for peace. They are preparing right now to put weapons in space, to build a national missile defense, they are preparing for Armageddon, World War III, whatever you want to call it. I think this is the time for America to start preparing for peace. So start preparing for a **world** without end; so start preparing or creating a **world** which we would be happy to turn over to our children…

…And the militarization of thought which has taken place in this society has robbed us of a capacity to be able to understand that we can create a nation which does not depend on arms for survival. With 50 members of Congress…I was able to create legislation to help put forward a Department of Peace that would serve to make non-violence an organizing principle in this society. As we confront the demons in our own society of domestic violence, spousal abuse and child abuse, we empower ourselves as a nation to truly be more effective in carrying the message of peace around the **world.**

As we address the issues in our own society of gangs in the schools, of police/community relations problems, of racial problems, problems against gays, we empower ourselves to be more expressive of the potential for peace in the **world.** As we do that, we then can work with other nations to grasp the dream that has eluded this nation and the nations of the **world** for so long but which really is a dream which relates to our human capacity, and that is the dream to work with the nations of the **world** to make war, itself, archaic. [Applause!] Who says we are stuck with war? Where is it written that we are stuck with war? Where is the law that says we have to be at war forever? We are being taken in that direction, but that is not resident with who we are as a people; that is not where our hearts are; that is not where the human spirit is...

… To have all of our commerce based on principles of bilateral trade, based on human rights, workers' rights and the environment. We can reclaim what it means to be Americans by working with the **world** community to lift up the **world**."

How great it is to hear one of our governmental representatives talk about non-violence, total nuclear disarmament, and peace. I join with Dennis Kucinich in proclaiming that war is archaic. I also agree with Kucinich's stance on other issues. I agree that we should break up agricultural monopolies and restore a strong, independent family farm system with ethical treatment of animals, fair prices for farmers, and healthy food for consumers. I strongly agree with Kucinich that we need universal health care with a single payer plan. With our present health care system, over 40 million Americans are uninsured and 30 million more have only minimal coverage. Those with coverage often pay exorbitant amounts for health insurance. Finally, I support Dennis because he is opposed to capital punishment. With a feeling of "Reverence for All Life," we can never justify killing another person.

These are only a few of the important reasons why I support Dennis Kucinich as he works to bring that still more excellent way of life and love into our world and our relationships with all that live. These are only a few of the reasons why—on Tuesday, February 17, 2004, in the Wisconsin Democratic Presidential Primary—with much excitement and pride, I penciled in my "X" on the paper ballot next to the name of Dennis J. Kucinich. Without a doubt it was the most meaningful and important vote of my entire life. Thanks Dennis!

May we all join in this great and noble endeavor of working to bring about a more peaceful, sensible, and caring world—a world more full of Reverence for All Life—during the days and years ahead.

Compassion for a Homeless Man
By Justin Walker

While he was a senior at Duke University, Justin Walker spent several months covering the 2004 Democratic Presidential campaign as part of an independent study project for his Political Science major. The Louisville, Kentucky, native drove over 10,000 miles following the campaign. We thank Justin for granting us permission to use this report from his Campaign Diary.

Date: Saturday, January 10, 2004
Location: Cedar Rapids, Iowa
Place: Parking garage with Dennis Kucinich

Saturday night, I found myself in a parking garage with Dennis Kucinich and a sleeping homeless man. This is our story.

It begins with me, a life-long Republican at an Iowa Democratic Party fundraiser. Four presidential candidates speak. Thousands of dollars are raised.

As we leave the ballroom, I ask Kucinich a question that mentions a homeless man sleeping in the stairwell of the hotel's parking garage. Kucinich immediately responds, "He's there now? I'll go visit him." And 20 minutes later, we meet at the garage's entrance – a congressman, an aide, a security agent and me.

The four of us walk down the dark stairwell. Kucinich stops. He doesn't want to frighten the sleeping man, and whispers to us to keep our distance. Three of us stand 10 steps above the concrete floor this sleeping man calls home.

Below, the Congressman stands motionless, staring at this man whose poverty is absolute. Is Kucinich thinking of his own past? As a boy, his family sometimes lived in cars. Tonight, Kucinich's face says more to me than any speech he's ever given. I believe that he is suffering right along with this helpless and hopeless sleeping man. It is 25 degrees out tonight. How cold was the boy in Cleveland who called cars home?

The Congressman finally kneels beside the man and leaves a gift. What will the homeless man buy with the significant amount of money Kucinich has left him? I'd like to think he is a Jean Valjean*, a discouraged man for whom one display of compassion and generosity will inspire a new beginning. I'd like to think he will not buy drugs or alcohol. I'd like to be less cynical.

Before I joined the campaign trail, friends quipped that I'd come back a Democrat. I doubt it. But I also doubt that I will ever forget the sleeping man whose name I never knew and whose face I never saw. Nor will I forget the look of compassion on the face of a motionless Dennis Kucinich, as he visited a man whom most of his party and most of his country would rather ignore.

Compassion comes from a Greek word meaning, "to suffer with."

* Jean Valjean is a character from Victor Hugo's novel *Les Miserables*.

Peace and Nuclear Disarmament
By Dennis J. Kucinich

The following speech was delivered by Congressman Dennis J. Kucinich on the floor of the United States House Of Representatives in Washington D.C. on March 20, 2002.

"Come my friends, 'tis not too late to seek a newer world"
--Alfred, Lord Tennyson

If you believe that humanity has a higher destiny, if you believe we are all ultimately perfectible, if you believe we can evolve, and become better than we are; if you believe we can overcome the nihilistic scourge of war and someday fulfill the dream of peace and harmony on earth, let us begin the conversation today. Let us exchange our ideas. Let us plan together, act together and create peace together. This is a call for common sense, for peaceful, non-violent citizen action to protect our precious world from widening war and from stumbling into a nuclear catastrophe.

The climate for conflict has intensified, with the struggle between Pakistan and India, the China-Taiwan tug of war, and the increased bloodshed between Israel and the Palestinians. The United States' troop deployments in the Philippines, Yemen, Georgia, Columbia and Indonesia create new possibilities for expanded war. An invasion of Iraq is planned. The recent disclosure that Russia, China, Iraq, Iran, Syria, North Korea and Libya are considered by the United States as possible targets for nuclear attack catalyzes potential conflicts everywhere.

These crucial political decisions promoting increased military actions, plus a new nuclear first-use policy, are occurring without the consent of the American people, without public debate, without public hearings, without public votes. The President is taking Congress' approval of responding to the September 11 terrorists as a license to flirt with nuclear war.

"Politics ought to stay out of fighting a war," the President has been quoted as saying on March 13, 2002. Yet Article 1, Section 8 of the United States Constitution explicitly requires that Congress take responsibility when it comes to declaring war. This President is very popular, according to the polls. But polls are not a substitute for democratic process. Attributing a negative connotation here to politics or dismissing constitutionally mandated congressional oversight belies reality. Spending $400 billion a year for defense is a political decision. Committing troops abroad is a political decision. War is a political decision. When men and women die on the battlefield, that is the result of a political decision. The use of nuclear weapons, which can end the lives of millions, is a profound political decision. In a monarchy there need be no political decisions. In a democracy, all decisions are political, in that they derive from the consent of the governed.

In a democracy, budgetary, military and national objectives must be subordinated to the political process. Before we celebrate an imperial presidency, let it be said that the lack of free and open political process, the lack of free and open political debate, and the lack of free and open political dissent can be fatal in a democracy.

We have reached a moment in our country's history where it is urgent that people everywhere speak out as president of his or her own life, to protect the peace of the nation and world within and without. We should speak out and caution leaders who generate fear through talk of the endless war or the final conflict. We should appeal to our leaders to consider that their own bellicose thoughts, words and deeds are reshaping consciousness and can have an adverse effect on our nation. Because when one person thinks: *fight!* he or she finds a fight. One faction thinks *war!* and starts a war. One nation thinks *nuclear!* and approaches the abyss.

Neither individuals nor nations exist in a vacuum, which is why we have a serious responsibility for each other in this world. It is also urgent that we find those places of war in our own lives, and begin healing the world through healing ourselves. Each of us is a citizen of a common planet, bound to a common destiny. So connected are we, that each of us has the power to be the eyes of the world, the voice of the world, the conscience of the world, or the end of the world. And as each one of us chooses, so becomes the world.

Each of us is architect of this world. Our thoughts, the concepts. Our words, the designs. Our deeds, the bricks and mortar of our daily lives. Which is why we should always take care to regard the power of our thoughts and words, and the commands they send into action through time and space.

Some of our leaders have been thinking and talking about nuclear war. In the past week there has been much news about a planning document which describes how and when America might wage nuclear war. The Nuclear Posture Review recently released to the media by the government:

1. Assumes that the United States has the right to launch a pre-emptive nuclear strike.
2. Equates nuclear weapons with conventional weapons.
3. Attempts to minimize the consequences of the use of nuclear weapons.
4. Promotes nuclear response to a chemical or biological attack.

Some dismiss this review as routine government planning. But it becomes ominous when taken in the context of a war on terrorism which keeps expanding its boundaries, rhetorically and literally. The President equates the "war on terrorism" with World War II. He expresses a desire to have the nuclear option "on the table." He unilaterally withdraws from the ABM treaty. He seeks $8.9 billion to fund deployment of a missile shield. He institutes, without Congressional knowledge, a shadow government in a bunker outside our nation's Capitol. He tries to pass off as arms reduction, the storage of, instead of the elimination of, nuclear weapons.

Two generations ago we lived with nuclear nightmares. We feared and hated the Russians who feared and hated us. We feared and hated the "godless, atheistic" communists. In our schools, we dutifully put our head between our legs and practiced duck-and-cover drills. In our nightmares, we saw the long, slow arc of a Soviet missile flash into our very neighborhood. We got down on our knees and prayed for peace. We surveyed, wide eyed, pictures of the destruction of Nagasaki and Hiroshima. We supported the elimination of all nuclear weapons. We knew that if you "nuked" others you "nuked" yourself.

The splitting of the atom for destructive purposes admits a split consciousness, the compartmentalized thinking of Us versus Them—the dichotomized thinking, which spawns polarity and leads to war. The proposed use of nuclear weapons pollutes the psyche with the arrogance of infinite power. It creates delusions of domination of matter and space. It is dehumanizing through its calculations of mass casualties. We must overcome doomthinkers and sayers who invite a world descending, disintegrating into a nuclear disaster. With a world at risk, we must find the bombs in our own lives and disarm them. We must listen to that quiet inner voice which counsels that the survival of all is achieved through the unity of all.

The same powerful humanity expressed by any one of us expresses itself through each of us. We must overcome our fear of each other by seeking out the humanity within each of us. The human heart contains every possibility of race, creed, language, religion, and politics. We are one in our commonalities. Must we always fear our differences? We can overcome our fears by not feeding our fears with more war and nuclear confrontations. We must ask our leaders to unify us in courage.

We need to create a new, clear vision of a world as one. A new, clear vision of people working out their differences peacefully. A new, clear vision with the teaching of nonviolence, nonviolent intervention and mediation. A new, clear vision where people can live in harmony with their families, their communities and with themselves. A new clear vision of peaceful coexistence in a world of tolerance.

At this moment of peril we must move away from fear's paralysis. This is a call to action: to replace expanded war with expanded peace. This is a call for action to place the very survival of this planet on the agenda of all people everywhere. As citizens of a common planet, we have an obligation to ourselves and our posterity. We must demand that our nation and all nations put down the nuclear sword. We must demand that our nation and all nations:

- Abide by the principles of the Nuclear Non-Proliferation Treaty.
- Stop the development of new nuclear weapons.
- Take all nuclear weapons systems off alert.
- Persist towards total, worldwide elimination of all nuclear weapons.

Our nation must:

- Revive the Anti-Ballistic Missile treaty.
- Sign and enforce the Comprehensive Test Ban Treaty.
- Abandon plans to build a so-called missile shield.
- Prohibit the introduction of weapons into outer space.

We are in a climate where people expect debate within our two-party system to produce policy alternatives. However, both major political parties have fallen short. People who ask "Where is the Democratic Party?" and expect to hear debate may be disappointed. When peace is not on the agenda of our political parties or our governments, then it must be the work and the duty of each citizen to the world. This is the time to organize for peace. This is the time for new thinking. This is the time to conceive of peace as not simply being the absence of violence, but the active presence of the capacity for a higher evolution of human awareness. This is the time to conceive of peace as respect, trust, and integrity. This is the time to tap the infinite capabilities of humanity to transform consciousness which compels violence at a personal, group, national or international level. This is the time to develop a new compassion for others and ourselves. It is necessary that we do so, for at this moment our world is being challenged by war and premonitions of nuclear annihilation.

When terrorists threaten our security, we must enforce the law and bring terrorists to justice within our system of constitutional justice, without undermining the very civil liberties which permit our democracy to breathe. Our own instinct for life, which inspires our breath and informs our pulse, excites our capacity to reason. Which is why we must pay attention when we sense a threat to survival. That is why we must speak out now to protect this planet and:

- Challenge those who believe in a nuclear right.
- Challenge those who would build new nuclear weapons.
- Challenge those who seek nuclear re-armament.
- Challenge those who seek nuclear escalation.
- Challenge those who would make of any nation a nuclear target.
- Challenge those who would threaten to use nuclear weapons against civilian populations.
- Challenge those who would break nuclear treaties.
- Challenge those who think and think about nuclear weapons, to think about peace.

It is practical to work for peace. I speak of peace and diplomacy not just for the sake of peace itself. But, for practical reasons, we must work for peace as a means of achieving permanent security. It is similarly practical to work for total nuclear disarmament, particularly when nuclear arms do not even come close to addressing the real security problems which confront our nation--witness the events of September 11, 2001.

It is practical to work to make war archaic. That is the purpose of HR 2459. It is a bill to create a Department of Peace. HR2459 seeks to make non-violence an organizing principle in our society. It envisions new structures to help create peace in our homes, in our families, in our schools, in our neighborhoods, in our cities, and in our nation. It aspires to create conditions for peace within and to create conditions for peace worldwide. It considers the conditions which cause people to become the terrorists of the future—issues of poverty, scarcity and exploitation. It is practical to make outer space safe from weapons, so that humanity can continue to pursue a destiny among the stars. HR 3616 seeks to ban weapons in space, to keep the stars a place of dreams, of new possibilities, of transcendence.

We can achieve this practical vision of peace, if we are ready to work for it. People worldwide need to meet with likeminded people, about peace and nuclear disarmament, now. People worldwide need to gather in peace, now. People worldwide need to march and to pray for peace, now. People worldwide need to be connecting with each other on the Web, for peace, now. We are in a new era of electronic democracy, where the World Wide Web, with its numerous websites and bulletin boards enable new organizations, exercising freedom of speech, freedom of assembly, freedom of association, to spring into being instantly. We need websites dedicated to becoming electronic forums for peace, for sustainability, for renewal and for revitalization. We need forums which strive for the restoration of a sense of community through the empowerment of self, through commitment of self to the lives of others, to the life of the community, to the life of the nation, to the life of the world.

Where war-making is profoundly uncreative in its destruction, peacemaking can be deeply creative. We need to communicate with each other about the ways in which we can work in our communities to make this a more peaceful world. I welcome your ideas. We can share our thoughts and discuss ways in which we have brought or will bring them into action. Now is the time to think, to take action and use our talents and abilities to create peace:

- In our families.
- In our block clubs.
- In our neighborhoods.

- In our places of worship.
- In our schools and universities.
- In our labor halls.
- In our parent-teacher organizations.

Now is the time to think, speak, write, organize and take action to create peace as a social imperative, as an economic imperative, and as a political imperative. Now is the time to think, speak, write, organize, march, rally, hold vigils and take other nonviolent action to create peace in our cities, in our nation and in the world. And as the hymn says, "Let there be peace on earth and let it begin with me."

This is the work of the human family, of people all over the world demanding that governments and non-governmental sectors alike put down their nuclear weapons. This is the work of the human family, responding in this moment of crisis to protect our nation, this planet and all life with it. As we understand that all people of the world are interconnected, we can achieve both nuclear disarmament and peace. We can accomplish this through upholding a holistic vision where the claims of all living beings to the right of survival are recognized. We can achieve both nuclear disarmament and peace through being a living testament to a Human Rights Covenant where each person on this planet is entitled to a life where he or she may consciously evolve in mind, body and spirit.

Nuclear disarmament and peace are the signposts toward the path of an even brighter human condition wherein we can, through our conscious efforts, evolve and reestablish the context of our existence from peril to peace, from revolution to evolution. Think peace. Speak peace. Act peace. Peace.

Prepare for America's Future
By Dennis J. Kucinich

As the war resolution to give President George W. Bush approval to use force against Iraq was being debated on the floor of the United States House Of Representatives on October 9, 2002, Congressman Dennis J. Kucinich presented the following statement on behalf of all of us who live and work for peace using non-violent methods.

Yesterday students held a peace rally on the west front of the Capitol. It may have been the first rally on the Capitol grounds in opposition to war with Iraq. I attended and I heard representatives of America's youth asking, "Why?:"

- Why war against the people of Iraq?
- Why assert military power, which threatens innocent civilians?
- Why war to settle differences?
- Why separate our nation from the world community?
- Why not give peaceful resolution a chance?

I looked at the faces of the young people at the peace rally. Fresh faces, hopeful, optimistic and challenging. Soon the voices of our youth will be heard across the nation. And we should pay them heed. They will be heard on campuses, in town halls, in marches. They will be raised to challenge and to confront senseless violence, mindless war, the death of innocents, the destruction of villages to save villages. Voices will be lifted up in urgency because the future knows when the place it needs to build could be destroyed. The future knows skepticism when promises of peace are wrapped in fire and brimstone.

Our young people opposing war represent a message from the future America, the America that can be, and with the upwardly spiraling aspirations of millions of Americans of all ages, the America that will be:

- The future America works to make nonviolence an organizing principle in our society.
- The future America works to make war archaic.
- It is a nation that lives courageously in peace, working to settle differences at home and abroad without killing.
- The future America comprehends the world as an interconnected whole. It understands that changes in transportation, communication and trade have made people throughout the world neighbors.
- The future America believes that each person is sacred. That each person makes a difference. That each choice we make affects others. That an injury to one person is an injury to all. That justice ought to be international and that vengeance is reserved to the Lord.
- It is an America where human rights and workers rights and environmental quality principles are one with the ark of the Human Covenant.
- It is a nation where each life is given an opportunity to unfold, where all have access to health care, to higher education, to jobs and to a secure retirement. Where the quality of life matters. Where people build families, build

communities, build an American community of our dreams, where our highest aspirations light the way to a better nation and to a better world.

- The future America is a nation which works to sustain life on earth. It champions protection of the global environment. It works with all nations to abolish nuclear weapons, chemical weapons and biological weapons.
- It is a nation which preserves the heavens for the restless human soul. And it rejects putting weapons in space because it knows the kingdom that will come from the stars should bring eternal peace, not war.
- While some voices clamor for war, a future America looks for deeper unity of all people worldwide and seeks not empire but harmony.

So to you, young America, I sing a hymn of praise because while some may want to send you marching off to fight yesterday's wars, you are advancing from the future, reminding us that our nation has a higher calling. Reminding us of the America that can be. Reminding us that there has to be a better way. Challenging us to find that better way. Joining with us to make straight the path of democracy.

This is a time for caution as we would face war, but it is also a cause for joy because the same reveille which sounds a battle cry and clangs the tocsins of war, brings forth legions of others enlisted in a holy cause to relight the lamp of freedom in our own land.

So come forth young and old. Prepare for America's future.

29

Fresh Voices

After reading the text of Congressman Dennis Kucinich's speech praising the actions of young people at a peace rally in Washington D.C., I decided I would like to have "the voices of our youth" represented in my book. To my great fortune, I did not have far to look. I asked our neighbors, Kestrel and Forest Jenkins—at the time aged 17 and 14 respectively—if they would be willing to write essays in response to Rep. Kucinich's speech. Much to my gratitude, both were willing to accept my assignment and wrote their essays during the Christmas Holiday break of the 2002-03 school year.

*I then found another possible source of youthful commentary even closer to home: right in my office, on my computer. While perusing one of my favorite websites on the Internet, Common Dreams (**www.commondreams.org**)--which is a great source for alternative and independent news reports with links to many other excellent websites—I came across a wonderful essay written by a 12-year-old girl named Charlotte Aldebron, from Presque Isle, Maine.*

The essay "What the American Flag Stands For" was indeed about the American flag. But it was by no means a patriotic, "flag waving" piece of work. It was intelligently critical. It was painfully accurate. It was very powerful. It was just what I was looking for. Charlotte subsequently became a very vocal opponent to our nation's military action in Afghanistan and Iraq, speaking to politicians and their staff and becoming a familiar face at peace rallies around Maine. The transcripts of some of her speeches also appeared on the Common Dreams site. I felt that her message very much embodied the spirit of Reverence for Life, so I contacted her via an email to her mother, Jillian Aldebron. The Aldebrons also were kind enough to give me permission to use these passages in the book, and for that I am very grateful.

I, like Rep. Kucinich, find it very heartening to know there is a new generation of people who do not believe everything that is spoon-fed to them in the mass media and instead are thinking for themselves and questioning the world we live in and the actions of world leaders. I am thrilled to find the spirit of Reverence for Life alive and well in our nation's youth.

Kestrel and Forest Jenkins

Kestrel Jenkins was a senior at the Galeville-Ettrick-Trempealeau Senior High School in Galesville, WI, when she wrote her essay. Currently she is enrolled at Hamline Universtiy in St. Paul, Minnesota. Forest Jenkins was a freshman at G-E-T Senior High when he penned his essay. He currently attends G-E-T Senior High. I would like to thank Forest and Kestrel for allowing their messages of peace to be printed in this book.

Peace First
By Kestrel Jenkins

In my mind, peace always needs to be considered as the first option in solving an international disagreement. Whether peace can actually be attained still remains unclear, but I feel that before any extreme measures are taken by going to battle, bombing, or initiating a war, our nation should examine and attempt all the peaceful solutions first.

The young people of our nation are the voice of our country's future. So, if peaceful ideas are promoted and encouraged to today's youth, hopefully we can gradually educate our nation to at least look to peace as an option before heading straight into negative solutions that usually end up leading to war.

I don't really understand why there is so little being said, at least around me, about the situation with Iraq. For instance, in my high school, the only way anything is discussed about the possibilities of war is through a history or government class. I never hear any of my fellow classmates talking about our nation's problems. It seems like the possibility of war doesn't even faze the people around me. I don't know if they don't care what our country decides to do, or if they think everything is under control and taken care of by President Bush, or if they maybe just don't think about it because they feel they can't change anything that is happening or that their voices will not be heard or listened to.

As for me, I feel that all U.S. citizens have the opportunity, the right, and the responsibility to voice their opinions about the actions that will affect the future of our nation. Maybe one voice can't make a difference in our nation's decisions, but on the other hand, one voice could possibly ignite the minds of others and encourage them to look into alternative ideas and solutions.

Therefore, as one single voice, all that I can honestly say is that for the betterment of the citizens in our country, along with the citizens of all countries around the world, peaceful options should be sought out and attempted before the decisions for physical fighting, battle, and killing create even more problems.

War is Not the Answer!
By Forest Jenkins

I believe that war is not a solution to international arguments. As to whether or not we should go to war with Iraq, I believe that non-violence is a solution that should be tested. In Congressman Dennis J. Kucinich's speech, he spoke about how youth are our nation's future. I agree with that and feel that everyone is important and can make a difference. Right now, youth are making a difference by holding peace rallies, protests, and debates to attempt to get people to consider peace before just wanting to go to war.

Where I live, the only time the peace and war subject is brought up in my school and among my peers is in history class. Most students sit back and don't say much, but the majority seem to want to go to war. Our teacher tries to keep us updated on this issue with current events so we have something to base our opinions on.

After spending a week in Costa Rica, which has no military power and where war isn't an issue to most people, I am curious to see if our government still wants to go to war. It will also be interesting to hear if my peers have changed their opinions at all.

I hope that more people will begin to consider peace as the best option. We need to help other nations such as Iraq instead of just destroying them. Some things we could do to help them are helping them get better medical care, housing, and financial support. Hopefully in the near future more people across the world will realize the advantages of peace, as I do, and understand how beneficial a world without war would be to us all.

Charlotte Aldebron

After she gained fame for her flag essay, Charlotte became a vociferous spokesperson for peace, speaking out loudly and clearly time and time again, questioning our nation's aggressive approach to international relations and calling for peaceful solutions based on understanding and compassion. Like so many of us, she has been appalled by the violent manner in which our nation's leaders have chosen to react to the challenges we face. Unlike many of us, she has had the courage to publicly voice her opinions. Her message has traveled around the world primarily by means of the Internet. We thank Charlotte and her mother, Jillian, for giving us permission to use the following passages so that we might spread her message to the readers of this book.

What the American Flag Stands For
By Charlotte Aldebron

Charlotte wrote the following essay on February 12, 2002, for a competition in her sixth-grade English class at Cunningham Middle School in Presque Isle, Maine. It brought her well-deserved acclaim when it was posted on the Common Dreams website (www.commondreams.org) on April 3, 2002.

The American flag stands for the fact that cloth can be very important. It is against the law to let the flag touch the ground or to leave the flag flying when the weather is bad. The flag has to be treated with respect. You can tell just how important this cloth is because when you compare it to people, it gets much better treatment. Nobody cares if a homeless person touches the ground. A homeless person can lie all over the ground all night long without anyone picking him up, folding him neatly and sheltering him from the rain.

School children have to pledge loyalty to this piece of cloth every morning. No one has to pledge loyalty to justice and equality and human decency. No one has to promise that people will get a fair wage, or enough food to eat, or affordable medicine, or clean water, or air free of harmful chemicals. But we all have to promise to love a rectangle of red, white, and blue cloth.

Betsy Ross would be quite surprised to see how successful her creation has become. But Thomas Jefferson would be disappointed to see how little of the flag's real meaning remains.

Is Anyone Listening?!
By Charlotte Aldebron

The following is a transcript of the speech Charlotte gave at a peace rally in Maine on October 26, 2002.

I've been speaking up a lot since September 11 [2001]. On February 12, I wrote an essay for school saying that we care more about the American flag than about living up to what it stands for. On March 22, I told [Maine Republican U.S. Senator] Olympia Snowe's staff in Presque Isle that you grown-ups were hypocrites because you tell kids to solve problems with words, while you kill people in Afghanistan. On March 28, I said the same thing to [Maine Republican U.S. Senator] Susan Collins in person. She told me that because we invaded Afghanistan, little girls can go to school and learn to read. Some choice: learn to read or have a mom and dad.

On April 3, the Common Dreams website posted my flag essay. It got lots of attention and was reprinted and read on the radio. I got 800 emails. I was surprised to get such a response because I'd started to believe that solving problems by talking was something only kids had to do, but that grownups could fight all they wanted—like they get to drink and swear, but kids can't.

On May 12, I spoke at the Peace Rally in Bath [Maine]. On May 20, I talked to [Maine Democratic State Senator] Chellie Pingree and [South Dakota Democratic U.S. Senator] Tom Daschle. I suspected that Tom Daschle was not paying attention because, with a glazed look in his eyes, he stuffed my flag essay in his pocket, unread. On June 22, I spoke at the Maine Green Independent Party Convention. Now here it is October 26, and I am giving another speech. That's really a bad sign because it means we still don't have peace. In fact, we're about to go and kill even more people. Well, I'm getting a little sick of hearing my own voice! HELLO—is anyone out there listening?!

I guess my own voice is too small to make a difference. So this time, I'll add the voices of other children, and maybe together we'll be loud enough. Children like Ali, who was three when we killed his father in the Gulf War. Ali scraped at the dirt covering his father's grave every day for three years calling out to him, "It's all right, Daddy, you can come out now; the men who put you here have gone away." And Luay who was 11 at the time and was glad he didn't have to go to school or do homework. He went to bed and got up whenever he felt like it. But today he has no education and still hears the explosions in his head.

And the children in Basra, southern Iraq, who today play in the dust while air raid sirens scream around them because we keep dropping bombs. And all the children in Iraq who will never grow up because they have leukemia and cancers from the depleted uranium in our missiles, and they can't get any drugs or radiation treatment because we won't let their country have them. I don't know the names of all these children.

Can you hear our voices yet? I'll add 10-year-old Mohibollah in Afghanistan, who was out collecting firewood for his family when he found one of those bright yellow soda-can-sized cluster bomblets with parachutes. What child could resist? He ended up with mangled flesh where his left hand used to be.

President Bush asked each American child to give a dollar to help Afghani children. Here is my dollar's worth: it is the voice of 6-year-old Paliko who was carried to the hospital still wearing her party dress for the wedding that we bombed for two hours, killing her whole family—by mistake. And 2-year-old Alia, who was dug out of the rubble where her family was crushed when we blew up their village—again by mistake. Afterward, our soldiers said they were sorry. Among themselves, they called the Afghans "rag heads." Like I said in my flag essay, we are better at caring about symbols than real people.

Can you hear us yet? Our government is paying for educational theater in Afghanistan that teaches kids to fight with pen and paper, not guns, and tells them to "join the educated culture of the world." They call it Mobile Mini Circus for Children. The performers are orphans who live just north of Kabul, in an orphanage filled with 2,000 victims of our air strikes, our greed, our comfort. When are *we* going to join the educated cultures of the world?

Maybe you'll hear the voices of Palestinian children: Sami, shot in the head by an Israeli soldier the day before his 12th birthday; 10-year-old Riham, killed in her schoolyard by an Israeli tank shell; and 14-year-old Faris, who told his 8-year-old brother Abdel to go home when he followed him out to buy groceries. Abdel refused, so he got to see the tank shoot his brother dead in the street. And the six Matar children, ages 2 months to 17 years—all killed when an Israeli pilot flying an American-made jet dropped a one-ton bomb on their home. The pilot was sent by Israeli Prime Minister Ariel Sharon, who our President calls a "man of peace."

Can you hear us yet? How about the voices of Israeli children? Like 14-year-old Raaya and 2-year-old Hemda, killed with their parents by a Palestinian suicide bomber when they went out to eat pizza; 9-month-old Avia, killed by Palestinians who shot and threw grenades at cars; and the 12 teenagers killed by a suicide bomber at a nightclub. Can you hear us now?

How many more children must suffer or die before you hear us? No offense, but I really don't want to have to make another peace speech ever again!

Take a Look at Me!
By Charlotte Aldebron

Charlotte gave this speech in Presque Isle on February 15, 2003, at a rally timed to coincide with the unprecedented international coordination of demonstrations held by 10 million people around the world to protest the pending U.S. invasion of Iraq.

When people think about bombing Iraq, they see a picture in their heads of Saddam Hussein in a military uniform, or maybe soldiers with big black mustaches carrying guns, or the mosaic of George Bush, Senior, on the lobby floor of Al-Rashid Hotel with the word "criminal." But guess what? More than half of Iraq's 24 million people are children under the age of 15. That's 12 million kids. Kids like me. Well, I'm almost 13, so some are a little older, and some a lot younger, some boys instead of girls, some with brown hair, not red. But kids who are pretty much like me just the same. So take a look at me—a good, long look. Because I am what you should see in your head when you think about bombing Iraq. I am what you are going to destroy.

If I am lucky, I will be killed instantly, like the three hundred children murdered by your "smart" bombs in a Baghdad bomb shelter on February 16, 1991. The blast caused a fire so intense that it flash-burned outlines of those children and their mothers on the walls; you can still peel strips of blackened skin---souvenirs of your victory---from the stones.

But maybe I won't be lucky and I'll die slowly, like 14-year-old Ali Faisal, who right now is in the "death ward" of the Baghdad children's hospital. He has malignant lymphoma—cancer—caused by the depleted uranium in your Gulf War missiles. Or maybe I will die painfully and needlessly like 18-month-old Mustafa, whose vital organs are being devoured by sand fly parasites. I know it's hard to believe, but Mustafa could be totally cured with just $25 worth of medicine, but there is none of this medicine because of your sanctions.

Or maybe I won't die at all but will live for years with the psychological damage that you can't see from the outside, like Salman Mohammed, who even now can't forget the terror he lived through with his little sisters when you bombed Iraq in 1991. Salman's father made the whole family sleep in the same room so that they would all survive together, or die together. He still has nightmares about the air raid sirens.

Or maybe I will be orphaned like Ali, who was three when you killed his father in the Gulf War. Ali scraped at the dirt covering his father's grave every day for three years calling out to him, "It's all right Daddy, you can come out now, the men who put you here have gone away." Well, Ali, you're wrong. It looks like those men are coming back.

Or maybe I will make it in one piece, like Luay Majed, who remembers that the Gulf War meant he didn't have to go to school and could stay up as late as he wanted. But today, with no education, he tries to live by selling newspapers on the street.

Imagine that these are your children—or nieces or nephews or neighbors. Imagine your son screaming from the agony of a severed limb, but you can't do anything to ease the pain or comfort him. Imagine your daughter crying out under the rubble of a collapsed building, but you can't get to her. Imagine your children wandering the streets, hungry and alone, after having watched you die before their eyes.

This is not an adventure movie or a video game. This is reality for children in Iraq. Recently, an international group of researchers went to Iraq to find out how children there are being affected by the possibility of war. Half the children they talked to said they saw no point in living any more. Even really young kids knew about war and worried about it. One 5-year-old, Assem, described it as "guns and bombs and the air will be cold and hot and we will burn very much." 10-year-old Aeser had a message for President Bush: he wanted him to know that "A lot of Iraqi children will die. You will see it on TV, and then you will regret."

Back in elementary school I was taught to solve problems with other kids not by hitting or name-calling, but by talking and using "I" messages. The idea of the "I" message was to make the other person understand how bad his or her actions made you feel, so that the person would sympathize with you and stop it. Now I am going to give you an "I" message. Only it's going to be a "We" message. "We," as in all the children in Iraq who are waiting helplessly for something bad to happen. "We" as in the children of the world who don't make any of the decisions but have to suffer all of the consequences. "We," as in those whose voices are too small and too far away to be heard:

- We feel scared when we don't know if we'll live another day.
- We feel angry when people want to kill us or injure us or steal our future.
- We feel sad because all we want is a mom and a dad we know will be there the next day.
- And, finally, we feel confused—because we don't even know what we did wrong.

Do We Really Have Free Speech?
By Charlotte Aldebron

Charlotte gave the following speech at a peace rally on April 19, 2003, in Augusta, Maine, in her continued effort to spread her important message.

The invasions of Afghanistan, and now Iraq, have given me a big lesson in freedom of speech—or, should I say, the difference between the idea of free speech and the reality of free speech. Yes, I can speak. But what does it matter if I have no place to speak? Or if I am ostracized? Or no one listens?

In early March, my social studies teacher switched the class topic to Iraq. He said Saddam Hussein's time to disarm was up. We had to get rid of him. He was a brutal dictator who gassed his own people. I raised my hand. I said that the U.S. gave Saddam Hussein chemical weapons, and the CIA helped him find the targets to use them on. My teacher snapped back, "Actually, Charlotte, you're wrong!" Then he turned away and refused to call on me again.

After the invasion, our class focused on combat. It was like a game. We got a hand-out on the Persian Gulf countries, called "The Players." We were given photos with short bios of top Iraqis, the team to beat. We got a map of the Gulf region with the size and location of all the armies and the weapons each possessed. We read an article about the threat of Iraq using chemical weapons against our troops.

My mother complained to the principal and the Commissioner of Education that we were being taught to glorify war, admire military strategy, and objectify the killing and maiming of human beings. The Commissioner responded that each school's curriculum was its own business. The principal answered that he thought the social studies lesson plan was "balanced and comprehensive." Yes, my mom was free to speak. In fact, she could scream her head off for all they cared. It wouldn't change a thing.

Meanwhile, in Science, we had to answer questions like, "What are the advantages of biological weapons?" I said there weren't any advantages because biological weapons kill people. How can death be an advantage? I was asked to give two examples of biological weapons. I said one was the smallpox on blankets we gave to Native Americans to kill them. The other was E. coli bacteria that have been found in McDonald's hamburgers. I said we could close the gap between the threat and the capability of biological weapons by signing the U.N. Chemical Weapons Convention and by hiring more meat inspectors. Somehow, our assignments never got corrected.

I should tell you that I am famous in some countries. My anti-war speeches have been translated into French, Spanish, Norwegian, Danish, Japanese, Korean, Vietnamese, Urdu, Bengali, and who knows what else. I have been featured in newspapers and on television and radio. A popular singer in Bombay read my speech at his sold-out concert. I've received over 3000 e-mails.

But in my own community, I am invisible. The principal won't let me read my speeches in school. The local papers won't print them. When a Japanese TV crew came to do a story on me, the principal barred them from the school. When they interviewed my classmates on the street after school, the principal came running angrily and demanded that they not use the footage. Of course, they were filming when he did this and, of course, they used the footage. The Japanese know what a bad idea war is because they have suffered the horrible consequences of our nuclear bombs.

I get encouraging e-mails from around the world telling me not to despair even if my own town and teachers and friends ignore me. Many say that I am very brave to speak out "in a country like the United States!" One such e-mail was from a Japanese man who, at age 9, saw the two friends he was walking with in Honshu on July 20, 1945, buried beneath the rubble of a building bombed by a P-51 Mustang fighter. He and his mother were miraculously spared. And there was the e-mail from the Jordanian mother duct-taping her windows with plastic sheeting to protect her children from possible chemical attack. And the Greek man whose parents were scarred for life by the Nazi occupation. And the Canadian who cannot understand calling human beings "collateral damage." And the man from Calcutta who hopes the warriors will come to their senses and put away their weapons. And the South Korean student who thinks it is wrong to sit at his desk and study when there are terrible crimes taking place. And the Iranian who cannot sanction the harming of innocents, even if they are the people of an "enemy" nation.

Because I am free to speak, these people have heard my voice and we have been able to share our desire for peace. Some of them live in countries where protesting is against the law. In the U.S., we are more subtle. We are more sophisticated. In the U.S., we can allow people to talk freely. We don't need to stifle speech to stifle dissent. We just have to block our ears.

30

Peace Poems

Poems have a magical way of capturing sentiments and ideas that may otherwise remain elusive and ethereal, and making them a viable part of reality. Whereas prose tends to be substance—rational and thought provoking, bricks and mortar—poetry is essence. It is fairy wings and angel dust. It is the stuff dreams are made of. And yes, dreams can come true. Every time we write about peace, read about peace, think about peace, and speak about peace, we send a wish for peace out into the universe and bring the world that much closer to peace. And so, it is our pleasure to bring you a few poems about peace.

Bree Breckel is a student at the University of Wisconsin - La Crosse. She is a member of the Campus Progressives, has helped to organize an Annual Festival Of Life event and is active in numerous peace and environmental projects.

Christine Meisenheimer is a poet and writer who lives at West Salem, Wisconsin. Her interests include activism and advocacy in peace, environmental and human rights issues, literacy, and the effects of global trade policies.

Ty F. Webster is co-author of this book and, every now and again, a poet.

Linda Jenkins is our good friend and neighbor. She might not claim to be a poet, but her passage proves that everyone can be a poet—even when they aren't necessarily trying to—and reminds us that we can make peace a part of our everyday lives.

We thank the poets for giving permission to share their poems with the readers of our book.

FLOW
By Bree Breckel

At the point
Where Earth and Sky become one
Here we lie tonight
As to where we are
We haven't a clue:
Anywhere
     Everywhere
Long grass flows around us like water
Surrounding us, swallowing us
Enveloping us in this being of Earth
     And Sky
     We pulse with the Heartbeat
Of Land and Air, of all this Life
A being defined by Energy
     [Matter is a state of Mind]
We lie, holding each other
Electri-cited by the rhythm
The Beating
     Thumping
          Throbbing
               Rhythm
It is Us and we are It
Nothing is apart in Life or Death
     We are awed by a breath
     Taking into our bodies this air
     Realizing it's been
     Through the lungs
     Of all our predecessors
Gandhi inhaled this air
It flew from the lungs of Hitler
Slipping the lips of Stalin
This air carried the words
Of Jesus

All before and all to come,
This air, these molecules, are all of us
Life flows over us
Around us
Through Us
Our bodies, we come to know,
Are not solid
Instead unnumbered aspects of Energy
Molecular Structure
And LIFE
In beautiful rhythmic collaboration
To create what we define as
"Me"
"We"
Skin separates us from nothing
These molecules, these atoms
The Air and Life that we are
Knows no color, no borders
Or boundaries
These molecules made Nazis
And Jews
The same molecules were the bodies
Of Lynch mobs
And hanged men
Every al-Qaeda member and every Iraqi
Breathes the same air as every American
LIFE
Is Non-Discriminatory
All these pieces of history
Are within Us All
And it's Always MOVING
What was Me is now You
What was You has joined the Sky
All that has been will always be
And all we have
Is NOW

Peace Is
By Christine Meisenheimer
(11/13/02)

Peace is like the
lining in a hummingbird's
nest – made of web strands.
Peace is like soft downy feathers
of a gosling – a baby kitten's fur –
a child's head or their cheek.
Oddly, peace looks like
joy. awe. love.
Peace
sounds like
the celestial hum
of the universe called
'music of the spheres'
It sounds like flutes – soft
breezes in a pine forest.
It can be silent and
comforting but
it is always
elusive
yet
p
o
s
s
i
b
l
e.
Peace
simply is.
Peace is profound.
To say peace is precious
is shallow. Peace
is essential.
Amen

A Wish
By Ty F. Webster

The sunset
This evening was epic:
Glowed purple-pinkly orange,
Dancing on canvas clouds
Like flames in God's fireplace,
Growing ever diminishingly dimmer,
Less vibrant,
Until all that was left of the conflagration:
A pale gray-blue—
Like a curtain pulled across a stage after the ballet—
While the first, faint star
Unveiled its twilight twinkle.
(Make a wish!)
I wish I may
I wish I might
Make more men and women watch more sunsets more often.
If all the GeorgeDubya Dumb-oldRumsfelds, the
OsamabiNapoleonHitlerAtillaSharonSaddams
Of the world would make it a habit to sit quietly and
View the beauty at the end of the day,
There would be far fewer wars.
Why plot a pinzer
Or map out a murderous massacre
When you can watch the sun set slowly
Instead?
What's so noble about going out in a blaze of glory
If doing so
Means you'll never get to see the sun do the same
Again?
Yes, if more men watched more sunsets more often,
We would be much nearer to the dawning
Of a brand new,
PEACEful Day.

What Sense?!
By Ty F. Webster

"Nadia was lying on a stretcher beside the stone mortuary slab. Her heart lay on her chest, ripped from her body by a missile which smashed through the bedroom window of the family's flat nearby in Palestine Street. Her father ... stood beside her corpse. ... 'A shell came down into the room as she was standing by the dressing-table,' Najem says. 'My daughter had just completed her PhD in Psychology and was waiting for her first job. She was born in 1970. She was 33. She was very clever."
--"The Saddest Story of All;" Anton Antonowicz; The Daily Mirror *(London, UK); Apr. 5, 2003.*

WHAT SENSE does it make to live in a world where powerful men with far more wealth than wisdom wage war in the name of "FREEDOM" in order to make big $$$ in big oil and war-industry factories, which produce metal mechanisms that crash through the walls of a house and separate the still-beating heart from the rest of the body of a beautiful, well-educated, loving daughter of a loving mother and father who have worked their entire adult lives to give their children a chance to BE SOMEBODY, to DO SOMETHING SPECIAL, only to have that dream ripped from them along with the heart ripped out of their daughter's chest, and buried in the cold, hard ground along with the beautiful woman in the non-descript, black wooden casket

WHILE --

At the very same moment on a quiet hilltop in the distant country where illegitimate leaders (the very same powerful men profiting from the war they have started in the name of "FREEDOM") are waging this illegal war -- the first flowers of spring rise up out of the newly-thawed ground, bow to the whispering wind and open their downy-soft, purple petals to gather the sun's life-giving rays?

WHAT SENSE?!

If any, then this:

The birth of HOPE:

The HOPE that just as purple pasque flowers poke up from the once-frozen ground, signaling the end of the cold, bleak, dark days of winter and the beginning of a time when the world will again be filled with warmth and light and color, so too, can there be a rebirth of a greater magnitude in the history of mankind: the coming of a time when war is but a distant memory, when "FREEDOM" means that people are free to live their lives to full fruition and not have them cut short by mean men with bad blood, a time when there are fewer "intelligent" people building "smart" bombs and more wise people building pathways to PEACE.

Enjoy Your Moments...
By Linda Jenkins

The following message was part of a December 2003 Holiday greeting that we received from our neighbors, Linda, Jim, Kestrel, and Forest Jenkins.

Happy holidays dear family and friends! As we gaze out our windows, we see so many wonders of winter. The Mississippi River is presently a sparkling white beauty. It came to a stop this week with chilling temperatures outside. This usually brings us down a bit, but this year we've been noticing really how outrageous it is with the sun shining on its crystal display. This phase of the seasons provides us with a quiet stillness that allows us to notice more. The bluffs are white with black silhouettes of maples, oaks, and birch that have lost their leaves. Red and gray squirrels, morning doves, blue jays, cardinals, nuthatches, chickadees, and tufted titmice are entertaining us at breakfast each day in return for our food offerings. This reminds us at this holiday season and beyond, the importance of working together to make "life" work more cooperatively. From our own small yard to our universe, may we work for more cooperation and peace. There are too many beautiful moments not to. ....

Above all, we would like to wish you and your loved ones love, peace, and good health this coming year. Enjoy your moments...

31

A New Renaissance

By John Webster and Ty F. Webster

A "renaissance" is defined as a transition, revival, rebirth, or new birth. Most often when we think of the word, we think of the Renaissance that took place in Europe in the fourteenth, fifteenth, and sixteenth centuries A.D.: a time when that part of the world emerged from the era of barbarism known as the Dark Ages and enjoyed a rebirth of learning and artistic endeavors.

A "rendezvous" is defined as an event in which a group of people comes together in a special place for a specific purpose. A rendezvous with Reverence for All Life can lead to a New Renaissance. In this case, the special place is our world. The group involved in this rendezvous includes all the people of the world. The event involves all people working together in an effort to create a New Renaissance based on the principles of Reverence for All Life.

Unfortunately, we live in a world rampant with violence, hatred, mistrust, and divisiveness. We live in a dark era when large groups of people hold vicious and malicious attitudes toward other groups of people they perceive to be different from themselves. Many of these groups of people possess powerful weapons or the knowledge and ability to cause vast destruction and inflict grave injury. It is a sad fact that if we do not change our approach—the very way that we view the world—and come to live peaceably together, we may all be in very grave danger. The New Renaissance we speak of is of a more pressing nature than the previous one, for this one is necessary if we are to ensure our continued survival.

This chapter features the ideas of Dr. Albert Schweitzer and U.S. Congressman Dennis Kucinich: two men who, in two different eras—one past and one present—devoted much time, thought, and action to the singular goal of generating a new human spirit that would usher in a new and greater Renaissance. Also involved in this chapter are the authors and readers. For ultimately, it is up to us to follow the lead of wise men such as Schweitzer and Kucinich and do our part to bring about the change in spirit they speak of. It is up to us, all of us, to come together in a world-wide rendezvous with Reverence for All Life.

Albert Schweitzer's New Renaissance

In his Nobel Peace Prize lecture of 1954, Dr. Schweitzer made a very interesting observation. He noted the sad fact that the amazing technological progress made by humanity was not being paralleled by a corresponding intellectual progress. As a result, mankind's very survival was in jeopardy. He summarized humanity's troubled plight:

Let us dare to face the situation. Man has become superman. He is a superman because he not only has at his disposal innate physical forces, but also commands, thanks to scientific and technological advances, the latent forces of nature which he can now put to his own use...However, the superman suffers from a fatal flaw. He has failed to rise to the level of superhuman reason which should match that of his superhuman strength. He requires such reason to put this vast power to solely reasonable and useful ends and not to destructive and murderous ones. Because he lacks it, the conquests of science and technology become a mortal danger to him rather than a blessing. . . .

Schweitzer continued his speech by detailing the horrors that technological advances allowed human beings to perpetrate upon other humans in the two World Wars:

The essential fact which we should acknowledge in our conscience, and which we should have acknowledged a long time ago, is that we are becoming inhuman to the extent that we become supermen. We have learned to tolerate the facts of war: that men are killed en masse—some twenty million in the Second World War—that whole cities and their

222

inhabitants are annihilated by the atomic bomb, that men are turned into living torches by incendiary bombs. . . .

He then scolded all of humanity for accepting the situation as inevitable and pointed out that on some level, all people were guilty of allowing these atrocities to happen. He proclaimed the necessity for a dramatic change of heart in all people to avoid repeating the same disastrous mistakes and to lead us to a time when there are no more wars. In his own words:

. . . We learn of these things from the radio or newspapers and we judge them according to whether they signify success for the group of peoples to which we belong, or for our enemies. When we do admit to ourselves that such acts are the results of inhuman conduct, our admission is accompanied by the thought that the very fact of war itself leaves us no option but to accept them. In resigning ourselves to our fate without a struggle, we are guilty of inhumanity.

What really matters is that we should all of us realize that we are guilty of inhumanity. The horror of this realization should shake us out of our lethargy so that we can direct our hopes and our intentions to the coming of an era in which war will have no place.

This hope and this will can have but one aim: to attain, through a change of spirit, that superior reason which will dissuade us from misusing the power at our disposal.(1)

Schweitzer proceeded, without naming it such, to call for a New Renaissance. He alluded to the European Renaissance and called for a similar but new and greater transformation in human spirit to bring us back from the brink of catastrophe:

The height to which the spirit can ascend was revealed in the seventeenth and eighteenth centuries. It led those peoples of Europe who possessed it out of the Middle Ages, putting an end to superstition, witch hunts, torture and a multitude of other forms of cruelty or traditional folly. It replaced the old with the new in an evolutionary way that never ceases to astonish those who observe it. All that we have ever possessed of true civilization, and indeed all that we still possess, can be traced to a manifestation of this spirit. . . .

223

. . . Today if we are to avoid our own downfall, we must commit ourselves to this spirit once again. It must bring forth a new miracle just as it did in the Middle Ages, an even greater miracle than the first.(2)

A few years later, in his article, "Albert Schweitzer speaks Out," published in *The World Book Year Book of 1964*, Schweitzer reiterated his stance, this time calling the New Renaissance by name and pointing to his philosophy of Reverence for Life as a means of salvation: "A new renaissance must come, and it must be much greater than the one that lifted the world out of the Middle Ages. This new renaissance must help mankind to advance from the pathetic sense of reality in which it lives, toward the spirit of reverence for life. Only through it can mankind be saved from destruction, from its senseless and cruel wars. It alone can bring about peace in the world."(3)

Dennis Kucinich's New Renaissance

Half a century after Schweitzer addressed the world from the Nobel pulpit, his words ring as true as ever. Sadly, humanity has not heeded his call. Still the earth is plagued by wars and violence. Even as I write these words, armed conflicts rage around the globe. Israel and Palestine continue their ages-old, tit-for-tat violence. Soldiers from my own country die almost daily in a bloody war in Iraq that has reportedly caused the death of no less than 100,000 Iraqi citizens and shows no signs of ending. North Korea tests high-powered ballistics and threatens that war will follow if the U.S. does not agree to a non-aggression treaty. China threatens violence on Taiwan if it declares independence from China. Terrorist groups make threats and promise violence against the United States and its allies. The incumbent U.S. President and his opponent in the 2004 election give further voice to hatred, promising to hunt down and kill the terrorists wherever they are hiding. On and on goes the destructive trend.

And equally as sad, there are very few leaders in the world questioning this state of affairs. It is as if the majority of our world leaders are convinced that human conflict is innate and unstoppable. Fortunately, there are exceptions. One such leader is Congressman Dennis Kucinich. Kucinich is one of the few voices of reason proposing that the way forward is not to meet threat with threat and violence with violence, but rather to change our ways of thinking so that we might avoid world-wide calamity and usher in a new era of peace and understanding. Interestingly, he employs some of the same language Schweitzer did in his lifetime. Kucinich, too, speaks of a New Renaissance.

In his 2002 speech, "A Second Renaissance," the Congressman called for the United States to lead the way toward a more peaceful world. The speech related these unique and insightful ideas:

The idea of America emerged from the intellectual energy, the heart energy and the spirit energy of the Renaissance...The quest for universal principles of justice, of human rights, of civil rights, of opportunity, of a meaningful future is what caused millions to see America as the light of nations. These universal principles are stars by which those who came to our shores sailed. These are stars which can guide us past the shoals of arms dealers and oil interests who today would crash our ship of state upon the rocks of war.

America has a higher destiny. As with generations past, our destiny can take us to places we have never been or can only imagine. Places of peace. Places of plenty. Places of hope. Places of love. We have a right to live our ideals. That is our birthright. We should not trade it for the pretensions of empire, nor for the delusions of grandeur, nor for all the gold in Fort Knox, all the tea in China, or all the oil in Iraq. America has a higher destiny. Today I want to speak to you about the America that can be...About a Second Renaissance which can begin in this nation, with this generation.

We are at a critical and creative moment in history where we have it within our power to change the world. It is about evolutionary politics which follows an evolutionary consciousness. We can do it by changing the way we look at the world. By contemplating and realizing the universal brotherhood and sisterhood of all persons. We can do it by tapping our own unlimited potential to think anew...I tell you there is another America out there. It is ready to be called forward. It is the

America of our dreams. It is the America of the flag full of stars. It is the America which is in our hearts and we can make it the heart of our world.(4)

And Kucinich has continued to speak out for a more peaceful, caring world. He employed this enlightened line of rhetoric frequently in his campaign for the 2004 Democratic Presidential nomination. For example, in an online message e-mailed to his supporters on September 21 (the International Day of Peace), 2003, he spoke these encouraging words:

We need to let people know that it is peace which is practical and war which is not. We need to let people know that it is peace which can enable prosperity and war which brings poverty...

...This is the moment where through a political campaign we can help America achieve a transformation, and we understand that such a transformation is necessary. With an administration [currently in office] that has inflicted upon this nation the consequences of thinking of unilateral policies and preemptive war, the thinking which has produced nuclear first strike policies and the building of new nuclear weapons, this is the time that we have to reclaim a more beneficent role for America and the world.(5)

Our New Renaissance

A rendezvous is meant to be an exciting event. It is with great excitement and a sense of urgency that we must strive toward a rendezvous with Reverence for All Life, toward the crucial transition which will establish "Peace" as our password and Reverence for All Life as the foundation of our civilization. As humans, we can help this New Renaissance become a reality. We can march to a different drumbeat than the slow, often destructive evolutionary beat of the non-human world and of the history of the human world to this point.

Because we can imagine new possibilities and know there is creativity in our midst that we have not even begun to fathom, we do not have to be tied down to old schools-of-thought that tell us, for instance, that hatred and violence are inevitable in human relations. We can begin to change our pre-conceived notions, and work for positive change. We can affirm that with an attitude of Reverence for All Life, we can march creatively, with a quickened step, toward a greater love and peace for all. As Schweitzer said in his Peace Prize address, "Many a truth has lain unnoticed for a long time, ignored simply because no one perceived its potential for becoming reality."(6)

Our New Renaissance involves making the potential for world peace a reality. It involves the transition from a world where people tend to act in accordance with what is best for "Me," to a world where people act in accordance with what is best for "We." It calls for a change from a world dominated by nationalism and ill will between the different peoples of the world to a united, peaceful world. It calls for a change in attitude that allows conflict to be solved through dialogue and cooperation rather than threats and aggression.

The key to our Renaissance is the spirit of Reverence for All Life. When it comes alive within us, this spirit will not allow wars to continue to pollute our world. Dr. Schweitzer put it this way: "Only the kind of thinking dominated by reverence for life can bring lasting peace to our world." Rep. Kucinich put it this way: "We must listen to that quiet inner voice that counsels us that the survival of all is achieved through the unity of all."

It is up to us to hear the wise words of men like Albert Schweitzer and Dennis Kucinich, perceive their potential for becoming reality, and begin to employ them in our own lives. The time has come for us to notice the truth of their words and work to bring about a New Renaissance. The "Second Renaissance" *can* come about if we all think and work together with a spirit of deep respect, love, and awe for all that lives.

As humans who know and affirm that we are life which wills to live, in the midst of life which wills to live, we can work together to rise above the indifference of the non-human world and of the cruelty inherent in so much of past human history. Our wills-to-live, urged forward by the universal will-to-live, can lead us to the new world we are searching for. It will be a world where the light of love causes all negatives such as hatred, racism, hunger, war, and selfishness to fade into the darkness of the past. In his book *The Philosophy of Civilization,* Dr. Schweitzer proclaimed, "I would be a humble pioneer of this Renaissance, and throw the belief in a new humanity, like a torch into our dark age."(7) Let us all strive together to pick up Dr. Schweitzer's torch and carry it forward into our own dark age. Let us become pilgrims united in an effort to bring to reality the rendezvous with Reverence for All Life that will guide us to a great New Renaissance.

Notes

1.) Dr. Albert Schweitzer; "The Problem of Peace in the World Today;" Nobel Peace Prize address, delivered November 4, 1954, in Oslo, Norway. Printed online at www.nobel.se/peace/laureates/1952/schweitzer-lecture.html; p.4-5.
2.) Ibid.; p. 6.
3.) Schweitzer; "Albert Schweitzer Speaks Out;" *World Book Yearbook of 1964*; p. 144.
4.) Dennis Kucinich; "A Second Renaissance;" Speech presented at the University of California, Berkeley; September 14, 2002.
5.) Kucinich; online message delivered on his website, www.kucinich.us; September 21, 2003.
6.) Schweitzer; "The Problem of Peace;" p. 8.
7.) Schweitzer; *The Philosophy of Civilization*; (1987) p. 84.

32

Wake Up Everybody; It's Game Time!

By John Webster

While living in Melrose, Wisconsin, I had the privilege of coaching the Melrose-Mindoro High School baseball team for a number of years. What a fun time that was for me. There were many memorable moments during my tenure as coach of the "Mighty Mustangs," but the start of one particular game especially stands out in my memory.

It was a home game at our ballpark at the Melrose-Mindoro High School. Warm-ups were over, the obligatory meeting between coaches and umpires at home plate was finished, my team had just taken the field, and the home plate umpire had just yelled the traditional "Play ball!" Everyone was ready for the first pitch when my shortstop suddenly pierced the anxious silence by shouting out as loudly as he could to his eight teammates on the field: "WAKE UP EVERYBODY; IT'S GAME TIME!"

What a great way to get the adrenaline flowing to start the game. What better way to make sure that everyone is awake and alert and has their minds firmly focused on the tasks at hand? Whenever I've thought about that wake-up call over the years, I've gotten excited and wanted to start a new game. But now I realize that in fact every single day we are all playing a very important game: the game of life. And I suggest that my shortstop's rally cry all those years ago is one that each of us should heed as we continue this great game. "WAKE UP EVERYBODY; IT'S GAME TIME!"

It is crucial to remember that this is not a practice game. The game of life is real, and the result counts. Each day is another inning, another portion of the game. Each portion is an event that will help determine what tomorrow's inning will be like and, ultimately, what the outcome of the game will be.

In the game of life, there are no spectators; we all are players. We don't have to worry about making the team, because all of us are already on the team. We each bring our own individual talents to the game, and those talents are important, whatever they may be. The success of any team depends upon the diversity of its members' talents.

We must also remember that not only are we all players in this great game of life, but more than that, we are teammates. This is not a game of "Us" versus "Them," of "the free world" versus "the evil empire," of whites versus non-whites, of rich versus poor. We are all partners on the same team. Every last one of us the world over is a teammate. We are all in it together, which means that we will either win together, or we will lose together. We will rejoice together, or we will cry together. We will move up the ladder of civilization together, or we will fall down together. We are one.

The game of life is not played with bats and balls. In fact, we, the players, get to choose the equipment we use. As human members of the team, we have some very important responsibilities. We can do many things our non-human partners cannot do. We can argue. We can hate. We can injure and retaliate for our own injuries. We can build guns and bombs and even weapons of mass destruction. And if we so choose, we can use these things and other "tools of ignorance" as the equipment for our game. This approach, however, can ultimately have only one result: GAME OVER!

Yet there is another option. We can choose as our equipment for the game "tools of enlightenment" such as peace, love, reason, compassion, compromise, forgiveness, sacrifice, service, and sharing. We can come to have respect for all of our teammates. We can play the game with the knowledge that "we are life which wills to live, in the midst of life which wills to live." In short, we can choose to play the game according to the rules of "Reverence for All Life." We are capable of adopting a reverential attitude that will allow love to work in special ways to bring about a world where all teammates co-exist peacefully and with full respect for one another and every living thing.

It is crucial that we begin to play the game of life according to the rules of "Reverence for All Life." After all, we must remember that there is only one ballpark: the world we live in. Every game is a home game. We must take great care of our home field, because there is no other park we can move to if we destroy the one we have. If we do not change our ways and begin to live for and love all of our partners, we may spoil the game of life and there may not be a meaningful game in the future that our children and grandchildren can be a part of. What an awesome responsibility we have!

To those of us who are not yet quite awake, I offer the rally cry one more time. "WAKE UP EVERYBODY; IT'S GAME TIME!" It is time to take all the Reverence for Life that we can squeeze into our very being and make our mark on the world. It is time to spread the message of Reverence for All Life by what we say and by the example of our very lives. All of our partners are waiting. They need our help just as much as we need theirs. Together, we can win this game!

<u>33</u>

A Second Job

By Ty F. Webster

Dr. Albert Schweitzer was a great man in many ways. But what made him exceptional is the fact that he whole-heartedly devoted his adult life to the service of his fellow human beings and all life forms in general. After much deep, rational thought, he came to the conclusion that the only way for humankind to alter its course toward certain disaster and probable destruction was to develop and embrace an attitude of Reverence for Life. And he subsequently made himself a living example of this way of thought in every aspect of his life. In essence, he made it his job to make the world a better place for all living things.

Some forty years after Dr. Schweitzer's death, the course of history is still downright frightening. We live in a world where Reverence for Life is a scarce commodity: a world with an ever-widening gap between the privileged rich and the underprivileged poor, an ever-quickening pace of destruction of our natural world and the creatures that inhabit it, a continued prevalence of the belief that economic wealth is more important than ecological health, a continued and growing mistrust and animosity between peoples of different ethnicities and religious beliefs all around the world, and even a newly declared "war on terrorism,"—a war that by definition will be endless and unwinable and will only accelerate all of these negative trends. What the world needs now more than ever are more people who are willing to incorporate reverential ideas into their daily lives, people who will follow Schweitzer's example and make it their job to bring about a greater attitude of Reverence for All Life in our modern world.

"But I already have a job," you protest. "I have an incredibly busy life with too many responsibilities and not enough time to do the things I'm already supposed to be doing. Now you want me to run off to the African jungle and start a missionary hospital?!"

That, of course, is not the idea. We do not have to travel to far away places or do anything particularly extraordinary to begin to incorporate a greater spirit of Reverence into our lives. In fact, as James Brabazon pointed out in the epilogue to the second edition of his biography about Dr. Schweitzer, Schweitzer himself would not advise us to. After all, Schweitzer's advice to his own granddaughter Christiane when she expressed a desire to go to assist him at his hospital in Lambarene, Africa, was this: "You can have your Lambarene anywhere."(1)

As a matter of fact, Schweitzer himself was aware that the vast majority of people are unable to commit the entirety of their lives to the service of others. He knew it is often difficult merely to get by in the day-to-day world and hard enough for people to provide for themselves and their families. He knew that it is impossible for everyone to enter vocations that have the well-being of fellow creatures as their main purpose. However, he was firm in his belief that all people are capable of helping each other and all living things in countless little ways wherever we happen to be and strong in his conviction that charity not only helps those who receive it, but also makes the givers better people in the process and subsequently makes the world a better place for everyone.

In an article printed in a 1949 issue of *Reader's Digest*, Schweitzer expounded upon the idea that we all can make it a primary concern to help others whenever and however possible. He pointed out that no matter what our primary vocation is, we all can make Reverence for Life our second, and possibly most rewarding, job. The article begins with these words:

Often people say: 'I would like to do some good in the world. But with so many responsibilities at home and in business, my nose is always to the grindstone. I am sunk in my own petty affairs, and there is no chance for my life to mean anything.'

This is a common and dangerous error. In helpfulness to others, every man [or woman] can find on his [or her] own doorstep adventures for the soul—our surest source of true peace and lifelong satisfaction.

To know this happiness, one does not have to neglect duties or do spectacular things. This career for the spirit I call 'your second job.' In this there is no pay except the privilege of doing it. In it you will encounter noble chances and find deep strength. Here all your reserve power can be put to work, for what the world lacks most today is [people] who occupy themselves with the needs of other [people]. In this unselfish labor a blessing falls on both the helper and the helped. Without such spiritual adventures the man or woman of today walks in darkness. In the pressures of modern society we tend to lose our individuality. Our craving for creation and self-expression is to that extent retarded.

What is the remedy? No matter how busy one is, any human being can assert his [or her] personality by seizing every opportunity for spiritual activity. How? By his [or her] second job: by means of personal action, on however small a scale, for the good of his [or her] fellow [humans]. . . .(2)

Certainly one way to directly assist our fellow creatures is to assist with organized welfare work. From Habitat for Humanity to the World Wildlife Fund to the United Way or Red Cross, to the many varied organizations working for peace around the globe, to local church or community organizations that assist with programs for youth or the elderly or the needy, to the many groups set up to help with various health related disorders, to any of the countless worthy causes all around the world—any time or money that we give is time or money well spent in the service of others. As Schweitzer pointed out in the article, "organized welfare work is, of course, necessary." But these organizations can only do so much. The rest is up to us. Wrote Schweitzer:

"We cannot abdicate our conscience to an organization, nor to a government. 'Am I my brother's keeper?' I most certainly am! I cannot escape my responsibility by saying the State will do all that is necessary...A charitable organization is a complex affair; like an automobile, it needs a broad highway to run on. It cannot penetrate the little bypaths; those are for men and women to walk through, with open eyes and hearts full of compassion."(3)

The gaps in organized welfare work, Schweitzer said, "must be filled by personal service performed with loving kindness."(4)

And we should remember that acts of charity need not involve sums of money. Schweitzer pointed this out, as well. "I hear people say: 'Oh, if I were only rich, I would do great things to help people," he wrote. "But we all *can* be rich in love and generosity. Moreover, if we give with care, if we find out the exact wants of those who need our help most, we are giving our own loving interest and concern, which is worth more than all the money in the world." And we will reap benefits of our own in return. As Schweitzer pointed out, "By some working of the universal law, as you give of love, you are given more love and happiness to go on with!"(5)

What we all need to begin doing, or doing more often, is whatever we can to make the lives of our fellow human beings— indeed of all living things—more bearable. Every day we are presented with many opportunities to assist other people. But our tendency is to "look out for number one," and miss these opportunities. Wrote Schweitzer, "Our greatest mistake, as individuals, is that we walk through our life with eyes closed and do not notice our chances. As soon as we open our eyes and deliberately search we see many who need help, not in big things but in the littlest things."(6)

Schweitzer presented several examples of this type of charity. For one, he spoke of a young man who, while riding a train on which Schweitzer was traveling through Germany, discovered that an old man on the same train was heading to a large city to visit his gravely ill son in the hospital. The man was distraught because it would be dark when he reached the city, and he did not know his way around. Upon hearing the old man's story, the boy—who knew the city well—volunteered to show the man the way to the hospital and catch a later train on to his own destination.

Indeed, there are countless examples of ways we all can help each other on a daily basis. For instance, we can make it a policy in our homes to be "bug friendly" and whenever possible usher unwanted creatures out of doors instead of thoughtlessly killing them. We can walk or ride bicycles more and drive our cars less, knowing that we are limiting pollution and environmental damage in the process. If we happen to be driving in rush hour traffic and see someone wanting to pull out of a driveway, we can fight the tendency to think, "No way, buddy; not in front of me you don't!" We can slow down, give the person a smile and let them into the flow of traffic. If we see a stranger looking lost in a town we know well, we can ask them if they need some directions. If a family member or co-worker is having a bad day and says something spiteful to us, we can fight the urge to respond spitefully in our own turn and instead give the person a word of encouragement. Anytime we see someone looking sad or distraught, we can give him or her an empathetic nod or a knowing smile. For as Schweitzer said in the article, "Often a friendly glance is like a single ray of sunshine piercing a darkness we ourselves may not even dream is there."(7)

These are mundane examples of minor things we can do to help each other get along in the world. There are thousands of similar examples I could give. But the actual examples are not important; in each case, what counts is the spirit of the action. When we do something nice for someone—be it a close friend, family member, or someone we do not know—we add to an overall spirit of caring and compassion in the world. We fight the presiding tendency to live only for ourselves. We follow Schweitzer's example and do our part to make the world a nicer place.

Given the current nature of things in our world, it is all too easy to despair. One needs only to crack open the newspaper to be overwhelmed by the rampant negativity in world affairs. It is very easy to become distraught, easy to think, "If only I could make a difference; but what can one person alone in the world possibly do?" The answer, as Schweitzer suggests, is exactly this: a great deal. No, we cannot single-handedly change the world. We cannot end wars, cure plagues, stop homelessness and poverty, save rainforests, et cetera all by ourselves. But every day we have ample opportunities to do small things that help to bring a little bit of light into whatever corner of the world we happen to be in. And when all the little corners of the world become light, darkness will have no more reign.

The important thing is that we get into the habit of doing "the little things," and not only once in a while, when it's convenient for us. We must create a frame of mind where helpfulness to and compassion for other living beings becomes second nature to us. We must reach a stage where we do not do nice things because we feel like we have to—because someone might be watching, and we want to look good—but because we want to. We must reach a stage where we act humanely at all times because it makes us feel good and because we know that we are doing our little part to bring about a more civilized, more humanized world. Whatever our vocation in life happens to be, we must answer Schweitzer's call to make Reverence for Life our second job. And it will be helpful to remember the benefits that we will reap by doing so—benefits that Schweitzer pointed out in the conclusion of his article:

You may think it is a wonderful life my wife and I have in the equatorial jungle. That is merely where we happen to be. But you can have a still more wonderful life by staying where you happen to be and putting your soul to the test in a thousand little trials, and winning triumphs of love. Such a career of the spirit demands patience, devotion, daring. It calls for strength of will and determination of love: the greatest test of a man [or woman]. But in this hard 'second job' is to be found the only true happiness.(8)

Notes

1.) James Brabazon; *Albert Schweitzer: A Biography* (2000); p. 500.

2.) Dr. Albert Schweitzer; "Your Second Job;" *Reader's Digest*; October 1949; p. 1-2.

3.) Ibid.; p.2.   4.) Ibid.; p. 4.   5.)Ibid.

6.) Ibid.; p.2.   7.) Ibid.; p.5.   8.) Ibid.

34

Make a Difference

By Ty F. Webster

"But however concerned I was with the suffering in the world, I never let myself become lost in brooding over it. I always held firmly to the thought that each one of us can do a little to bring some portion of it to an end."
--Dr. *Albert Schweitzer;* Out of My Life and Thought.

Desiring to bring about positive change in the world is one thing. But it is entirely another to genuinely work to actualize change or to know exactly what to do to begin to make it happen. Making Reverence for All Life our second, if not our first, job is a pretty thought, a grand ideal. But how exactly do we go about making this theoretical idea a practical reality? What can we do to revolt against the pervading spirit of thoughtlessness Dr. Schweitzer spoke of? How can we help to bring about the New Renaissance? In other words, what practical steps can we take on a daily basis to make a difference?

These are questions the authors have often considered during the process of writing this book. We both have our own ideas, and we also feel strongly that every person has their own valuable and insightful notions about measures that can be taken to bring about a world more filled with Reverence. With this thought in mind, my father came up with the idea of making our own list of suggestions for things we feel anyone can do to bring about a more reverential world, and he subsequently asked some friends and family members to contribute to our list. I think we've made a good start of it.

Dad initiated the list with these ideas:

❑ We can use a plastic cup or glass with an envelope or sturdy piece of paper as a lid to capture insects (flies, ants, bugs, spiders, etc.) we don't want in the house and take them outside and set them free. The life cycle of some insects is not very long. Allowing an insect to live another day may mean half a lifetime for the little creature.

❑ While driving, we can slow down when we see an animal on or near the road ahead. May it become as much of a habit for us to slow down for animals as it should be for us to slow down when a child is near the road.

❑ Choose to walk on a sidewalk or path instead of on the grass, whenever possible. Then our footsteps will not crush the grass and the creatures that might be living there.

❑ We can eat less meat. Even one (or more) fewer meat meals a week can make a difference. It will be better for us, for the animals, and for the world.

❑ We can purchase produce grown on family farms, rather than on large corporate farms, whenever possible.

❑ We should walk more and drive less. But if we must drive, we can buy our gas at Citgo stations. Citgo is a U.S. firm that is a wholly owned subsidiary of Venezuela's state-owned oil company. Whereas most oil company's profits benefit the rich and the corporate, Venezuela uses some of its oil revenue to provide health care, literacy and education, and subsidized food for its citizens. There are more than 14,000 Citgo stations in the U.S. Find the ones closest to you by going to the following website: http://www.citgo.com/CITGOLocator/StoreLocator.jsp.

❑ We can save energy by hanging our clothes out to dry rather than drying them in an electric or gas-powered dryer.

❑ We can remember not to leave water or other liquids in open containers outside or inside where small creatures (mice, bugs, etc.) can fall in and drown. This will also keep the mosquitoes from multiplying so rapidly.

❑ Whenever possible, we can give undivided attention (be totally present) to each individual human and non-human life we encounter every day. We can take time to look and listen for ways to promote and nurture what is best for each partner in any given situation. We can pause to celebrate and enjoy life in the moment as our individual wills-to-live strive for wholeness and become one in our sharing of Reverence for All Life. This can be as true when our relationship involves a bug or flower as when it involves another person.

My sister, Steffi, was here on vacation from Europe when Dad was compiling the list, and she added these great ideas: (Technically, Steffi is my sister-in-law, but I don't see what the law really has to do with it. I've heard the term "sister-in-love" before and like that one, but I still prefer "sister," because in my eyes, that's what she is.)

❑ Be tolerant toward people of different race, color or religion.
❑ Listen to each other and try to understand the other's point of view, even if we don't necessarily agree with it.
❑ Understand that every being (human, animal, or plant) has a role and job to do in this world.

Dad put a notice on the employee bulletin board at the restaurant where we work asking our co-workers to contribute to the list. Our good friend and co-worker, Terry Dahmen, accepted the challenge and took the idea home to his wonderful wife, Ann. The Dahmens came up with these creative ideas:

❑ Recycle and reuse.
❑ Use fluorescent light bulbs, which last up to five years longer than regular light bulbs.
❑ In the winter, turn your thermostat down to 69 degrees and wear a sweater; turn it down to 65 degrees while sleeping.
❑ Turn off all lights that are not needed and use a timer on outdoor Christmas lights to save electricity.
❑ Use a homeowner wind generator. They are available now and are relatively inexpensive. Your unused energy can be sold back to the electric companies.
❑ Walk or ride a bicycle instead of driving cars short

distances.

- Eliminate plastics as much as possible, especially in your kitchen where food comes in contact with them. These petroleum-based products are carcinogens and can't be disposed of safely in our environment because of their toxicity.
- Buy organic foods to keep our food chain safe.
- Spend more time exploring the outdoors and less time being consumers.
- Spend less, save more.
- Purchase soaps that don't have antibiotics in them. Antibiotic soaps have been proven to be ineffective in normal hand washing (you would need to wash your hands for 5-10 minutes for the antibiotic to work) and not safe for our health, as they contribute to antibiotic immunity. There is a doctor's organization in Wisconsin that is trying to get antibiotics out of all lotions and soaps that people use in their homes and offices.
- Use cloth shopping bags for groceries rather than plastic. Take your own to the store.

Ann liked the idea of our list so much, she passed it on to her friend, Jane Barko, who added these insightful suggestions:

- Teach our children to be non-violent.
- Recycle, recycle, recycle. Walk whenever possible rather than drive. Conserve energy. Smile. Pray.
- Talk peace. The more people that talk peace, the sooner peace will become a reality.

And now it's my turn. Here it goes:

1.) I feel that one of the primary things we can do to evoke positive change is to realize that we all, each and every single one of us, can make a difference in this world. Author Nathaniel Altman pointed out in his profound book, *Ahimsa: Dynamic Compassion*, that one of the greatest obstacles we all face in our lives is the feeling that we, as such a miniscule part of such a great big world, are powerless to bring about change in the world. As he puts it: "Many of us would like to believe that our life is experienced in isolated, watertight compartments and that the way we conduct our daily affairs does not have a significant impact on the society in which we live."

I agree with this statement, and also with Mr. Altman's follow-up statement, which cautions us to be careful not to spread negativity to those around us:

In reality, however, our effect on others is far greater than many realize. Every day we usually have some form of contact with between fifty and one hundred people, whether at home, at work or school, while shopping or visiting friends. When seen in this light, a negative thought, a careless word, or a selfish action can have a strong potential for causing harm to others. In many cases, people we encounter may respond to a negative expression, and like a chain reaction, can spread their own hurtful action to others during the course of the day. Within a matter of hours, one cruel or thoughtless word on our part can literally affect hundreds of others, just as a stone thrown into a pool will affect every molecule of water in that pool. . . We can see how this daily accumulation of disharmony can add to the total store of accumulated disorder in the world. Thus the quality of our relationships contains the seeds for powerful change in the world. (1)

And while Altman uses this idea in a cautionary manner to warn us away from negative activity, I would suggest that the same concept holds true for positivity. Any time we have a positive thought or take a positive action, the spirit of that thought or action will ripple through the people and environment around us. At any given moment, we have the potential to add to the accumulated harmony of the world, the opportunity to help to sow the seeds for powerful positive change in the world.

In other words: Be nice. Smile. Make it a habit to say and do nice things to everyone around you as often as possible. It will make you feel better, and the likelihood that the people you encounter will follow your example is very high. You might even be surprised to find out how much positive energy you get back from family, friends, and even people you don't know, when you make a habit of being positive to them.

2.) Another very important thing we all can do to make a difference is to stay informed. We need to make an effort to find independent news sources in order to keep ourselves apprised of world events presented from an unbiased perspective, or at the very least, be sure to examine both sides of the pertinent issues of the day. This is not an easy task, as many news sources, especially major corporate news conglomerates such as the few that dominate the U.S. media, tend to tell us what they want us to hear rather than the whole truth. This is a very dangerous situation because, as Schweitzer's biographer James Brabazon points out, "A public that believes itself to have a free press and an open government is far more vulnerable to insidious propaganda than one that has learned to regard its rulers as barefaced liars."(2)

Accusing the "free press" in this country of slinging insidious propaganda might be a bit harsh. Then again, maybe not…One of many possible examples I would point to is the fact that one major U.S. cable television news channel—during their coverage of the events in the days *before* our country started dropping bombs on Iraq, while the (albeit pitifully limited) debate of whether or not to go to war was still going on—deemed their coverage "America at War." I find that to be pretty insidious.

And really, whether we want to admit it or not, most news sources in our country are going to put a spin on world events that are favorable to our country. Witness a recent headline in my local daily, which generally speaking, is not extremely biased. The headline came after another tragic day of fighting in Fallujah, Iraq. It read: "U.S. Forces Kill 150 Iraqi Insurgents." It seems to me, the headline could just as easily have said: "U.S. Forces Slaughter 150 Heroic Iraqi Freedom Fighters." Or maybe, to be more accurate and less biased: "150 Fathers and Sons of Dearly Loved Ones Killed in Iraq."

Whatever the case, my point is this: because there are two sides to every story, we need to search for independent sources that provide unbiased news, or at least reports that present the other side of the story. Fortunately, there are sources that do just that. However, they won't be delivered to your doorstep every morning. I personally recommend the following:

Common Dreams. Found on-line at **www.commondreams.org**. The goal of this national, non-profit, privately funded citizens' organization is to bring progressive Americans together to promote progressive visions for America's future. As stated on the site, the Common Dreams "Newscenter" presents "an eclectic mix of politics, issues and breaking news with an emphasis on progressive perspectives that are increasingly hard to find in our corporate-dominated media." It supplies a clearinghouse of news reports from around the globe on pressing issues that affect us all.

Democracy Now! A national, daily, independent, award-winning news program airing on over 225 stations in North America. Its website, **www.democracynow.org** , gives a state-by-state listing of radio stations that broadcast the program. According to the website, the show "provides our audience with access to people and perspectives rarely heard in the U.S. corporate-sponsored media, including independent and international journalists, ordinary people from around the world who are influenced by U.S. foreign policy, grassroots leaders and peace activists, academics and independent analysts."

Alternet. Another good resource for information you won't find in mainstream outlets. Alternet is a comprehensive online information source that, as its website says, "provides readers with crucial facts and passionate opinions they can't find elsewhere." Find it at **www.alternet.org**.

Fighting Bob. At **www.fightingbob.com,** you'll find an online magazine that provides an educational forum for writers, viewpoints, and topics not welcome on the pages and airwaves of most mainstream media outlets. It focuses on issues in Wisconsin, but also tackles national and international issues.

Cursor. At **www.cursor.org** you can find a good summary of current and breaking news from around the world with links to published newspaper and magazine articles and also to other great independent and alternative news sources.

Indy Media. www.indymedia.org. Indy Media bills itself as "a collective of independent media organizations and hundreds of journalists offering grassroots, non-corporate coverage" of news from around the world.

Check these sources out and pass on what you learn to friends and family members. Many of the articles on the websites listed above can be easily e-mailed. This way we can all stay better informed and attempt to fight our way through the prevailing propaganda. As Dr. Schweitzer once said: "In the long-run even the most efficiently organized propaganda can do nothing against the truth." (3)

3.) Contrarily, take time off from the news. Yes, it is very important to stay informed. But it's a sad fact that most news reports tend to be dominated by negative stories, and it is very possible to spend too much time dwelling on all the negatives in the world. That makes it much more difficult to avoid negativity and spread positive feelings to those around you.

Dr. Schweitzer once told his friend Norman Cousins, "I am worried about present-day journalism. The emphasis on negative happenings is much too strong. Not infrequently, news about events marking great progress is overlooked or minimized. It tends to make for a negative and discouraging atmosphere. There is a danger that people may lose faith in the forward direction of humanity if they feel that very little happens to support that faith. And real progress is related to the belief by people that it is possible."(4)

So turn off the TV. Take a day off from the newspaper or your Internet news source. Go for a walk in a park or nature preserve. Soak up some sunshine. Smell the flowers. Call or visit a friend or family member you haven't talked to in a while. Read a positive book or some poetry. Create your own good news.

4.) Another direct measure we can all take to make a difference in our world is to support organizations that are working to preserve our natural environment and make the world safer and healthier. It is crucially important that we do this now because of the recent trend in government policy to weaken existing environmental protections. In recent years, critical environmental legislation has been weakened, including the Clean Water Act and Clean Air Act; policies in our national parks and forests have been altered to allow for more intensive logging and oil drilling; and efforts have been made to debunk the dangers of global warming and climate change. All of these measures have been implemented with a figurative tip of the cap to big business and with disregard for the sanctity of natural ecosystems and the creatures that live therein, and also for the health and well-being of the public in general. Our best, and possibly only, hope to stop these trends is to become involved in grassroots movements to counteract them.

Fortunately, there are many organizations that help us to do just that, organizations that are working to offset the damage done by these policies and to change the policies themselves. It is critically important that we all do everything we can to help these organizations. Many national (and international) environmental organizations have very informative websites that allow us to stay in tune with the pressing issues of our times and, in some cases, to take direct action on specific issues. I personally find it quite empowering to be an "online activist," sending letters of protest or concern to crucial people at crucial times with a few simple clicks of my computer's "mouse" from the convenience of my home.

There is no shortage of environmental groups. Seek them out; join the ones that you like; and do all you can to support their efforts. Here are descriptions and the Internet addresses of a few of my favorites:

246

Environmental Defense Fund (EDF); www.edf.org: a leading non-profit organization representing more than 400,000 members. EDF is "dedicated to protecting the environmental rights of all people, including future generations." Among these rights, EDF lists "clean air, clean water, healthy food and flourishing ecosystems." EDF is, in essence, an environmental law firm for all of us, taking legal action on our behalf to protect our environment.

Natural Resources Defense Council (NRDC); www.nrdc.org: Another organization that takes a legal approach, protecting our environmental rights through action in the courts. According to the NRDC website, they "use law, science and the support of more than 1 million members and online activists to protect the planet's wildlife and wild places and to ensure a safe and healthy environment for all living things."

The Nature Conservancy; www.tnc.org: This organization's mission is "to preserve the plants, animals and natural communities that represent the diversity of life on Earth by protecting the lands and waters they need to survive." The Conservancy buys land and works with communities, businesses, governments, partner organizations, and individuals to preserve lands in their natural conditions. Given the trend of the federal government to soften protection of national wilderness areas and open them to such damaging activities as livestock grazing, oil drilling, and timber cutting, supporting The Nature Conservancy is especially important if we are to ensure that fully-protected, natural areas continue to be a part of our world.

World Wildlife Fund; www.worldwildlife.org: With 5.2 million members world-wide, this organization directs international efforts toward three global goals: saving endangered species, protecting endangered habitats, and addressing global threats such as toxic pollution and climate change.

Sierra Club; www.sierraclub.org: 700,000 members support America's oldest grassroots environmental organization in its mission to: 1.) Explore, enjoy and protect the wild places of the earth. 2.) Practice and promote the responsible use of the earth's ecosystem and resources. 3.) Educate and enlist humanity to protect and restore the quality of the natural human environment. 4.) Use all lawful means to carry out those objectives.

Earthjustice: www.earthjustice.org: The legal arm of the Sierra Club, Earth Justice is a non-profit public law firm dedicated "to protecting the magnificent places, natural resources, and wildlife of this earth and to defending the right of all people to a healthy environment." They work to "bring about far-reaching change by enforcing and strengthening environmental laws."

EarthSave: www.earthsave.org: This organization educates people about the powerful effects our food choices have on the environment, our health and all life on Earth, and encourages a shift toward a healthy, plant-based diet.

True Majority: www.truemajority.org: While not strictly an environmental organization, this grassroots education and advocacy group supports many environmental causes. A recent effort that caught my attention is their support of a project called Exxpose Exxon, a collaborative campaign by 12 of the nation's largest environmental and public interest advocacy organizations (including NRDC and the Sierra Club) to educate and activate Americans in regard to the ExxonMobile company's efforts to drill in The Arctic National Wildlife Refuge, prevent action on global warming, and encourage America's dependence on oil.

An "action alert" e-mail from TrueMajority alerted me to the facts that in spite of making a record profit of $25 billion in 2004, ExxonMobil is still not paying the full amount it owes fishermen and natives hurt by the Exxon Valdez oil spill sixteen years ago, is the only oil company that hasn't succumbed to public pressure and bowed out of a group lobbying Congress to open The

Arctic National Wildlife Refuge to drilling, and has spent $15 million since 1998 to deny the existence of global warming. The alert allowed me to e-mail ExxonMobil's CEO and notify him of a.) my disapproval of the company's immoral practices and b.) my intention to join a boycott of ExxonMobil's products. I'll continue to follow my father's advice to fill my tank at Citgo stations when I can; but when I can't, I won't be stopping at any Mobil stations!

5.) We can also make a huge difference in the world by flexing our "Reverential" muscles as consumers. Let's face it. We live in a world where money is king. Many of our most important decisions in life are made at least partially on a financial basis. But we must remember that we, as consumers, do not have to respond to the whims and desires of the huge corporations that run the economy. We do not have to settle for the cheap junk that dominates our retail landscape, products that often are produced in unethical ways, such as those reported by the international goodwill organization, Oxfam, early in 2004.

Oxfam's report, printed in the British newspaper the *Independent*, highlighted the fact that many global retailers are "systematically inflicting poor working conditions on millions of women workers" by conducting price wars to "feed ever-rising consumer expectations of cheap produce." The report referenced a study of employment conditions in twelve countries which supply items to international brands such as Walmart, and found that the largely female workforce in many countries "is working longer hours for low wages in unhealthy conditions and failing to reap any of the benefit from globalization."

In order to combat this situation, we can make it a point not to buy products from companies that support non-reverential practices, to seek out companies that do act ethically, and to find items that are produced in a beneficial, non-harmful manner. Capitalism is based on supply and demand, and when more of us consumers begin to demand more "earth-, people-, and animal-friendly" products and back those demands by putting our money where our mouths are, corporations will be forced to listen and supply us with those products at a more affordable price.

One of the easiest and best ways we can currently support "green" products is by making a point to buy organically-grown food whenever possible. John Robbins, the founder of the aforementioned EarthSave organization, points out in his book, *The Food Revolution*: "The advantages of organic agriculture are many, including reduced soil erosion, greatly improved soil health, far less contribution to global warming, and dramatically reduced water pollution. And there are nutritional advantages, too..." (5)

And fortunately, the organic foods industry is proving to be a model example of consumers changing global markets for the better. The Worldwatch Institute reported in the year 2000: "Driven by rising consumer demand and growing dissatisfaction with conventional farming practices, the organic industry is soaring." Robbins reports in his book that "By the turn of the millennium, more than 17 million acres worldwide were planted with organic foods...[and] the number of acres dedicated to organic farming was 10 times what it had been only 10 years previously. (6)

By supporting the organic foods industry—shopping at natural foods cooperatives or grocery stores that stock organic items and making it a point to buy organic as often as possible— we can assure that earth (and animal) friendly agricultural practices become the rule rather than the exception.

But we should not limit our "green" consumer choices only to food. We should use our buying power to sway the market toward "green" products in other categories. From more fuel-efficient cars and energy-efficient appliances to less harmful cleaning and personal hygiene products, we should make it a point to buy "green" whenever possible. Again, shopping at natural food coops is a good way to gain access to such products. And there are some good websites to guide us in our search, as well:

Eco Mall; www.ecomall.com: The site bills itself as: "Earth's largest environmental living center. Your first stop to shop for green products that are good for people <u>and</u> the environment." It allows you to shop hundreds of websites that offer environmentally friendly products and services, from pet and baby products to alternative energy products, to eco-friendly travel and investment options. It also gives access to interesting news articles and activism alerts, fun on-line activities for children, and a local resource database to help you find information about all things "green" in your local area.

Pristine Planet; www.pristineplanet.com: This site provides consumer reviews of earth conscious and socially responsible organizations, products, and services, and provides direct links to the websites of each one.

6.) Ms. Barko already mentioned this one in her portion of the list, but I so wholeheartedly concur that I want to reiterate: Talk Peace! Speak out for peace. Write your congressional representatives asking them to end armed conflicts and use their positions of power to bring about a more peaceful world. Write letters to the editor of your local papers and give greater voice to peace. Talk to your friends and family members about what you can do to bring about greater peace in the world. And take action on your ideas. Support local and national peace rallies and organizations.

It is very easy to become discouraged and think that there will never be an end to wars and aggression. But the more people talk peace, the more people will hear peace, and the more likely it will become that yet more people will begin to work toward making world peace a reality.

When Dr. Schweitzer first contemplated whether to add his voice to the worldwide effort to bring about peace and nuclear disarmament, he asked himself these questions: "Should I make a statement at all?" and, "What good would it do?" After careful consideration, he concluded: "This crisis intimately concerns the individual. The individual must therefore establish a connection with it . . . the leaders will act only as they become aware of a higher responsibility that has behind it a wall of insistence from the people themselves. I have no way of knowing whether I can help in this. Perhaps I may be justified in trying."(7)

Clearly, Dr. Schweitzer did make a great deal of difference, and I think the same can be true for all of us if we dare to stand up and speak our conscience: if we dare to make our voices heard. Certainly, we will be justified in trying.

7.) Embrace a more vegan or vegetarian diet, or at least make your diet less meat-centric. Read the ensuing chapter, ("Why Did I Eat Meat"), or better yet read John Robbins books, *Diet for a New America* and *The Food Revolution*, from cover to cover. Make it a point to eat less meat. It really might just be the single biggest thing we can do to live a life that is more in line with Reverence for All Life.

8.) Finally, add your own ideas to this list. Take a moment to sit and think about things that you could do, and hope that others would do, to make the world a better place. Better yet, make it a family project. Get your mom and dad, your brothers and sisters, your grandparents and children together and make a nice, long list. Turn off the TV and enjoy some quality time together in your circle of love. Family time is precious time. Have fun with it. Smile, laugh, have a prize for whoever comes up with the most or best ideas. And when you're done, email your list to us at **reverence@triwest.net**. If we ever get around to writing another book, maybe it will be a compilation of all the great ideas we get from all of you!

Notes

1.) Nathaniel Altman; *Ahimsa: Dynamic Compassion* (1980); p. 30-31.
2.) James Brabazon; *Albert Schweitzer: A Biography* (2000); p. 457.
3.) Albert Schweitzer; *Peace or Atomic War* (1958); p.16.
4.) Brabazon; p. 457.
5.) John Robbins: *The Food Revolution: How Your Diet Can Help Save Your Life and Our World* (2001); p.370.
6.) Ibid.; p. 365.   7.) Brabazon; p.457.

35

Why Did I Eat Meat?

By John Webster with Ty F. Webster

For the first fifty-plus years of my life I was a meat eater. Why? I don't really know. Until several years ago I had never given it much thought. I grew up on a farm, and we always had meat dishes at two if not three meals a day. It was a way of life I never questioned. I ate meat. It was a habit; everyone else did it; and that's just the way it was. If a meal were really going to be a meal, it had to include a meat dish of some kind.

But then, during those years when I was celebrating birthdays in my fifties, I began to think about the possibility of not eating meat. One reason was that our eldest son, Jay, in college at the time, became a vegetarian and would come home talking about the advantages of a vegetarian diet. I found the idea a bit strange, but Jay had some interesting points. Soon thereafter I read John Robbins' book, *Diet for a New America: How Your Food Choices Affect Your Health, Happiness and the Future of Life on Earth.* Suddenly it dawned on me: I do not have to eat meat in order to partake of a healthy diet. And I also realized that what I choose to eat can make a big difference in a number of ways to the world around me.

I was already familiar with the old adage, "You are what you eat." But I began to realize that the same holds true for our planet. In a sense, the Earth is what we eat. It is in fact possible to eat ourselves out of house and home, and that is exactly what the "privileged" people of the world are doing with our meat-based diets. I realized that I could make a significant contribution to the well-being of the world by embracing a vegetarian diet. So I said, "This is one thing I can do; I will no longer eat meat of any kind." And I have not touched an ounce of meat since, thanks in no small part to my special partner. Liz shops the groceries and prepares the meals at our house, and her cooperation with my decision to go vegetarian has been a blessing. As I came to learn more about Albert Schweitzer's ethic, I was happy to realize that the dietary choice I had made before I became familiar with his concept of Reverence for Life was very much in tune with it.

Now you might be asking the very same question I once asked: Why would anyone want to be a vegetarian? There are a number of very valid reasons, many of which are presented in John Robbins' aforementioned book, *Diet For a New America* (Stillpoint Publishing, 1987), and his more recent book, *The Food Revolution: How Your Diet Can Help Save Your Life and Our World* (Conari Press, 2001) [for brevity's sake, these books will subsequently be referenced as *"NA"* and *"FR."*]. I highly recommend both of these books and wish that they were required reading for everyone. In them, Robbins eloquently and graphically presents some very sound, well-researched evidence that tells why it is in our best interest to move away from a meat-based diet.

Better for the Environment: Perhaps the best reason to move toward a more vegetarian diet is the fact that meat production is a huge contributing factor in the increasingly woeful state of the earth's natural environment. The processes involved in raising animals for food are highly damaging to our environment in a number of different ways.

One of the biggest environmental problems that humans will face in this century will be a scarcity of fresh water. We are using water at ever-increasing rates, and the meat industry is a huge culprit. According to Robbins, over half the total amount of water consumed in the United States goes to irrigate the land that grows food for livestock. The production of one pound of meat uses up to 100 times more water than the production of a pound of wheat. Whereas it takes over 4000 gallons of water to produce a day's food for one meat-eater, for a lacto-ovo vegetarian (one who eats egg and dairy products) it takes only 1200 gallons; and for a vegan (one who eats no animal products) it takes only 300 gallons. Robbins points out: "It takes less water to produce a year's food for a pure vegetarian than to produce a month's food for a meat-eater." (*NA*; p.367)

The amount of water used to produce a single pound of beef in California (water usage for meat production varies somewhat by location) is more than what would be saved if a person stopped showering for six full months! (*FR*; p.237) Robbins highlights the contradiction of the trend of Americans wanting to save water and the reality of the average American diet:

> Everywhere you look today...people are seeking to conserve water. You see people washing their cars less often. People are installing low-flow showerheads and sink fixtures, and low-flow toilets...The vigilant turn off the water at the sink when brushing their teeth, except to rinse the brush, and when shaving, except to rinse the blade. These measures are prudent and helpful, but all of them combined don't save anywhere near the amount of water you would save by shifting toward a plant-based diet. (*FR* ; p.235)

Meat production also contributes heavily to dangerous water pollution. The amount of waste produced by livestock is staggering. Robbins writes: "Every 24 hours, the animals destined for America's dinner tables produce 20 billion pounds of waste. That is 250,000 pounds of excrement per second. The livestock of the United States produce twenty times as much excrement as the entire human population of the country!" (*NA*; p.372) And whereas human waste is strictly controlled and treated at sewage facilities, most livestock waste is neither treated nor regulated and tends to wind up in local water supplies. Says Robbins: "Astoundingly, the meat industry single-handedly accounts for more than three times as much harmful organic waste water pollution as the rest of the nation's industry combined! A new direction for America's diet-style would do more to conserve and clean up our nation's water than any other single action." (*NA*; p.373)

It would also go a long way toward saving the world's forests, which, as Robbins reminds us, are crucial to our existence: "We need our forests. They are vital sources of oxygen. They moderate our climates, prevent floods, and are our best defense against soil erosion. Forests recycle our water. They are homes for millions of plants and animals. They are a source of beauty, inspiration, and solace to millions of people." (*NA*; p.362) They are also being chopped down at an alarming rate. In the U.S. alone, over 260 million acres of forest have been converted to land for livestock production.

But the real damage has been done to the world's rainforests. These ancient forests are home to no less than half of all species on earth, account for a large portion of the world's oxygen supply, and provide the raw materials for one quarter of all our medicines. And they are being destroyed at a rate the equivalent of a football field every second. What is the biggest factor in the clear-cutting of rainforests? You guessed it: conversion to land for cattle grazing. (*FR*; p. 255)

Clearing the rainforests also greatly contributes to global warming. But that is only one way that the meat-production industry influences the greenhouse effect. Robbins points out that production of food for a meat-based diet is much less energy efficient than that for a vegetarian diet. A detailed study sponsored by the U.S. department of Interior and Commerce determined that "the production of meats, dairy products and eggs accounts for one-third of the total amount of all raw materials used for all purposes in the United States." And the production of grains, vegetables, and fruits consumes less than 5% of the raw materials needed for the production of meat. One of the main raw materials in question is fossil fuel, the burning of which releases huge quantities of carbon dioxide, a greenhouse gas, into the atmosphere. (*NA*; p.374) Also, the Worldwatch Institute has estimated that livestock account for 15 to 20 percent of all global methane emissions, another important factor in global warming. In fact, a report published in 1999 by the Union of Concerned Scientists concluded that the two most damaging things that U.S. residents do to our climate are "drive vehicles that get poor gas mileage and eat beef."(*FR*; p.267-8)

Life on earth is entirely dependent on a very fragile, natural balance, and the statistics tell a clear tale: embracing a vegetarian diet is a great way to help protect the earth's environment from irreparable damage.

Better for People: Another reason to embrace a vegetarian diet is because meat production plays a huge roll in human starvation around the world. There are over 1.2 billion underfed and malnourished people in the world (*FR*; p.290). That means that one out of every six people on earth is going hungry. The problem, however, is not a lack of food. It is the fact that so much food is being fed to livestock to support the world's meat habit. In fact, nearly 40 percent of the world's grain is fed to livestock. (*FR*; p.284) In the U.S.—where 56 million acres of farmland produce hay for livestock while only 4 million acres produce vegetables—livestock eat 70 percent of our nation's grain and cereals. The number of human beings who could be fed by the grain and soybeans eaten by U.S. livestock: a staggering 1.4 billion! (*FR*; p.292)

Plus, it turns out that feeding grains to livestock is a very inefficient use of food. According to Robbins, "By cycling our grain through livestock, we not only waste 90 percent of its protein; in addition, we sadly waste 96 percent of its calories, 100 percent of its fiber, and 100 percent of its carbohydrates." (*NA*; p.352)

Yet there is a worldwide trend toward using grain to feed livestock. This has been a great disadvantage to the underprivileged of the world. Robbins cites a Worldwatch Institute report: "Higher meat consumption among the affluent frequently creates problems for the poor, as the share of farmland devoted to feed cultivation expands, reducing production of food staples. In the economic competition for grain fields, the upper classes usually win." In El Salvador, for instance, beef exports increased more than six fold between 1960 and 1980. But at the same time, increasing numbers of small farmers lost their livelihood and were pushed off their land, and today 72 percent of Salvadoran infants are underfed. (*FR*; p.287) There are similar trends in nations the world over. In Guatemala, 75 percent of children under five are malnourished, but Guatemala exports 40 million pounds of meat to the U.S. every year! (*NA*; p.352)

We must remember that every time we eat meat, we are playing a role in this process. Dr. Walden Bello, the Executive Director of the Institute for Food and Development Policy and a leading expert on global food realities notes:

Every time you eat a hamburger you are having a relationship with thousands of people you never met...And many of these people are hungry. The fact is that there is enough food in the world for everyone. But tragically, much of the world's food and land resources are tied up in producing beef and other livestock—food for the well-off—while millions of children and adults suffer from malnutrition and starvation. (*FR*; p.291)

Embracing a vegetarian diet not only shows reverence for the environment, it shows greater reverence for humanity, as well.

Better for You: Another plus for a vegetarian diet is that it has been proven to be much healthier for the human body than a meat-based diet. Robbins states the case:

Eating the standard American diet that's based on meat and dairy products, with plenty of white flour and white sugar, one-third of the women and one-half of the men in the U.S. population die of heart disease. Meanwhile, medical research is telling us that vegetarians and vegans (vegetarians who consume no dairy products or eggs) not only have far less heart disease, but also have lower rates of cancer, hypertension, diabetes, gallstones, kidney disease, obesity, and colon disease. They live on average six to ten years longer than the rest of the population, and in fact seem to be healthier by every measurement we have of assessing health outcomes. (*FR*; p.14)

He also points out that although the National Cattlemen's Beef Association and the National Dairy Council tell us repeatedly that we put our health at risk if we do not consume their products, impartial researchers and nonprofit public health organizations such as the World Health Organization, the American Institute for Cancer Research, the American Heart Association, the Physicians Committee for Responsible Medicine, the National Cancer Institute, and the Center for Science in the Public Interest all have done research that provides a different perspective.(*FR*; p.15)

According to Robbins' well-researched data presented in *FR* (gleaned from many different respectable sources), the average blood cholesterol level of vegetarians is 14 percent lower than non-vegetarians. For vegans it is 35 percent lower. (p.19) Non-vegetarians have triple the incidence of high blood pressure compared to vegetarians, and 58 percent of patients with high blood pressure are able to completely discontinue use of their medications after adopting a low sodium, low-fat, high fiber vegetarian diet. (p.29) And because vegetarian diets are heavy in fruits, vegetables and high-fiber, low-fat foods, they can help to protect against cancer. According to William Castelli, M.D., the director of the Framingham Health Study at the National Heart, Lung, and Blood Institute, "A low-fat plant-based diet would not only lower heart attack rate about 85 percent, but would lower the cancer rate 60 percent. (p.47)

As it turns out, in addition to showing reverence for the environment and fellow humans, eating a vegetarian diet also reflects a higher level of reverence for one's own life!

Better for the Animals: One final big reason to move toward a vegetarian diet is because of the lack of reverence for the lives of most animals that are raised and slaughtered for human consumption. Historically, most animals were raised on family farms in reasonably harmonious environments. But today most meat that makes its way to our tables comes from huge factory farms where the animals are treated merely as profitable commodities. Robbins points out:

Much changed with the advent of intensive factory farming. Modern technology has made possible a shift in the time-honored responsibility livestock producers had for the welfare of their animals.

Starting in the last half of the twentieth century, it began to be not only possible, but economically advantageous, to raise animals in conditions that are completely unnatural and unhealthy and that frustrate virtually all of their urges and instincts.

Although extreme crowding of animals greatly increases the rates of the animals' illnesses and deaths, it nevertheless also raises profits. Even when more than 20 percent of pigs and chickens die prematurely in today's intensive husbandry systems, for instance, producers find their profits increased by such practices. (*FR;* p. 169)

The very numbers of animals killed for human consumption are staggering. Eight billion chickens, 90 million pigs, and over 30 million cattle are slaughtered in the U.S. alone *every year.* And the vast majority of these creatures are raised in cramped, horribly overcrowded, and unsanitary conditions on massive animal factory "farms." Up to 30,000 chickens may be crammed into a single building. Most pigs are fattened for market in total confinement in small cages inside of huge buildings where they never see the light of day. Most beef cattle have similar fates in the cramped confines of massive feedlots. And all of these creatures are force-fed to get them up to market weight as quickly as possible. Robbins points out that although it traditionally took a chicken 21 weeks to reach a 4-pound market weight, today it takes them only seven weeks, and the rapid obesity causes many serious diseases and premature deaths.(*FR* p.195)

Peter R. Cheeke, a professor of animal science at Oregon State University, is quoted elsewhere in *FR*: "One of the best things modern animal agriculture has going for it is that most people...haven't a clue how animals are raised and processed...the less the consumer knows about what's happening before the meat hits the plate, the better."(p. 171)

A lot of people would like to justify the unethical treatment of livestock by claiming that they are just stupid animals. Many of these people, however, don't know much about farm animals. In *FR*, Bernard Rollin, a Colorado State University expert on animal farming, points out that chickens are not stupid birdbrains:

Contrary to what one may hear from the industry, chickens are not mindless, simple automata but are complex behaviorally, do quite well in learning, show a rich social organization, and have a diverse repertoire of calls. Anyone who has kept barnyard chickens also recognizes their significant personality. (p.190)

Robbins points out that both pigs and cows are rather amazing creatures, as well. "Pigs actually have one of the highest measured I.Q.'s of all animals, surpassing even the dog," he writes. "They are friendly, sociable, fun-loving beings...Did you know that pigs recognize people, remember individuals clearly, and appreciate human contact when it is not hostile?" (*NA*; p.75) About cows, he writes: "The truth is that cows have a special kind of intelligence and sensitivity. But because they are such patient, gentle souls who rarely hurry or make a fuss about things, we tend to think they are dumb, and don't recognize their unique presence." (*NA*; p.103)

Having grown up on a family farm, I can attest to the intelligence and unique personalities of farm animals. They are indeed creatures with wills-to-live like our very own. So the influence of Reverence for All Life on my own life reassures me that my choice to become a vegetarian was a good one. After all, if I almost always do all that I can to avoid intentionally hindering an ant, a spider, or any other creature that may be within my circle of influence, why would I choose to hinder the life of an animal by having it killed so that I can eat it?

Fortunately, as Robbins points out, I am not alone. More and more people are coming to the same conclusions I have, and I truly feel that the world is a better place because of it. I agree with his statement: "In our time, there is an awakening sense of compassion toward animals. We can run from it. We can deny it. We can mock those who stand for it. But when we choose to eat with conscience, I truly believe that our world becomes a kinder safer place for us all." (*FR* ; p.226)

So, as it happens, besides being better for the environment and better and healthier for people, a vegetarian diet also shows a much higher level of reverence for the well-being of animals. To quote John Robbins one final time:

> It is increasingly obvious that environmentally sustainable solutions to world hunger can only emerge as people eat more plant foods and fewer animal products. To me it is deeply moving that the same food choices that give us the best chance to eliminate world hunger are also those that take the least toll on the environment, contribute the most to our long-term health, are the safest, and are also far and away the most compassionate toward our fellow creatures. (*FR*; p.302)

I know that not everyone will choose to stop eating meat entirely as I have. However, if I have caused some folks to think about the possibility of eating less meat, they will be doing something more than I did during the first fifty-some years of my life. Giving up meat completely is a somewhat drastic step for those who have eaten meat their entire lives. But if everyone would plan to eat at least one or two fewer meat meals each week, or if we could all commit to eat half of the meat we now eat, and if those who are currently vegetarian but not vegan could commit to eating a few vegan meals per week, together we could all begin to make a big difference in the world. By choosing to eat with a greater awareness and consciousness of how our dietary choices affect the world and the people and creatures in it, we can begin to bring about a world with a much higher level of Reverence for All Life.

And as for those who think that a vegetarian diet has to be boring and flavorless—and also for those of you looking for vegetarian recipes to add to the ones you already use—keep reading. In the next few pages, you'll find some relatively quick and easy and *very* tasty vegetarian recipes. Enjoy!

Vegetarian Recipes

Compiled by Elizabeth Webster

Alexandra's Taste-Good-Gratin   Serves 6-8

This recipe was created for us by Jay's sister-in-law, Alexandra Kruschwitz, in Wegberg, Germany and has been adapted to American measurements and products. Ingredients are mainly a matter of preference and cooking times are approximate.

5-6 medium Potatoes, scrubbed
4-6 cups Vegetables: Cauliflower, Broccoli, Carrots, Onions, etc.
    Cook potatoes, cool, peel, and slice into greased, 3-quart flat casserole dish. Cut vegetables into chunks. Cook with a little bit of salt until tender-crisp. Drain, and layer over potatoes.
<u>Sauce</u>:
3 Tbs. Butter
3 Tbs. Flour
2 cups Milk
Pepper, Salt, Nutmeg
4-8 oz. Herb-flavored Cream Cheese (depending on consistency)
1-2 eggs (optional)
    Melt butter, stir in flour, cook for 1-2 minutes, stirring constantly. Do not allow to brown. Slowly whisk in milk and cook over medium heat, stirring constantly until sauce is thickened. Add pepper, salt, and nutmeg to taste.
    Stir cream cheese into hot sauce until thoroughly melted. Remove from heat and cool. Whisk in eggs. (If not using, add another tablespoon each of flour and butter to thicken. In this case, it is not necessary to allow the sauce to cool.) Pour over vegetables in casserole dish.

1-2 cups Sharp Cheese, grated
    Sprinkle cheese over top. Bake at 400° F. for 35-45 minutes until heated through and cheese is melted and golden brown.

Stewart's Stew

Serves 6-8

*This recipe came to us from our neighbor and good friend, Linda
Jenkins. We like to use the baked/flavored tofu products available
in the refrigerator section of our area food coop.*

1½ lbs. Tofu, firm / extra firm, cut into ¾"–1" cubes
½ cup Soy Sauce, or reduced-sodium Tamari
     Combine and marinate for at least 15 minutes

5-6 medium Potatoes, chopped
6 Carrots, chopped
4 medium Onions (or desired number), chopped
½ tsp. Salt (optional)
2 quarts Water
     Combine in a 5-quart saucepan and boil until vegetables are
almost soft.

1 cup unbleached White Flour
½ tsp. Salt
1 tsp. Pepper
     Combine in a plastic bag. Shake to mix. Drain soy sauce
into the cooking vegetables. Place tofu in the bag and shake to coat
well.

     Brown the breaded cubes in ½ cup oil. Be careful not to
knock off the breading when turning the cubes.

     Add the browned cubes to the almost soft vegetables. Mix
any left-over flour mixture into a smooth gravy with a little of the
broth, then stir into the stew. Continue simmering until vegetables
are soft.

Without-Turkey Pie   Serves 6

Possibly the best potpie you'll ever taste. You won't miss the meat.

<u>Crust:</u>
⅓ cup Butter, softened
¾ cup Sour Cream
1 Egg
1 cup All-purpose Flour
1 tsp. Baking Powder
½ tsp. Dried Sage
    Combine first 3 ingredients and beat at medium speed until smooth. Add next 3 ingredients and blend at low speed until well mixed. Spread batter evenly over bottom and sides of lightly oiled 9½" deep-dish pie plate.

<u>Filling:</u>
⅓ cup Carrot
⅓ cup Onion
⅓ cup Green Pepper
⅓ cup Red Pepper
⅓ cup Celery
1 package (8 oz.) Seasoned Baked Tofu or Flavored Seitan cut into small cubes
1¼ cup thick White Sauce (Butter, Flour, Milk) seasoned with 2 Tbsp. Chicken-less Broth Powder or 2 tsp. Poultry Seasoning (or use a 10 ¾ oz. can low-salt Cream of Mushroom Soup and add the seasoning)
1½ c. Cheddar Cheese, shredded

Chop and combine vegetables in mixing bowl. Stir in tofu or seitan and seasoned sauce. Place in crust and sprinkle with grated cheese.
Bake at 350° for about 1 hour until firm and golden brown. Let stand 15 minutes before serving.

Leek and Potato Soup   Serves 6-8

This is a good "starter" recipe. Add any other vegetables you have on hand and adjust flavorings as desired. Substitute thyme and dill for the marjoram and rosemary. For a cream soup, stir in sour cream or thickened cream or low-fat milk or soy milk. The possibilities are as varied as your imagination suggests.

1½ lbs. Leeks
1½ lbs. Potatoes
1½ lbs. Carrots
1-2 stalks Celery
1 Tbsp. Olive Oil
1 Tbsp. Butter
Chop vegetables. Sauté until heated through in the oil / butter mixture in a 5-6 quart saucepan, stirring occasionally.

3 quarts Water
⅓ cup (approx.) Meatless Chicken-flavored Broth Powder
Add water and enough flavored broth powder to give rich flavor. Bring to boil, lower the heat and simmer until vegetables are soft (about 25 minutes).

½ tsp. Summer Savory
½ tsp. Marjoram
pinch of Rosemary
1 Tbsp. Dried Parsley
Salt & Pepper to taste
Add seasonings, simmer another 30 minutes and serve.

If smoother soup is desired, puree ½ or more of the cooked soup in blender; reheat before serving.

Max's Southwest Tofu Club w/ Spicy Chili Sauce   Serves 4

Chef Maximillian Wilda of the Historic Trempealeau Hotel came up with this recipe while studying at a Le Cordon Bleu Culinary Institute in Mendota Heights, MN. A version of it was published in Vegetarian Times *magazine.*

Marinade:
½ cup lime juice;   1 tsp. sugar;   2 Tbs. fresh cilantro;
2 Tbs. chili powder

Tofu Club:
14 oz. pkg. extra firm tofu
8 slices of your favorite sandwich bread
1 medium-sized ripe avocado, thinly sliced
2 cups bean sprouts, blanched
1 red bell pepper and 1 green bell pepper, seeded and thinly sliced
1 red onion, thinly sliced crosswise
1 large tomato, thinly sliced crosswise

Dressing:
1 cup plain yogurt
½ cup canned green chilies   ¼ cup enchilada sauce
1 Tbs. minced garlic   1 Tbs. grated ginger
2 Tbs. cilantro, chopped   2 Tbs. chili powder
2 Tbs. cayenne   1 tsp. kosher salt, to taste

1.) To make the Marinade: Mix together the marinade ingredients in a mixing bowl.
2.) Slice the tofu into 8 uniform slices. Put the tofu slices into marinade and refrigerate for 1 to 4 hours.
3.) To make the Dressing: Mix together the ingredients in a mixing bowl and set aside.
4.) To assemble the Tofu Club sandwiches: Toast the bread slices lightly. Remove the tofu from the marinade, and blot dry with paper towel. Spread dressing on each piece of toast, and lay the toast on a flat surface. On one slice, place two slices of tofu and the vegetables, and top with a second slice of bread. Repeat until all the ingredients are used up.

Vegetarian Chili   Serves 6-8

This is basically a "dump and taste" recipe. As our son Jay, who "invented" this recipe said, "Meat in chili is not all it's cracked up to be." Use whatever vegetable and seasoning combinations strike your fancy and let them cook slowly to bring out and meld the flavor.

Vegetables:
3-4 Carrots
1-2 Onions
1 large Green Pepper
1 Tbsp. crushed Garlic
　　　Chop vegetables coarsely, add garlic, and cook in 1-2 Tbsp. olive oil in soup pot over low heat until softened but not browned.

Seasonings:
1-2 Tbsp. Chili powder
2 Tbs. Meatless Beef-flavored Broth Powder
2 Tbs. Dried Parsley
1-2 tsp Basil
1-2 tsp. Dried Oregano Leaves

Beans & Tomatoes:
3 cans (15 oz. each) cooked Beans: Pinto, Kidney, & /or Black
3 cans (15 oz. each) Diced Tomatoes
Tomato Juice (or condensed Tomato Soup, thinned) enough to give desired consistency
　　　Add seasonings, beans, tomatoes, and juice to vegetables (amounts are approximate, increase or decrease as desired).
　　　Simmer at least ½ hour before serving. Like all soups, flavor improves with time. Serve with a crusty bread or hot cornbread.

"Sloppy Joe" Barbecue Sandwiches   Serves 6

This is one of those recipes that has myriad variations, just as the original versions made by our mothers and grandmothers with a pound of hamburger and whatever combination of soups and seasonings did. A visiting friend once remarked, "I know John doesn't eat meat, yet I saw he was eating the barbecue, how can that be?" You just might be fooled, too.

1 Tbsp Olive Oil
1 medium Onion, chopped
1lb. Non-meat Ground Beef Substitute or Crumbles
1 10½ oz. can Condensed Cream of Tomato Soup
1-2 Tbsp. Worcestershire Sauce
Pinch of Sugar
1-2 Tbsp bottled Barbecue Sauce (Optional)

Sauté onion in oil in 10" skillet. Add beef substitute and heat until it begins to brown; stirring to prevent sticking.

Stir in remaining ingredients. Simmer on low-heat, covered, for at least 30 minutes. Stir occasionally to prevent sticking.

Spoon onto hamburger buns.

Hummus   5 (1/2-cup) servings

There are as many variations of hummus as there are cooks who make it. Ann Dahmen, another creative friend, sent this super-simple recipe. Serve with chips, crackers or veggies as a dip or spread on pita or other bread in a sandwich.

2 cups Garbanzo Beans (Chick Peas)
¼ cup Olive Oil

1 Tbsp. Lemon Juice
½ Tbsp. Sesame Oil
1 Tbsp. Parsley Flakes
½ Tbsp. Garlic, chopped
¼ cup Onion, diced
¾ tsp. Cumin
¼ tsp. Cayenne Pepper
1 Tbsp. low-sodium Soy Sauce

Drain the garbanzo beans and put all of the ingredients into a food processor. Process on high for 10 seconds, scrape the sides and process on high for another ten seconds. That's all folks!

Although none of the recipes included here came from them, there are three recipe books I often draw upon when I'm looking for a good, and usually simple, dish to prepare. As a friend commented, "I've never made a recipe from [one of these] that wasn't good." Granted, I haven't made them all. However the ones that have sounded good, when I've tried them, have always lived up to expectation.

The Enchanted Broccoli Forest...and other timeless delicacies
Mollie Katzen, 1982, Ten Speed Press, P.O. Box 7123, Berkeley, CA 94707

Quick Vegetarian Pleasures
Jeanne Lemlin, 1992, Harper Perennial, NY

Vegetarian International Cuisine: An Essential Cookbook
From the Chefs of the Cheese Factory Restaurant, 1997, The Cheese Factory Restaurant Cookbook LLC, 132 Hines Terrace, Wisconsin Dells, WI 53965

Appendix

A Process Perspective of God and Creation

By John Webster

'Actual entities'—also termed 'actual occasions'—are the final real things of which the world is made up. There is no going behind actual entities to find anything more real.
--Alfred North Whitehead; Process and Reality; *Macmillan Publishing Co. Inc.; New York, 1929; p. 23.*

We cannot know anything, and nothing can make the slightest difference in our lives unless it be an event or some possibility carried by an event.
--Henry N. Wieman; The Source of Human Good; *Southern Illinois University Press; Carbondale, Illinois; 1946; p. 8.*

... God may be spoken of variously as the ground of wholeness, the character of reality in its wholeness, the dynamic reality making for wholeness. *... God is the Wholeness-Reality fundamental to the universe in its dynamic, relational, evolutionary fullness and open-endedness, and fundamentally implicated in man's arriving, surviving, becoming, dying, and hoping.*
--Harvey H. Potthoff; God and the Celebration of Life; *Rand McNally & Company; Chicago; 1969; p. 192.*

Process theologians believe that freedom is an inherent feature of reality. The universe is the becoming of events that are self-creative, from quarks to human minds. Without freedom there would be no world
--C. Robert Mesle; Process Theology: A Basic Introduction; *Chalice Press; St. Louis; 1993; p. 59.*

To the mix of ideas forming the foundation of a "process" perspective of creation, including those just referenced, I would add the following ideas brought to us by Dr. Albert Schweitzer. Dr. Schweitzer is not usually listed among process thinkers, yet I find many of his ideas very compatible with process thought.

"The most immediate fact of man's consciousness is the assertion: 'I am life which wills to live, in the midst of life which wills to live'.... As in my will-to-live there is ardent desire for further life and for the mysterious exaltation of the will-to-live which we call pleasure, while there is fear of destruction and of that mysterious depreciation of the will-to-live which we call pain: so too are these in the will-to-live around me, whether it can express itself to me, or remains dumb." --Out of My Life and Thought; *1933; pp.186-87.*
"The essential nature of the will-to-live is determination to live itself to the full. It carries within it the impulse to realize itself in the highest possible perfection." --The Philosophy of Civilization; *1987; p.282.*

Many of my ideas concerning life and creation have been developed from a "process" perspective of thought. "Process thought" suggests that reality is made up of a network of events, all of which are interrelated. As it works out, my introduction to process thought serves as a good example of the interrelation of events. Alfred North Whitehead, who is known as the father of process theology, was a professor at Harvard University from 1924 to 1937. One of his students at Harvard during the 1935-36 school year was a young man by the name of Harvey H. Potthoff. One of my favorite instructors at The Iliff School of Theology in Denver, Colorado, was Dr. Harvey H. Potthoff. During my years at Iliff, I participated in as many of Dr. Potthoff's classes as possible, picking up ideas about process philosophy along the way. And now I share with the readers of this chapter some of my own ideas about a process view of the world. I take pride in proclaiming a relationship with the process school of thought. It is a relationship I have found to be especially functional and meaningful.

This chapter is not meant to be an introduction to, nor an explanation of, process philosophy or process theology. What follows is simply a collection of thoughts and ideas which I hope will cause you, the reader, to think about what you believe to be important for your own life and all of creation. When we think about God, we need to question everything we believe and have been told about God. Always use reason when searching for God. If we are searching for the God that is Real, it is crucial that we think and use reason in our searching. Never be afraid to question what you believe. As this questioning goes on, those ideas and beliefs that continue to make sense and be meaningful are the ones for us to keep and to celebrate.

If you believe in God, I invite you to think about your beliefs. Make your own list of ideas about God that are most important and meaningful to you. Never be afraid to entertain some new ideas about God. It is not unhealthy for our list of ideas about God to be constantly changing and growing.

If you do not believe in God, or are unsure whether or not you do, I invite you to come along on this theological journey just for the fun of thinking about some different ideas. Thinking about what seems to be most important for us and our world can be exciting even if you do not find any ideas that are keepers. But if you should find even a few ideas that make sense and seem worth keeping, the time you have spent will have been worthwhile.

Some Ideas and Questions to Think About

What is God? When we discover that which is ultimately most important for us and all of creation, we are getting close to the God that is Real. We believe that "love" is important. It has been said that "God is love." Does God use the "gentle persuasion of love" to urge us to choose the best possibilities available?

Everything is made up of events (units of process). The basic units of creation are events or happenings (Whitehead called them 'actual entities' or 'actual occasions') that are always in the

273

process of becoming. All events are interrelated. Life is made up of events. Your life, every life, is an event made up of many smaller events. All the people who have ever lived come together to help make you and me: the many become one and are increased by one. This is the on-going pulse of creation. We are each a unique new event which then becomes a part of the many that come together to help mold the next new event. In other words, when events end, they become a part of the past, which help mold the new events constantly in the process of becoming. Therefore, all the events that have ever happened come together to help make you and me. (Does this mean that all the creatures that are alive and have ever lived are our relatives and ancestors? What better reason to have Reverence for All Life?) Since reality is made up of events that are always in the process of becoming, nothing in our world is static or unchanging. Everything in our world is always dynamic, changing, flowing, growing, pulsing, throbbing, striving to become.

The process of creation brings to every event a spectrum or range of possibilities that are appropriate for that event. I propose that God is vitally involved in each event's range of possibilities as the concepts of will-to-live, novelty, freedom, and the urge-toward-wholeness suggest.

The will-to-live is important! "We are life which wills to live, in the midst of life which wills to live." The will-to-live connects us with every other person in the whole world. And not only with every other person, but with all that lives. Think of it! We are one! We are one with people, flowers, dogs, cats, pigs, birds, bugs, trees, and everything else that lives. Might the will-to-live, a vital part of everything that is alive, involve a spark of creativity that urges and lures every event to become the most it can be? If so, might this mean that the will-to-live includes a dynamic reality making for wholeness? Might the will-to-live along with an evolving will-to-love in human lives urge us to reach out with reverence to all life within our circle of influence?

The creation of each new event involves novelty. Every event is different. Some events are very different from past events. Novelty is important. Without novelty the process of creation would be stymied. Where does novelty come from? As the many become one and are increased by one, is it perhaps the new one added to the many that helps bring novelty to the next event? Is "novelty" God at work in each new event?

Each event has some degree of freedom to help mold its own destiny. Freedom is important. Without freedom the process of creation would collapse into sameness. Might freedom involve the presence of God within each event that is in the process of becoming? Freedom and novelty are both important and often work together in the quest for uniqueness and wholeness. Each event is bound inextricably in a relationship with every other event. Past events, freedom, novelty, the will-to-live, and the urge-toward-wholeness help to make us what we are. Might the past events, freedom, the novelty, the will-to-live, and the urge-toward-wholeness actually be God at work in our midst? Does this mean that we can never say, "I, alone, did that?" Events are always created in, and because of, a great network of relationships. Nothing exists in the isolation of being disconnected. Does this also mean that we cannot say, "God, alone, did that?" With freedom also comes tragic possibilities that can't be controlled.

I would suggest that what we discover to be most important in our process of creation is ultimately ethical. The will-to-live along with an attitude of Reverence for All Life is important. Schweitzer suggests that "good" means to maintain life, to further life, to bring developing life to its highest value. "Evil" means to destroy life, to hurt life, to keep life from developing. Might the will-to-live that ultimately leads to the will-to-love and the will to reach out with reverence to all life be God at work in our lives and in the life of the world? As Schweitzer said on page 270 of *Out of My Life and Thought (1933),* "The ethic of Reverence for Life is the ethic of Love widened into universality."

275

Where is God? God is wherever the will-to-live is active in our universe. The will-to-live is in the midst of all life events. This means that God is in the midst of life wherever life is found. Might the will-to-live that is related to each of us and to every creation that is alive be very closely related to God or even be the God that is real? Might the *Universal-Will-To-Live* be a meaningful concept to use when we talk about God? Might the will-to-live bring to us a hope and a yearning for a still more excellent way? If so, the essential nature of the will-to-live is a dynamic reality making for wholeness.

Is God present even where there is no life? God is wherever events are happening. Is the will-to-live present in events even when life is not present? Might the will-to-live always be waiting to come alive whenever the conditions become right? All events are related and God is within each event.

Something to ponder: Before there was any life on earth, where was the will-to-live? Does everything have to be somewhere? Was the will-to-live with God? Did the will-to-live originate with the first forms of life on earth? Perhaps there was life existing in other parts of the universe long before life existed here. If so, was it sparked by the same universal will-to-live that is present in our lives? If life does exist in far away parts of the universe (and it probably does) is the same God present with life there that is present with us here? Is the will-to-live something very basic to the nature and reality of God?

Is it reasonable to assume that the will-to-live is active only in events (units of process)? Might it be that God is totally within the network of events that make up our universe and is a vital part of every event? This means that God is always as near to us as our own self and our closest partners. God is not way out beyond (disconnected from) the process of events that make up our universe.

If all events are interrelated and God is present within each event, does this not mean that you and I are related to God and to each other? The process of creation brings to all our new events a number of possibilities, and God urges us from within and lures us from without (from other events) to choose the most positive ones. God brings us the freedom to choose. We have something to say about what we will become even though much of each new event is determined by past events. God also brings the gift of novelty to each new event. God urges and lures us toward the more positive possibilities using the gentle persuasion of hope and love. God is the dynamic reality making for wholeness. When some possibilities close for us, other possibilities will open up.

As we live, God is with us. God is always with us. When we die, does God continue to be with us? In death, do we continue to be with God? Might it be that in death we lose our immediate location yet retain a universal location (being related to all events) that is now present with a greater awareness and intensity to those we have known and loved? When we die, we continue to be with those whom we have known and loved who are still alive. Even in death, we continue to be a part of the many that help to make the one that is new. In life, everything that we do is a possibility for someone else. Therefore, we should make sure our lives incorporate the ethic we want the future to embrace, as we will become the events from the past that will help mold the future.

Interesting questions to ponder. We may think of God being in the midst of each event. Might God be an event? If God is an event related to every other event, does God change as new events take place? If we look to the whole universe as being one very large event that is ever in the process of becoming, perhaps God is an event that parallels the universe in scope and unendingness. Whatever the case, I submit that God is an unending presence in the midst of this great event, made up of many smaller events, that we call the universe. In life and in death might we too become unending parts of the universe and God's eternal presence?

The world that we live in is dynamic, relational and becoming in nature. The world is made up of events which are always changing, interconnected, and evolutionary. The will-to-live constantly lures and urges events to become the best possible.

Our will-to-live relates us to God. Our will-to-live filled with an attitude of Reverence for All Life can enable new creative possibilities to open up for us and our partners as we, along with God, urge and lure creation to a higher level of harmony. When the going gets rough and the world seems to crumble in on us, we may sometimes stop and wish that God were with us. We need to realize that God IS with us. If something special needs to be done to make the situation a little more bearable, we may be the very ones God is urging to do it. God urges and lures us to be caretakers of all life within our circle of influence. We are life which wills to live, in the midst of life which wills to live. This means that we should do all that we can to care for and urge all our partners to become the best they can be. This is our will-to-live striving for wholeness and oneness with all that lives. It is our Reverence for All Life at work.

God is not like a powerful Caesar who rules over the world. God is more like the quiet power of the will-to-live that is at the center of every life-event urging it to be the best it can be. Perhaps God is more like a quiet urge that challenges each person to become aware of his or her oneness with all that lives. Perhaps God is always urging the will-to-live to also become the will-to-love.

What is the Kingdom of God? If God is within every event, might the Kingdom of God be made up of all the events that are now being created and that have ever been? Might the Kingdom of God involve Reverence for All Life, meaning that it encompasses not only Christians, but all people, and not only people, but all that lives and has ever lived?

The Kingdom of God is not supernatural, but very natural. Might we say that the Kingdom of God encompasses the universe (the totality of all that is)? The universe is a very large dynamic event made up of many smaller events. All events are interrelated and therefore have a continuity that does not contradict the integrity of being related. God cannot, all of a sudden, usher in a new world order that is completely disconnected from the present world. Yet, step-by-step, human beings, working in harmony with one another, with all of nature and with God, while embracing an ethic of Reverence for All Life, can move from violence to non-violence and from conflict to peace. Should we fail, we will surely perish from the face of the earth. Christians are fortunate to be able to experience and use the spirit, the will, and the ethic of Jesus as we go about Kingdom building. Jesus said, "Follow Me". We, too, can be a person using the spirit, the will, and the ethic of Jesus to bring about a still more excellent way of life.

The Kingdom of God is present now. The Kingdom of God is always coming. We are a part of this Kingdom. Nothing can separate us from the Kingdom of God. God urges our will-to-live to be filled with Reverence for All Life, so that the Kingdom for us may come into being with a greater harmony, intensity, and wholeness than ever before.

If God is "the dynamic reality making for wholeness" and all events are interrelated, might it be that the wholeness of any one life is related to the wholeness of every other life? Might this mean that we cannot move up the ladder of wholeness until all life within our circle of influence is also able to move up that ladder with us? This movement up the ladder of wholeness can happen only when all humans are grasped by the spirit of Reverence for All Life and we reach out as caretakers to help all of our partners.

The process of creation is real. As humans with the ability to think, we can know a great deal about this process. At the same time we realize there also is much we do not as yet know or understand. As some people evaluate the process that brings us the gift of life, they will sort out the things which seem most important and choose to associate those aspects of the process with God. Others of us may find the process to be very real and meaningful and not choose, for various reasons, to talk about God at all. What is most important for each one of us is to realize that the sustainability of our corner of the world may depend on many people developing an attitude of Reverence for All Life. May this ethic of "Reverence for All Life" become a universal religion that causes a true **civil**ization to evolve upon the face of our earth, where non-violence and peace are at the center of each human life.

We are one! The reality of Reverence for All Life can become a vital part of each of our new moments (events) and urge our will-to-live to become one with all other wills-to-live. This oneness and reverence for life could help to end all racism, hatred, revenge, retaliation, and wars within our relationships with one another and help us heal our troubled relationship with our environment.

When we think and talk about God, let us consider the realities of freedom, novelty, adventure, beauty, wholeness, will-to-live, will-to-hope, will-to-love, will-to-relatedness, and Reverence for All Life.

What is Possible?
By John Webster

Everything that is real is made up of events or units of process. The process of creation brings to every event of life a range of possibilities that are appropriate for that event. Not everything is possible for every life event. It is not possible for an elephant to fly. It is not possible for a bird to write a book. However, it **is** possible for a human being to know that everything that lives has the will-to-live just as he or she has. Every life has a range or spectrum of possibilities that is constantly changing as that life moves from one event to the next. The possibilities for any event range from the very desirable to the very undesirable. Our will-to-live urges us toward the most positive possibilities.

The will-to-live of any life event (be it human or non-human) urges that life to be the best, most whole, that it can be.

As human beings, we are never fully aware of all the possibilities for a given event in our lives. We are, however, free to some degree to make choices that will help to determine which possibilities become real in any given life event. Our will-to-live often urges us toward the novelty that is lurking in our set of possibilities for an event. The process of creation allows the new to burst forth in meaningful ways. There are always possibilities available which we can not yet even imagine, involving a still more excellent way of love and life.

Consider, for example, the set of possibilities that might be open to a student taking an exam in a class at school. We might project that the most positive outcome would be to get an "A" and the most negative to get an "F." The worst possibility, however, might be for the student to choose not to prepare and then get caught cheating on the exam, while the greatest possibility might be the flashing into being of a meaningful new idea for the student while he/she is thinking about the questions in the exam. Always, there is the urge and lure toward the most creative of possibilities.

It is important that we be aware of the range of possibilities that are available for our world, our earth, as we participate in the process of creation. As humans, we have a greater range of possibilities available to our events of life than are available to non-human life. This is because of our greater ability to think, to learn, and to use reason, and because our will-to-live can also become a will-to-love. This means, too, that even as we have more opportunities to do good, we also have more possibilities to be destructive. Our goal must be to use the ethic of Reverence for Life to bring about a more sustainable world by becoming caretakers of all life in greater ways than ever before.

As thinking beings who can know that every living creature has the will-to-live just as we do, we have much to say about what will happen to our world. If we continue to choose to use violence in the form of weapons of war, we will continue to help move our world to one of the most negative possibilities available. On the other hand, if we embrace an attitude of Reverence for All Life and set an example of non-violent living for others to see, we can help move our world toward positive possibilities for peace: possibilities that involve continued life rather than death.

At this moment, when the United States of America is involved in a so-called endless war on terrorism, there remains a possibility that this war and all terrorism can come to an end, and that all other wars can be avoided. It is a long shot, but none-the-less, we need to realize that peace is a possibility. PEACE IS POSSIBLE!!! An attitude of Reverence for All Life has the potential to set in motion for our world many new creative possibilities which, when they become real, can open still more possibilities than we have ever before dreamed to be possible. Peace is possible because there are people with the power that comes from using the ethic of Reverence for All Life.

We also need to be aware of events which can lead to possibilities for a greater sustainability for all life in our world, such as those involving a greater use of renewable energy, a more usable network of mass transit along with the will to use it, a commitment to limit the spread of pavement that replaces plant life, the will to preserve the forests, the will to do more with less.

Living every event of life with an attitude of Reverence for All Life will urge us to be aware of possibilities available to all of the partners that come into our circle of influence. Living with an attitude of Reverence for All Life can lift us above the indifference that is generally a part of non-human life and all too often a part of human life. We may have the opportunity to help a more creative possibility become real for one of our partners. We may be able to somehow encourage or enable our partners to be the best that is possible. Our partners in turn may lure us to greater heights. Let us remember that it is good to maintain and to encourage life, and it is bad to destroy or obstruct life. We should never destroy or obstruct life unless it is absolutely necessary. Let us remember, we are life which wills to live, in the midst of life which wills to live. The will-to-live filled with Reverence for All Life is what we need.

Bibliography and Recommended Readings

Listed here are sources that we have referenced or used in the research for this book. Most of the books can be found at used book stores. We have found the website www.abebooks.com useful in locating out-of-print books. We find it works best to order books direct from the individual stores. We have also been able to find books by and about Albert Schweitzer, both new and used, at Amazon *and* Barnes & Noble *websites.*

Following the bibliography, we have provided short synopses of some of our favorite Schweitzer resources. If you have questions about any of these resources or know of additional Schweitzer resources that are helpful, please let us know. The authors may be contacted online at **reverence@triwest.net***.*

Schweitzer Bibliography

Anderson, Erica. *Albert Schweitzer's Gift of Friendship*. Harper & Row, Publishers. New York. 1964.

---------. *The Schweitzer Album*, Harper & Row, Publishers. New York. 1965. (A Portrait in Words and Pictures. Additional text by Albert Schweitzer).

---------. *The World of Albert Schweitzer: A Book of Photographs*. Harper & Brothers Publishers, New York. 1955. (Text and Captions by Eugene Exman.)

Anderson, Erica & Atwood, Ann. *For All That Lives* (with the words of Albert Schweitzer). Charles Scribner's Sons. New York. 1975.

Arnold, Melvin & Joy, Charles R. *The Africa of Albert Schweitzer* (with a concluding essay by Albert Schweitzer). Harper & Brothers. New York. 1948.

Augustiny, Waldemar. *The Road to Lambarene*. Translated by William J. Blake. Frederick Muller Ltd. London. 1956.

Bergel, Kurt & Alice R., (Translators and Editors). *Albert Schweitzer and Alice Ehlers: A Friendship in Letters*. University Press of America, Inc. Lanham, MA. 1991.

Berman, Dr. Edgar. *In Africa With Schweitzer*. Harper & Row. New York. 1986.

Brabazon, James. *Albert Schweitzer: A Biography*. G. P. Putnam's Sons. New York. 1975. Second Edition, Syracuse University Press. 2000.

Clark, Henry. *The Ethical Mysticism of Albert Schweitzer*. Beacon Press. Boston. 1962.

Cousins, Norman. *Albert Schweitzer's Mission: Healing and Peace*. W. W. Norton & Company. New York. 1985.

--------- *Dr. Schweitzer of Lambarene*. Harper & Brothers, Publishers. New York. 1960.

Daniel, Anita. *The Story of Albert Schweitzer*. E. M. Hale and Company. Eau Claire, WI.1957.

Feschotte, Jacques. *Albert Schweitzer An Introduction*. Beacon Press. Boston. 1955.

Franck, Frederick. *Days With Albert Schweitzer*. Henry Holt and Company. New York. 1959.

---------. *My Friend In Africa*. The Bobbs-Merrill Company, Inc. New York. 1960.

Free, Ann Cottrell. *Animals, Nature and Albert Schweitzer*. The Albert Schweitzer Fellowship, The Albert Schweitzer Center, The Animal Welfare Institute, The Humane Society of the United States. 1982.

Gollomb, Joseph. *Albert Schweitzer: Genius in the Jungle*. The Vanguard Press, Inc. New York. 1949.

Greene, Carol. *Albert Schweitzer-Friend of All Life*. Childrens Press. Chicago. 1993.

Hagedorn, Hermann. *Prophet In The Wilderness*. The Macmillan Company. New York. 1948.

Jilek-Aall, Louise, M.D. *Working With Dr. Schweitzer*. Hancock House Publishers. Blaine, WA. 1990.

Joy, Charles R., (Editor). *Albert Schweitzer: An Anthology*. Beacon Press. Boston. 1947.

---------. *Music In The Life Of Albert Schweitzer*. Beacon Press. Boston. 1951.

Ice, Jackson Lee. *Albert Schweitzer: Sketches for a Portrait*.

University Press of America, Inc. Lanham, MD. 1994.
----------. *Schweitzer: Prophet Of Radical Theology.* The
Westminster Press. Philadelphia. 1971.
Kraus, Oscar. *Albert Schweitzer: His Work and His Philosophy.*
Adam & Charles Black. London. 1944.
Langfeldt, Gabriel. *Albert Schweitzer: A Study Of His Philosophy
Of Life.* George Braziller. New York. 1960.
Marshall, George N. *An Understanding of Albert Schweitzer.*
Philosophical Library. New York. 1966.
Marshall, George N. & Poling, David. *Schweitzer: A Biography.*
The Johns Hopkins University Press. Baltimore. 1971.
Meyer, Marvin & Bergel, Kurt, (Editors). *Reverence for Life: The
Ethics of Albert Schweitzer for the Twenty-first Century.*
Syracuse University Press. Syracuse, NY. 2002.
Miller, David C. & Pouilliard, James, eds. *The Relevance of
Albert Schweitzer at the Dawn of the 21st Century.* University
Press of America, Inc. Lanham, MD. 2000. (Papers presented at
the International Albert Schweitzer Colloquium held Aug. 23
and 24, 1990 at the United Nations.)
Montague, Joseph Franklin, M.D. *The Why Of Albert Schweitzer.*
Hawthorn Books, Inc. New York. 1965.
Mozley, E. N. *The Theology Of Albert Schweitzer for Christian
Inquirers* (With an Epilogue by Albert Schweitzer). The
Macmillan Company. New York. 1951.
Ostergaard-Christensen, L. *At Work With Albert Schweitzer.*
Beacon Press. Boston. 1962.
Picht, Werner. *Albert Schweitzer: The Man and his Work.* George
Allen & Unwin LTD. London. 1964.
Pierhal, Jean. *Albert Schweitzer: The Story of His Life.*
Philosophical Library, Inc. New York. 1957.
Roback, A. A. (Editor). *The Albert Schweitzer Jubilee Book.* Sci-
Art Publishers. Cambridge, MA. 1945.
----------. (Editor). *In Albert Schweitzer's Realms: A
Symposium.* Sci-Art Publishers. Cambridge, MA. 1962.
Robles, Harold E. *Albert Schweitzer: An Adventurer for Humanity.*
The Millbrook Press. Brookfield, CT. 1994.

Schick, Edwin A. "Schweitzer's Mission Remembered." *Currents in Theology and Mission.* Feb. 1988; vol.16, no.1, (Pages 36-41).

Schweitzer, Albert. *African Notebook,* translated by Mrs. C. E. B. Russell. Indiana University Press. Bloomington. 1958.

----------. "Albert Schweitzer Speaks Out." *World Book Year Book of 1964.* (Pages 133-148).

----------. *The African Sermons.* Ed. and tr. by Steven E. G. Melamed, Sr. Syracuse University Press. Syracuse, NY. 2003.

----------. *The Animal World of Albert Schweitzer.* Ed. and tr. by Charles R. Joy. The Ecco Press. Hopewell, New Jersey. 1950.

----------. *Christianity and the Religions of the World.* Henry Holt and Company. New York. 1923.

----------. "The Ethics of Reverence for Life." *Christendom,* vol.1, no.1. 1936. p. 225-39.

----------. *Goethe: Four Studies,* tr. by Charles R. Joy. The Beacon Press. Boston. 1949.

----------. *Goethe: Five Studies,* tr. by Charles R. Joy. The Beacon Press. Boston. 1961.

----------. *Indian Thought and Its Development.* The Beacon Press. Boston. 1936.

----------. *J. S. Bach: Volume I.* Dover Publications, Inc. New York. 1966.

----------. *J. S. Bach: Volume II.* Dover Publications, Inc. New York. 1966.

----------. *The Kingdom of God and Primitive Christianity.* The Seabury Press. New York. 1967.

----------. *Memoirs of Childhood and Youth.* The MacMillan Company. New York. 1963.

----------. *The Mystery of the Kingdom of God: The Secret of Jesus' Messiahship and Passion.* Tr. by Walter Lowrie. Prometheus Books. Buffalo, NY. 1985.

----------. *The Mysticism of Paul The Apostle.* The MacMillan Company. New York. 1955.

----------. *On Nuclear War and Peace.* Ed. By Homer A.

Jack. Brethren Press. Elgin, IL 1988.

----------. *Out Of My Life & Thought: An Autobiography.* Henry Holt and Company. New York. 1933.Later edition: The Johns Hopkins University Press. Baltimore. 1990.

----------. *Peace or Atomic War?* Henry Holt and Company. NY. 1958.

----------. *The Philosophy of Civilization.* Prometheus Books. Buffalo, New York. 1987.

----------. *A Place for Revelation: Sermons on Reverence for Life.* Macmillan Publishing Co. New York. 1988.

----------. *The Primeval Forest* (Including *On The Edge Of The Primeval Forest* and *More From The Primeval Forest*). Pyramid Books. New York. 1947.

----------. *The Psychiatric Study Of Jesus.* The Beacon Press. Boston. 1948.

----------. *The Quest of the Historical Jesus: A Critical Study of Its Progress from Reimarus to Wrede.* The Macmillan Company. New York. 1964.

----------. *The Quest of the Historical Jesus.* (First Complete Edition, Edited by John Bowden). Fortress Press. Minneapolis. 2001.

----------. "Religion in Modern Civilization" (Two articles summarizing his Hibbert Lectures given in the autumn of 1934). *The Christian Century.* November 21 and 28, 1934.

----------. *Reverence For Life* (An Anthology of Selected Writings, Ed. by Thomas Kiernan). Philosophical Library. New York. 1965.

----------. *Reverence for Life.* (Selected sermons). Harper & Row, Publishers. New York. 1969.

----------. *The Story Of My Pelican.* Photographs by Anna Wildikann, Tr. by Martha Wardenburg. Hawthorn Books, Inc. New York. 1965.

----------. *The Words of Albert Schweitzer.* New Market Press. New York. 1984.

----------. "Your Second Job" *Reader's Digest.* October 1949. (Pages 1-5).

Schweitzer, Albert and Bresslau, Helene. *The Albert Schweitzer-Helene Bresslau letters 1902-1912*. Ed. by Rhena Schweitzer Miller & Gustav Woytt. Syracuse University Press. Syracuse, New York. 2003.

Schweitzer, Albert and Mellon, William Larimer. *Brothers in Spirit: The Correspondence of Albert Schweitzer and William Larimer Mellon, Jr.* Tr. by Jeannette Q. Byers. Syracuse University Press. Syracuse, NY. 1996.

Seaver, George. *Albert Schweitzer: Christian Revolutionary.* Harper & Brothers, New York. 1944.

----------. *Albert Schweitzer: The Man and His Mind.* Harper & Brothers Publishers. New York. 1947.

Simon, Charlie May. *All Men Are Brothers: A Portrait of Albert Schweitzer.* E. P. Dutton & Company, Inc. New York. 1956.

Urquhart, Clara. *With Doctor Schweitzer In Lambarene.* George G. Harrap & Co. London. 1957.

Additional Bibliography

Altman, Nathaniel. *Ahimsa: Dynamic Compassion.* Quest Books. Wheaton, IL. 1980.

Kingsolver, Barbara. *Small Wonder.* HarperCollins. New York. 2002.

Leopold, Aldo. *A Sand County Almanac.* Oxford University Press. New York. 1968.

Robbins, John. *Diet for a New America.* Stillpoint Publishing. Walpole, NH. 1987.

----------. *The Food Revolution.* Conari Press. Boston, MA. 2001.

Recommendations for Learning More about Schweitzer

It is our hope that the Schweitzer chapters in our book might spark an interest in learning more about this very unique person. Students may find the life and ethic of Albert Schweitzer an interesting topic for a research paper or thesis. Following are some suggestions that we recommend as helpful possibilities for your continuing journey into the world of Schweitzer.

Erica Anderson's Books and Video
(Our favorites. All are great ways to learn about Dr. Schweitzer)

The book *Albert Schweitzer's Gift of Friendship* by Erica Anderson is a delightful read. Anderson went to Lambarene to make a documentary film about Schweitzer's life and work. Seven years in the making, the film won an Oscar for best documentary at the Academy Awards in 1958. In the book, the author tells of the many tribulations that had to be overcome in making the film, and gives much insight into the life and work of Dr. Schweitzer.

Anderson became close friends with Schweitzer, visiting him in Lambarene and at his European home in Günsbach many times. She is well qualified to bring us an in-depth look at the "real" Albert Schweitzer. After reading this book (or even before) you may be interested in viewing the film, which is available in video form.

The film *Albert Schweitzer* won an Academy Award for Best Documentary Feature in 1958. Produced and Directed by Jerome Hill; written by Thomas Bruce Morgan; cinematography by Erica Anderson. Available as a home video from VCI Home Video (800-331-4077), or order it online from the Website at **www.vcientertainment.com/product.asp?title=ALBERT%20S CHWEITZER**.

Schweitzer fans will find this film especially meaningful, as it gives a real-life glance at Albert Schweitzer in person. The video features a day in the life of the Schweitzer Hospital at Lambarene, with Dr. Schweitzer telling the story and showing viewers around his grand creation, and also shows Schweitzer in his European home in Günsbach, France. His youth is portrayed in still pictures and reconstructed scenes, which feature his sister and grandson. This video is well worth the $15 plus postage.

We also highly recommend two books of photographs by Erica Anderson: *The World of Albert Schweitzer* and *The Schweitzer Album*. Both provide excellent photo documentation of Dr. Schweitzer's life and work.

Books and Articles by Albert Schweitzer

"Albert Schweitzer Speaks Out." Article published in *World Book Year Book of 1964*. (Pages 133-148)
This article is a great first-person summary of Dr. Schweitzer's life and message. It is the best brief summary that we have found. It contains golden nuggets of Schweitzer's wisdom, such as the following passage: "Ethics up to now had been incomplete because it had held that its chief concern was merely with the relationship of man to man. In reality, however, ethics must also be concerned with the way man behaves toward all life. In essence, then, man can be considered ethical only if life as such is sacred to him--both in people and in all creatures that inhabit the earth."

It is well worth the time and effort to locate this volume, as the summary of events of 1963 found in it are also interesting. If you don't have a copy of this book in your local library, it can be found on the used book website **www.abebooks.com**.

Out Of My Life & Thought: An Autobiography.
This autobiography is a great way to become acquainted with Schweitzer and get a first-hand account of his life and message. However, we need to remember that Dr. Schweitzer completed this book in 1931, before recording a further 34 years of active service to all that lives; therefore, it is not a full account of this very talented person's lifetime achievements.

Memoirs of Childhood and Youth.
In May of 1923, Schweitzer visited his friend Oscar Pfister in Zurich. Pfister persuaded Albert to talk about memories from his early days. This short book gives the reader a wealth of

interesting information about Schweitzer's boyhood and ends with some inspirational reflections that are truly profound. A must-read for the Schweitzer student.

The Philosophy of Civilization.
This book includes two parts (Part I – *The Decay and the Restoration of Civilization*; Part II – *Civilization and Ethics*) and is one of Schweitzer's most important works. Chapter 26 gives a significant summary of Schweitzer's ethic.

Reverence for Life.
A collection of sermons delivered by Dr. Schweitzer at the Church of St. Nicholas in Strasbourg, where he was a minister for a number of years. The sermons span the years 1900 to 1919 and include his farewell to his congregation before his initial departure for Lambarene, as well as his first sermon after being released from a French internment camp at the end of World War I. In a February 16,1919, sermon, Schweitzer talks to a large group of people for the first time about his important African discovery of "Reverence for Life." This book provides a glimpse of Albert Schweitzer the minister and how important the spirit and ethic of Jesus was to his life and message.

A Place for Revelation: Sermons on Reverence for Life.
Another collection of sermons delivered by Dr. Schweitzer at St. Nicholas. In these sermons, Schweitzer takes an in-depth look at his ethic of Reverence for Life and applies the concept to everyday life. He also touches on such ethical issues as property, forgiveness, and gratitude.

The Primeval Forest (Including *On The Edge Of The Primeval Forest* and *More From The Primeval Forest*).
On The Edge Of The Primeval Forest and *More From The Primeval Forest* can be found as separate volumes. However, it is convenient to have them in the same book. The first volume is Schweitzer's account of his initial arrival in Africa with his wife

and the establishment of the jungle hospital at Lambarene. It begins in 1913 and continues until the Schweitzers returned to Europe as war prisoners during WWI.

The second volume is Schweitzer's account of returning to Lambarene in 1924 to reestablish the hospital. In these pages the reader cannot help but sense the conditions that existed in that part of Africa at the time and the amazing work that Albert Schweitzer accomplished. The accounts also allow the reader to experience the personality of the author coming to life in words from the text that he wrote. We recommend these books, as they take the reader to the heart of the spirit, dedication, and sacrifice of the author. A quick, favorite excerpt: "Joy at the success of it is not what I feel; rather I feel myself humbled, and ask myself how I earned the privilege of carrying on such a work, and in such a work attaining to success."

Schweitzer Biographies

Albert Schweitzer: A Biography. James Brabazon.

Brabazon presents the most complete and well-written Schweitzer biography of which we are aware. A thorough, well-researched, and studiously presented account of the many amazing details of Dr. Schweitzer's incredible life. A wonderful resource for any Schweitzer student or fan. The second edition, published in 2000, has several chapters with additional information that is not found in the first edition.

Albert Schweitzer: An Introduction. Jacques Feschotte.

Because Jacques Feschotte was a friend and neighbor of Albert Schweitzer, he brings a unique perspective of Schweitzer and the Alsatian village of Günsbach—his European home. Included in this book are two addresses by Albert Schweitzer that can only be found in this publication: "Childhood Recollections of Old Colmar," and "The Problem of Ethics in the Evolution of Human Thought," which was delivered on his installation as a member of the French Academy in 1952. We recommend this book and urge Schweitzer students to grab it when you can find it.

All Men Are Brothers: A Portrait of Albert Schweitzer. Charlie May Simon; photographs by Erica Anderson. This book was intended for the young people of America, but it is worthwhile reading for all. Charlie May Simon did her homework well. She visited Günsbach twice and also visited Lambarene in Africa in 1953 and again in 1955. Although she could not speak German or French, the author had these opportunities to observe Dr. Schweitzer going about his daily activities. After reading the manuscript for the book, Schweitzer wrote the author saying, "I found it very sympathetic in its simplicity. One feels that you know the atmosphere and that you know me as I really am."

Albert Schweitzer: An Adventurer for Humanity. Harold E Robles.
Robles wrote this book especially for young people, but persons of all ages will find it a valuable resource. It is a precise and well-written account of Schweitzer's life and message. The preface was written by Dr. Schweitzer's daughter, Rhena Schweitzer Miller. The book has a number of great photos.

The Words of Albert Schweitzer; Selected by Norman Cousins.
A short anthology of quotes from various Schweitzer works, with an introduction by Norman Cousins and some good photographs. A great intro to the world of Schweitzer.

Books and Articles About Dr. Schweitzer by People who Visited or Worked at His Village Hospital

These books provide information about the village community established by Albert Schweitzer at Lambarene and meaningful insights about the character and ethic of the man in charge. They give the reader a feeling that he or she has been to Lambarene and has experienced the ethic of Reverence for Life in action.

Working with Dr. Schweitzer: Sharing His Reverence for Life. Louise Jilek-Aall, M.D.

The author worked at Lambarene for several months during 1961 when Dr. Schweitzer was 86 years of age and still very much in control of his hospital. This is one of our favorite books. It has some great pictures of the Doctor and his hospital village. The best place to order the book is from Hancock House Publishers: **www.hancockhouse.com**. You can also read it online at http://**www.mentalhealth.com/books/lja/lja-toc.html**.

My Days with Albert Schweitzer. Dr. Frederick Franck.

Dr. Franck, a dentist-artist, visited Dr. Schweitzer's hospital at Lambarene in the spring of 1958 and worked there for several months. With the written word and art sketches in this book, Franck does a remarkable job of portraying the reality of everyday life in and around the hospital village and of Dr. Schweitzer the man. We recommend this book as one that every Schweitzer student should read.

With Doctor Schweitzer In Lambarene. Clara Urquhart.

Urquhart knew Albert Schweitzer well, made a number of trips to Lambarene, and is quite qualified to write this book. There are a number of great photos taken at the Schweitzer hospital. Another book you should buy when you can find it.

Dr. Schweitzer of Lambarene. Norman Cousins.

Cousins traveled to Lambarene to visit Dr. Schweitzer early in 1957 in an attempt to persuade the Doctor to use his influence to help bring to the world's attention the evils of nuclear testing and nuclear weapons. Mr. Cousins was successful, as Schweitzer spent much time during the next several years proclaiming the anti-nuclear message to the world. This is another book that brings to us the unique story of the Lambarene village hospital community and its unique demonstration of the reality of Reverence for Life.

At Work With Albert Schweitzer. L. Ostergaard-Christensen.

The author, a Danish surgeon, spent several months in Africa in 1958 working with Dr. Schweitzer. His book helps present the heart-warming story of the Lambarene community of reverence.

The Africa of Albert Schweitzer. Melvin Arnold & Charles R. Joy (with a concluding essay by Albert Schweitzer).

The authors spent several weeks in Africa with Schweitzer and also spent time at his European home at Günsbach. This is one of the earliest accounts of Schweitzer's African hospital. The book is well-written and has some stories and insights not found in other places. Grab this book if you can.

Albert Schweitzer's Gift of Friendship. Erica Anderson.

Note the description of this book under the heading "Erica Anderson's Book and Video" above.

In Africa With Schweitzer. Dr. Edgar Berman.

Dr. Berman was a temporary replacement for the chief surgeon at the Schweitzer community clinic at Lambarene during the fall of 1960. His book provides another interesting look at the goings-on of the jungle hospital.

Books that Bring the Message of "Reverence for Life" to Children

My Friend In Africa . Frederick Franck.

This is a great book for children. If you have children at your house, I urge you to hunt down a copy. Dr. Franck writes about an African boy, Bolo, who was a patient at Dr. Schweitzer's hospital because of an ulcer on the heal of his foot. The story tells how the boy, who dreams of becoming a doctor when he grows up, learns to overcome many of the superstitions and taboos that were a part of his family and tribe. It also portrays the life at the hospital and the attitude of reverence for all of the animals as well the people there. Unless you are lucky enough to find an updated edition of the book, you may not know that Bolo did indeed grow up to become a doctor (a fine surgeon who also teaches surgery to a whole new generation of African doctors).

Albert Schweitzer, Friend of All Life. Carol Greene.

This book presents a very brief summary of Dr. Schweitzer's life and work. There are lots of great pictures in this little book. It can often be found in public libraries.

For All That Lives. Erica Anderson & Ann Atwood.

A brief summary of Schweitzer's ethic of "Reverence for Life" that can be meaningful to both children and adults. Erica Anderson's pictures of Albert Schweitzer and his African experience are interwoven with Ann Atwood's nature photographs and meaningful quotations by Dr. Schweitzer to bring a fresh and inspirational summary of Schweitzer's message. This book is a masterpiece, and I would suggest that every person and family make an effort to locate and purchase a copy.

The Story Of My Pelican. Albert Schweitzer.

Three young pelicans were once brought to Dr. Schweitzer by native Africans. Schweitzer named them Parsifal, Lohengrin, and Tristan. Parsifal became Schweitzer's favorite and lived at the hospital for many years. He often spent the nights outside the window of the room where the Doctor worked and slept.

Anna Wildikann, one of the doctors at the hospital, took pictures of Parsifal and gave them to Dr. Schweitzer for a birthday gift. Soon thereafter, Dr. Wildikann was leaving the hospital. Schweitzer knew that she needed a car for her new work. Therefore, he sat down and wrote the biography of Parsifal in one night, so that the words could go with the photographs to make a book from which she could use the royalties to buy the car. We now have a delightful account of a pelican, a doctor, and his hospital. The story is told in the first person by Parsifal himself: "I am the pelican, the hero of this book...At night, I love more than anything else to be near where he is and mount guard over him... Sometimes he stops writing and talks softly to me in the night. Those night hours spent with him are very precious to me." We highly recommend this book for both children and adults.

Internet Resources

http://www.schweitzer.org/english/aseind.htm
The official homepage of the International Albert Schweitzer Association. This site has much information about Schweitzer and his message of "Reverence for Life" and shows pictures of Schweitzer's European home at Günsbach and gives other interesting information.

http://www.schweitzerfellowship.org
Website for The Albert Schweitzer Fellowship. Founded in 1940, the Fellowship continues to promote Dr. Schweitzer's legacy. The Fellowship sends senior medical students from the U.S. to work at the Schweitzer Hospital in Lambarene, and also runs a Fellows Program, in which students in health professions and related fields carry out direct service projects in underserved communities in the U.S. The Fellowship welcomes donations to carry on their important work.

http://www.christianeengel.com
Christiane Engel is a grandchild of Dr. Schweitzer. She has followed in her grandfather's footsteps by becoming a medical doctor and virtuoso musician. She has been especially inspired not only by the life of her grandfather, but also by her favorite composer, Wolfgang Amadeus Mozart, whose music she has used as a healing tool in her medical practice. She plays piano concerts around the world, generally for charitable causes. Her website lists

her concert schedule and has an interesting gallery of photos, including some taken with her grandfather.

http://www.pcisys.net/~jnf/
This website, established and maintained by Jack N. Fenner, is extremely well-done and useful. Fenner has listed a large number of books by and about Schweitzer and provided publisher information, a short review, a selection of quotes, and the table of contents of each book. The website also provides links to other important Schweitzer sites.

http://www.nobel.se/peace/laureates/1952/schweitzer-lecture.html
The full text of *The Problem of Peace*, Dr. Schweitzer's Nobel Lecture of November 4, 1954, can be found here.

http://www.awionline.org/schweitzer/as-idx.htm
Ann Cottrell Free's book, *Animals, Nature and Albert Schweitzer* can be found online in its entirety at this site.

http://www.mentalhealth.com/books/lja/lja-toc.html.
Working With Dr. Schweitzer: Sharing His Reverence for Life by Louise Jilek-Aall, M.D. (see review above) is one of my favorite books. You can read it online here.

http://www.wartburgseminary.edu/uploadedfiles/ Schweitzerstory.doc.
Dr. Edwin A. Schick's *Albert Schweitzer: A Voice For The Twenty-First Century* can be downloaded here. Dr. Schick, professor emeritus at Wartburg Theological Seminary in Dubuque, Iowa, honors the life and thought of Dr. Schweitzer in this thoughtful composition.

Periodicals with Articles by and about Dr. Schweitzer

Christendom, **vol.1, no. 1; 1936; p.225-39.** "The Ethics of Reverence For Life."

The Christian Century; **vol. 51, November 28, 1934; pp. 1519-21.** "Religion and Modern Civilization."

Life, **October 6, 1947;** "The Greatest Man in the World: That is what some people call Albert Schweitzer, jungle philosopher."

Life, **July 25, 1949.** Article about Schweitzer's visit to America.

Life, **February 19, 1965, pp 82-94.** "The White Wizard's 90th: An Inquiring Visit to Dr. Schweitzer." by Hugh Moffet. This article gives an extensive view of the hospital at Lambarene during Schweitzer's last days there. It gives a good overview of Schweitzer's philosophy and has many excellent color photos of the doctor and his hospital village.

Time, **July 11, 1949, pp.68-74.** "Reverence for Life." The article, written shortly after Schweitzer's one and only visit to the U.S., gives a good overview of Schweitzer's adult life and his philosophy, and has several good black-and-white photos of Schweitzer and his hospital.

Wisdom, **February 1956; pp.27-33.** "Saint of our Century" by George Seaver; plus "From the Wisdom of Albert Schweitzer," quotes from the writings of Dr. Schweitzer, with photos.

Multimedia Presentation

Words of Albert Schweitzer and the Music of Bach.

We highly recommend this multimedia musical dramatization. Written by Thurston Moore, this acclaimed production premiered in Nashville, Tennessee, in October 1995 and is now presented in various locations worldwide. The production uses a marvelous blend of historical slides, classical music, and spoken narrative to portray the life and work of Dr. Schweitzer. For more information and to find a list of scheduled presentations, visit the Tennessee Players website: **http://www.tennesseeplayers.org/sbproduction.html**

A Final Word

By Ty F. Webster

There's something about a river. An unnamable something that speaks to the very heart of our being. Maybe it's because our bodies are made mostly of water. Maybe it's because of the way our lives mimic the flow of a river: leaving its source in a weak trickle, then constantly flowing—at times rushing furiously, at others meandering lazily—toward its ultimate destiny. Maybe it's because of the direct link that a river provides to nature in a world that has become so artificial in so many ways.

Whatever the case, I consider myself fortunate to have lived along the shores of the Mississippi River while working on this book. It is little surprise to me that Dr. Schweitzer ultimately found his inspiration for Reverence for Life while on a river journey. Many are the times that I have looked to "my" river for inspiration, when I have found that the ceaseless flow of the "Mighty Miss" has helped the flow of abstract ideas in the dark recesses of my mind make their way to the light of day. My final words of this book are a perfect example.

For weeks I had wanted to write a conclusion to *Reverence for ALL Life*. I had a pretty clear concept of what I wanted to say, but the words had all the flow of a backwater slough. Then, on a recent evening at about sunset, I threw my kayak in the river and paddled across the main channel to the calm, shallow waters on the other side. It was a beautiful evening: warm but not hot, with just the hint of a breeze to stir the sunset reflection on the river into mesmerizing pink-orange ripples. Flocks of small birds and an occasional waterfowl flew past overhead. Little green dragonflies skimmed along the water beside me. The occasional splashes of fish jumping added a touch of percussion to the chorus of crickets and cicadas. The blooming lotus flowers swayed softly, as if waving good-bye to the day. I paddled a little and floated a lot, soaking up the serene scene as sunset faded away to dusk.

As I paddled back homeward through the encroaching darkness, a sudden movement from a treetop on a nearby island caught my eye. With almost breathless awe, I watched as the silhouetted form of a bird so large it could only have been a bald eagle winged silently away into the darkness. Something stirred in those dark recesses of my mind.

Back at home I turned on the computer and settled into my chair to see if I could capture any of the thoughts running around in my head. But I made the mistake of first going online to check my e-mails. As is so often the case, the news wasn't good. The headlines on my homepage told me that fourteen more of my countrymen had been added to the long list of those killed in action in Iraq. No mention was made of how many Iraqi's suffered the same fate that day. My "Inbox" provided no reprieve from the heavy news. An E-mail from one environmental group alerted me to the fact that due to global warming the 37 remaining glaciers in Glacier National Park will completely melt by the year 2030 if temperatures continue to rise at the current rate. Another informed me there is a very great danger that the U.S. Congress will vote this fall to allow oil drilling in The Arctic National Wildlife Refuge, one of the last pristine pieces of natural environment left on the planet and crucial habitat for many endangered species.

The vision of the silhouetted form of a creature winging silently away came back to me. This time, though, it wasn't an eagle. It was the Lorax: the sad, lonely creature that, in Dr. Seuss' children's story, flew away through a hole in the smog after the entrepreneurial Onceler ignored all of the Lorax's warnings and pleas and let his factory chop down all of the trees and pollute the waters and skies to the point that all of the animals had to leave and try to find new homes.

A poignant Schweitzer quote (from the epilogue to *Out of my Life and Thought)* came to mind, as well: "I am also pessimistic about the current world situation. I cannot persuade myself that it is better than it appears to be. I feel that we are on a fatal road, that if we continue to follow it, it will bring us into a new 'Dark Ages.'" Indeed, such a short time after viewing such an inspirational sunset, I found myself brooding over the fact that humankind might just be entering into a figurative sunset of our own making.

At almost the same moment, though, my eyes came to rest on a photograph I keep near my desk. I snapped it while in Berlin, Germany, last winter. It is a picture of one of the only remaining intact portions of the Berlin Wall. Most of that concrete dividing line between Communist East and "Free" West has been torn down in the city that was at the epicenter of the Cold War. Only a couple of short stretches remain, serving as a reminder of the great tension and division that once ruled the day there, and standing as testament to humankind's ability to evoke dramatic change, even in the worst of situations. And Berlin is such a perfect example: where for so many years there was division, now there is unity, where armed conflict, now peace.

This particular portion of the remaining Wall has been painted with images and slogans of peace and hope by artists from around the world. The bit I snapped the photo of contained a simple yet profound message, painted in block lettering, black on white, in both German and English. In German, it reads: "VIELE KLEINE LEUTE DIE IN VIELEN KLEINEN ORTEN VIELE KLEINE DINGE TUN KÖNNEN DAS GESICHT DER WELT VERÄNDERN." In English: "MANY SMALL PEOPLE WHO IN MANY SMALL PLACES DO MANY SMALL THINGS CAN ALTER THE FACE OF THE WORLD."

As it always does, the sight of this photo raised my spirits, reminded me that there is still hope. It also, on this occasion, reminded me of a couple of my favorite Schweitzer quotes:

"I am convinced, intellectually convinced, that the human spirit in our time is capable of creating a new attitude of mind: an attitude based on ethics." --Nobel Peace Prize Address.

"In my view, no other destiny awaits mankind than that which, through its mental and spiritual disposition, it prepares for itself. Therefore I do not believe that it will have to tread the road to ruin right to the end. If people can be found who revolt against the spirit of thoughtlessness and are sincere and profound enough to spread the ideals of ethical progress, we will witness the emergence of a new spiritual force strong enough to evoke a new spirit in mankind. Because I have confidence in the power of truth and of the spirit, I believe in the future of mankind." -- Epilogue to *Out of My Life and Thought*.

It also brought to mind the moral of Dr. Seuss' *Lorax*: the meaning of the word, "UNLESS," which the Lorax left behind as a warning before he flew away. As the Onceler pointed out, it means, "UNLESS someone like you cares a whole awful lot, nothing is going to get better. It's not."

And then one final quote came to mind, words from John Robbins' *The Food Revolution*:

"We will not, of course, turn things around merely because we do a few convenient things to save the Earth. But as more of us do the things that matter, as more of us lead by example, others will find themselves pulled along. One step leads to the next. As more of us find ways of expressing our love for the Earth, others will be swept up in the power of our caring and the integrity of our example."

And then I knew what it was I wanted to say by way of conclusion to *Reverence for ALL Life*. It's this: It is up to us, ALL OF US working together, to evoke a new spirit in humankind, to bring about a world more full of reverence for all life. Because if we are afraid to speak up or act out, or if we decide that the problem is too big for us—that nothing we do can really make a difference—then we *are* on a fatal road to a new Dark Age. But if we all pull together with an attitude of reverence for all life and do the many small things in the many small places—if we begin to follow the lead of those acting with reverence and start to set our own examples of reverence, if we all begin to speak of reverence to our friends, teach reverence to our children, dedicate our lives to a greater reverence—then as surely as the Mississippi River flows to the Gulf of Mexico, we *will* witness a new spirit in humankind, and a continued future for all that lives.

In Conclusion

It may be rather easy to dismiss the ethic of Reverence for Life as being sentimental and naïve. Who wants to be concerned about all humans and, especially, about all non-human life, as well? Why worry about the well-being of homeless children in Guadalupe or microbes on a penguin's wing in Antarctica? Don't we all have enough to worry about already?

Yet, **unless** we develop reverence for **all** human partners we will surely destroy ourselves in the midst of our warring nuclear madness and economic greed. And **unless** we also develop reverence for the well-being of all our non-human partners, we will soon wear out our environmental welcome as global warming, vanishing species and rainforests, pollution, and lack of food and usable water make continued human life (us) on earth obsolete.

So, in conclusion, perhaps we can afford to be a touch sentimental and naïve as we join together in deep respect, love, and awe for all that lives. **Might it just be our only hope for survival?** Does anyone have a more hopeful way to offer?

Therefore, may we dedicate our lives to the great ethic developed and demonstrated by Dr. Albert Schweitzer. Reverence for Life is a way of living that can bring PEACE and sustainability to us and to our world. May we take Dr. Schweitzer's example out into the communities of our world to heal and help all that lives!

The authors welcome your ideas, comments, and questions concerning the material presented in this book. We would be glad to answer, if we can, questions concerning the resources we have used in our study of the life and thought of Dr. Albert Schweitzer.

Contact information:
John or Ty F. Webster
W25128 Sullivan Rd.
Trempealeau, WI 54661
reverence@triwest.net

Photo Credits

The photographs in this book are from the following sources:

p.iii: Dr. Albert Schweitzer at Lambarene, Africa (**1**); **p.v**: Dr. Schweitzer and his daughter Rhena in Africa (**2**); **p.viii**: John, Elizabeth, and Ty F. Webster at a Dennis Kucinich political rally (**3**); **p.xiv**: Günsbach (**4**); **p.57**: Dr. Schweitzer on "the rocks" above Günsbach, France, with Günsbach in the background (**5**); Dr. Schweitzer on "the rocks" (**6**); Dr. Schweitzer at age 21 (**7**); **p.58**: Dr. Schweitzer overlooking the Ogowe River near Lambarene, Africa (**7**); **p.59**: Dr. Schweitzer with patient at the hospital in Lambarene; *and* Dr. Schweitzer with Sizi the cat; *and* Dr. Schweitzer with Parsifal the pelican (**8**); **p.60**: Dr. Schweitzer at the piano *and* Dr. Schweitzer sermonizing at Lambarene (**8**); **p.61**: Dr. Schweitzer in Africa (**5**); Head shot of Dr. Schweitzer (**1**); **p.62**: Dr. Schweitzer's living quarters at Lambarene; *and* Dr. Kokou tends to a young patient; *and* Georges leads an outreach program (**9**); **p.63**: The Albert Schweitzer monument at "the rocks" above Günsbach (**4**); **p.81**: John Webster with his father, Orville *and* John Webster with his mother, Helen (**6**); **p.82**: Paul Doescher and Ol' Mouser (**6**); **p. 87**: John and Elizabeth Webster with wedding party (**6**); **p.91**: Jay and Stefanie Webster wedding photo (**4**); **p.93**: Jay and Stefanie Webster, with Rev. John Webster officiating at their wedding (**6**); **p.105**: Jay and Stefanie Webster's German Wedding reception guests (**6**); **p.108**: The Websters with BMW (**4**); **p.109**: Schweitzer birthplace (**4**); **p.110**: Schweitzer's home in Günsbach (**4**); **p.111**: Schweitzer in doorway (**6**); Websters in doorway (**4**); **p.112**: Günsbach church (**4**); **p.113**: Günsbach (**4**); **p.114**: Webster - Kruschwitz family photo (**6**); **p.119**: Moonbeam (**4**); **p.121**: Moonbeam and John Webster (**6**); **p.125**: John Webster with sheep (**6**); **p.128**: Calliope the Christmas tree, with Tipper the cat (**4**); **p.135**: Fawn (**3**); Turkeys (**10**); **p.137**: Sunset at Trempealeau Wildlife Refuge (**4**); **p.142**: Dancing whooping cranes (**6**); **p.173**: Dennis Kucinich headshot (**4**); **p.191**: Dennis Kucinich campaign speech (**4**); **p.200**: Forest and Kestrel Jenkins (**10**); **p.203** Charlotte Aldebron giving speech (**11**); **p.208** Charlotte Aldebron at computer desk (**11**); **p.219**: Pasque flower (**4**).

(**1**) By Christiane Engel, courtesy of Rhena Schweitzer Miller; (**2**) By Erica Anderson, courtesy of Rhena Schweitzer Miller; (**3**) By Ann Dahmen; (**4**) By Ty F. Webster (**5**) By Erica Anderson, used with the permission of the Albert Schweitzer Fellowship; (**6**) From the authors' personal collection; (**7**) From the Albert Schweitzer Papers, Special Collections Research Center, Syracuse University Library, used with the permission of The Albert Schweitzer Fellowship; (**8**) By Erica Anderson, from the Albert Schweitzer Papers, Special Collections Research Center, Syracuse University Library, used with the permission of The Albert Schweitzer Fellowship; (**9**) Courtesy of the Albert Schweitzer Fellowship; (**10**) By Linda Jenkins; (**11**) Courtesy of Charlotte and Jillian Aldebron.

John Webster is a retired United Methodist minister who served churches in the Kansas West and Wisconsin Conferences for many years. He received a Bachelor of Arts degree from Arizona State University and Master of Divinity and Master of Sacred Theology degrees from the Iliff School of Theology at Denver, Colorado. John lives with his wife Elizabeth in Trempealeau, WI.

Ty F. Webster holds a Bachelor's degree in English from Carroll College in Waukesha, WI. When he is not roaming around the world as an amateur international goodwill ambassador, he lives in Trempealeau, WI.

The Authors would like to thank...

Rhena Schweitzer Miller for her input, encouragement, and graciousness; Dr. Lachlan Forrow and Ian Stevenson of the Albert Schweitzer Fellowship for their support and suggestions; Zoe Kiefer at the Fellowship for her assistance; Nicolette Schneider at the Syracuse University Library for her help facilitating the use of Schweitzer photos; Amy Vossbrinck for liaising between the authors and Rep. Dennis Kucinich; David Andrews for his willingness to provide us with the beautiful artwork for the front cover; Megan Gjersvig for letting us use "Earth Tree" on the back cover; everyone who contributed to or allowed us to include their works in the book; Dorothy Prell for all of her guidance in the publishing process; Sue Knopf for her skillful design work on the cover; Brandy Toberman at United Graphics, Inc. for her help with the printing process; Stefanie Webster, Jay Webster, Brett Unruh, and Jamie Buehner for their proofreading efforts; everyone at the Trempealeau Hotel for all of their interest in and support of our project; all of our friends and family who provided the same; and, especially, Elizabeth Webster for all of her assistance and loving support, and for generally putting up with the authors during this whole process. *Reverence for ALL Life* would not have been the same book without the help from all of you.